CAUSAL
ANALYSIS

CAUSAL ANALYSIS

David R. Heise

A WILEY-INTERSCIENCE PUBLICATION

JOHN WILEY & SONS, New York · London · Sydney · Toronto

Library of Congress Cataloging in Publication Data

Heise, David R.
  Causal analysis.

  "A Wiley-Interscience publication."
  Includes bibliographies and index.
  1. Social sciences—Statistical methods. 2. Social
sciences—Mathematical models. 3. Econometrics. I. Title.

HA29.H46   300'.01'51953   75-20465
ISBN 0-471-36898-9

Printed in the United States of America

10 9 8 7 6 5 4 3 2 1

To
my Students

PREFACE

This book focuses on the study of linear systems and represents an effort to organize a broad range of information about this topic in a fairly elementary fashion. Writing in the 1970s, I have had the privilege of drawing key ideas from the work of philosophers, engineers, and methodologists in the life sciences. Some innovations are added here, but the central intention is not so much to break new ground as to cultivate that which already is tilled and so instill a wider awareness and appreciation for this field and its products.

The book is addressed to a fairly wide audience of practicing social scientists, students, and interested laymen. Rather than compromise ideas in order to reach this wide audience, I have relied heavily on the pedagogical device of causal diagrams. These diagrams allow one to visualize and comprehend even some of the more intricate topics in social science methodology, and following rules for manipulating diagrams allows almost anyone to carry out many mathematical analyses with the precision of an algebraist. The pedagogical advantage offered by causal diagrams may suggest that they are a "rough and ready" approach to systems analysis. This is not the case. Causal diagrams with their set of rules in themselves constitute a form of mathematics. Such diagrams are employed daily by practicing scientists and engineers.

The teacher examining this book may wonder where it fits in a traditional curriculum. Statistics are discussed in detail, but the emphasis here is on statistical description of social systems rather than on the usual statistical inference from samples to populations. Substantive topics are analyzed in examples and in exercises, but the specific examples of models range over most of the field of sociology and comprehend a number of theoretical perspectives. Nevertheless, as a text on model building this volume can be employed in methodology and statistics courses that focus on the use of data for testing and elaborating theories and it can serve as an auxillary source in courses on theory construction.

Over the last decade numerous colleagues and students have helped to prepare me to write this book. Four were especially important teachers: Edgar Borgatta, George Bohrnstedt, Arthur Goldberger, and Dennis Willigan. James A. Davis, Duncan MacRae, Jr., and Ronald Burt provided valuable criticisms of early drafts of some chapters. So also did many anonymous student readers, including one wag (since identified as Donna Cowan) who suggested titling the book, "Studies in Arrow-Dynamics." Gert Rippy typed the original manuscript for use in courses at Chapel Hill.

In a more personal direction I have enjoyed rich support from Elsa Lewis and Stephen Heise, whose vitality and wit repeatedly reentered me from regions of abstraction while I was writing this book.

DAVID R. HEISE

Department of Sociology,
University of North Carolina, Chapel Hill
May 1975

CONTENTS

Prologue   **1**

Chapter 1.   Causality and Causal Analysis   **3**

Causal Ordering,   3
Operators, 6
Definition of Causality, 11
Causal Inference, 12
Flows, 17

  Additivity, 19
  Proportionality of Effect, 19
  Negative Multipliers, 20
  Terminology Conventions, 22

Linearity, 23

  Interpreting Structural Coefficients, 26

Causal Systems, 27

  Multiple Causes, 27
  Multiple Effects, 30
  Mutual Causation, 31

Sources and Additional Readings, 33
Exercises, 35

Chapter 2   Causal Diagrams and Flowgraph Analysis   **38**

Diagramming Causal Relationships, 38

Complexities in Diagrams, 41

Branches, 41
Loops, 42
Self-Loops, 43
Missing Arrows, 43
Disturbances, 44
Nonlinear Relations, 46

Flowgraph Analysis, 48

Equation Formation, 49
Structural-Equation Representations, 51
Reduction Rules, 52
Additional Interpretations of the Rules, 55
Flowgraphs with Loops, 56
Touching Paths, 61
Reduction with Loops, 62
Reduced Form of a System, 67
Semireduction, 67
Extensions of Flowgraph Analysis, 73

Research Applications, 73

Critical Cases, 73
Explanation, 74
Prediction, 75
Interdiction, 75

Sources and Additional Readings, 76
Exercises, 77

Chapter 3   Statistical Concepts   **82**

Distributions, 82

Graphs of Distributions, 83
The Mean, 85
Variance, 87

Joint Distributions, 88

Graphs of Joint Distributions, 88
Covariance, 95
The Correlation Coefficient, 96

Linear Regression, 98

   Residual Variance, 101

Multiple Regression, 103
Standardized Coefficients, 105
Regression and Causal Inference, 107
Sources and Additional Readings, 108
Exercises, 109

Chapter 4   Path Analysis   **111**

Flowgraph Modifications, 112

   Loop Reduction, 112
   Input Covariances, 113
   Disturbance Covariances, 114

Analyzing Statistical Coordination, 114

   Coordinating Paths, 114
   Covariance Analysis, 120
   Analysis of Correlations, 124
   Standardized Versus Unstandardized, 126

Analyzing Statistical Diversity, 127
Path Analysis and Algebraic Derivations, 131
Gating Mechanisms, 132
General Implications, 135

   Sources of Diversity, 135
   Coordination of Outcomes, 138
   Correlations in Loops, 140

Sources and Additional Readings, 142
Exercises, 142

Chapter 5   Identification and Estimation   **148**

Regression Analyses and Identification, 150

   The Need for Theory, 152

Recursive Systems, 153

   Ordinary Least Squares (OLS), 155

Nonrecursive Systems, 160

   Instrumental Variables, 160
   Instruments and Identification, 165
   Two-Stage Least Squares, 168
   Calculating Procedures, 172
   Graphical Interpretation of 2SLS, 172
   Identification Problems, 175
   Identifiability, 177
   Full-Information Methods, 181
   Self-Loops, 182
   Lagged Variables as Instruments, 184

Factors Affecting Estimates, 185

   Sampling Error, 185
   Strength of Relations, 186
   Measurement Imprecision, 188
   Specification Errors, 191

Elaboration in Social Research, 193
Zero Coefficients, 194
Sources and Additional Readings, 195
Exercises, 197

Chapter 6   Dynamic Considerations   **205**

Simple System Dynamics, 206

   Causal Lags, 206
   Elementary Dynamic Patterns, 208
   Feedback Effects, 213
   Higher Order Feedback, 219
   Complex Inputs, 223

Dynamic Confounding in Static Analyses, 225

   Equilibration, 226
   Equilibration Time, 227
   Time-Varying Inputs, 231
   Dynamics of Lagged Variables, 234

Static and Dynamic Variance, 235
Sources and Additional Readings, 237
Exercises, 238

Answers to Exercises   **245**

Chapter 1, 245
Chapter 2, 250
Chapter 3, 258
Chapter 4, 262
Chapter 5, 271
Chapter 6, 286

Index   **295**

CAUSAL
ANALYSIS

PROLOGUE

GHAZALI SAYS:

According to us the connexion between what is usually believed to be a cause and what is believed to be an effect is not a necessary connexion; each of two things has its own individuality and is not the other, and neither the affirmation nor the negation, neither the existence nor the non-existence of the one is implied in the affirmation, negation, existence, and non-existence of the other—e.g., the satisfaction of thirst does not imply drinking, nor satiety eating, nor burning contact with fire, nor light sunrise, nor decapitation death, nor recovery the drinking of medicine, nor evacuation the taking of a purgative, and so on for all the empirical connexions existing in medicine, astronomy, the sciences, and the crafts. For the connexion in these things is based on a prior power of God to create them in a successive order, though not because this connexion is necessary in itself and cannot be disjoined—on the contrary, it is in God's power to create satiety without eating, and death without decapitation, and to let life persist notwithstanding the decapitation, and so on with respect to all connexions.

I SAY:

To deny the existence of efficient causes which are observed in sensible things is sophistry, and he who defends this doctrine either denies with his tongue what is present in his mind or is carried away by a sophistical doubt which occurs to him concerning this question. For he who denies this can no longer acknowledge that every act must have an agent. The question whether these causes by themselves are sufficient to perform the acts which proceed from them, or need an external cause for the perfection of their act, whether separate or not, is not self-evident and

Reprinted from *Averroes' Tahafut Al-Tahafut* (*The Incoherence of the Incoherence*), translated by Simon van den Bergh (London: Luzac & Company Ltd., 1954), Volume I, pages 316, 318, with permission of the E. J. W. Gibb Memorial Trust and the publishers.

requires much investigation and research. And if the theologians had doubts about the efficient causes which are perceived to cause each other, because there are also effects whose cause is not perceived, this is illogical. Those things whose causes are not perceived are still unknown and must be investigated, precisely because their causes are not perceived. . . .

AVERROES (1126–1198 A.D.)

1 CAUSALITY AND CAUSAL ANALYSIS

The notion of causality applies whenever the occurrence of one event is reason enough to expect the production of another. Causal thinking relates to activity because occurrence of an event implies some form of change. Causal analysis procedures, however, usually focus on configurations of events—over time or at a single time—rather than on changes as such. Causation generates event patterns, and studying the patterns can provide insights into the causal relationships that generated them.

Causal thinking is applied regularly in everyday experiences, especially when objects are manipulated or changed from one state to another. Perhaps this is why manipulation seems so important in the establishment of causal relations and why causal explanations seem to provide not only a sense of understanding but also of potential control. Causal explanations can be abstracted beyond manipulations or at least to the point at which manipulations are purely hypothetical; for example, it might be said that the sun's gravitational field causes certain peculiarities in the motions of the planets even though there is no possibility of experimental proof. With the concept generalized this way it is possible sometimes to examine causality non-experimentally by using existing patterns in events.

The possibility of causal analysis and inference without manipulation is crucially important in the social sciences in which so many political, practical, and ethical problems narrow the possibilities of implementing classical experiments. Thus our first goal is to define causality generally enough so that the concept will apply even when manipulative control is unattainable.

CAUSAL ORDERING

Events are the starting point in causal analysis. An event is the occurrence of a particular state, or a configuration of states, in some entity. Mere changes

3

in location or physical orientation of an entity constitute elementary events. Events may also be defined in more abstract terms and be signaled by changes in observable characteristics, by changes in rate of activity, or by dispositional changes (i.e., changes in the potential for other events).

The notion of causality becomes relevant when events are ordered and structured in certain ways. First of all, saying that one event causes another requires that the first event—call it C—produces an expectation for the occurrence of the second event, E. A similar expectation does not exist in the reverse direction. If, for some reason, we know only that E has occurred, we have no special reason to believe that C will occur or even necessarily has occurred beforehand. These points can be summarized in tabular form, as shown in **1.1**.

1.1

		E	
		occurs	does not occur
C	occurs	yes	no
	does not occur	yes	yes

"Yes" means that "this combination can exist" and "no" means "this combination cannot exist." The pattern corresponds to the statement that "C causes E," which implies more specifically that "C cannot occur without E occurring."

The table in **1.1** might be read as follows: occurrences of C imply occurrences of E but occurrences of E do not imply occurrences of C; or occurrences of C are sufficient but not necessary for occurrences of E.

The notion that C implies E is crucial to causal thinking but by itself it is not enough to capture the essence of causality. Implication merely relates the possibilities of various cooccurrences of events without any restrictions on their timing or physical organization; for example, without taking timing and organization into account, the pattern in **1.1** might be interpreted alternatively as "occurrences of C develop out of occurrences of E."

Consideration of temporal ordering clarifies the way in which the logical implication is to be read. Effects do not occur before their causes. A cause always precedes its effect in the sense that the causal event always begins before the effect begins. By combining the logical and temporal criteria we obtain a more adequate conception of causality. One suspects the existence of a causal relationship when occurrence of one event implies later occurrence of another.

The addition of the temporal-priority condition distinguishes causal from developmental relationships in which one event implies another but the second occurs before the first. These two types of relationship are illustrated in **1.2**.

1.2 A causal relationship is one in which occurrence of a first event is a sufficient condition for the occurrence of a later event.

Time

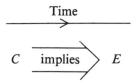

C implies E

A developmental relationship is one in which occurrence of a first event is necessary for the occurrence of a later event.

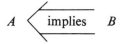

A implies B

Causality does *not* require the absence of E when C is absent. There may be no occurrence of C at an earlier time, yet E occurs anyway. In essence this allows that E may be caused by events other than C. So, although it is true that "an effect does not occur before its cause," we must recognize that an effect may be produced by one of its causes before the occurrence of another of its causes. Hence, to be precise, the first diagram in **1.2** should receive the following interpretation: C causes E only if an occurrence of E is invariably found after an occurrence of C, even if E were not in evidence beforehand.

A combination of the conditions of logical and temporal ordering provides a better statement concerning causality than either condition alone but the result is still inadequate. For one thing, this formulation would allow us to imagine that any event causes any other event under the untestable presumption that the second event invariably follows the first "somewhere in the universe." We need to recognize explicitly that causality operates under physical constraints. Moreover, causal relations do not invariably hold even in restricted domains unless some minimal conditions are fulfilled, and this, too, needs to be recognized.

OPERATORS

Causation depends on an extraordinary tuning of reality at a particular instant such that one event transmutes into another. The special organization required for causality is evident in a commonly cited example—a match that produces an explosion. Burning matches ordinarily do not cause explosions. Explosions result only when a lighted match is introduced into a room partly filled with flammable gas or is otherwise put in contact with properly packed explosive material. Structured circumstances are also involved in even the commonest physical instances of causality; for example, force causes motion in a body only if the body is adequately rigid (one cannot push a cube of air) and only if it has mass (a shadow has form but cannot be lifted). Applied to elementary mechanics, this notion of causality depending on extraordinary and transient circumstances seems esoteric because the required physical conditions are so ubiquitous, stable, and familiar that we take them for granted. The dependence of causation on preexisting structures is important, however, in studying social life in which the required structures are often absent. Even a fairly general sociological proposition like "external threats cause group cohesion" is applicable only to certain kinds of people (e.g., not infants) with some minimum of group identification and structure. Without the requisite conditions threats may cause other reactions such as panic or no reaction at all.

A material structure or structured process that implements a causal relation is called an *operator*. Causal transmutation of events cannot take place without an appropriate operator and the operator must exist before the transmutation it supports. A causal relation need not depend uniquely on a single operator. Both biological systems and human manufacturing systems routinely produce classes of essentially equivalent structures that implement the same relationships. Also, causal relations can frequently be implemented by operators with different internal structures (e.g., a car works whether it has a piston engine or a rotary engine). Thus a causal relation is dependent developmentally on the existence of a class of operators.

An operator consists of organized components. The components themselves are operators in that they are structures that serve to transmute one event to another; for example, an automobile has both an engine and a transmission and each of these parts is itself an operator for converting one kind of event into another. Moreover, because each component of an operator is an operator, it, too, can be analyzed into its subcomponents. Theoretically the process of analysis can be continued indefinitely. This analyzability of operators corresponds to analyzability of causal relations; that is, the transmutation of event C into event E can be analyzed in terms of a set of intervening causal relations manifested within the operator and implemented by the operator's components. These relations, in turn, can be analyzed into a still more discriminate set of constituent causal relations. In principle this analytic process can be continued indefinitely. Thus causes and effects are linked by continuous chains of intervening events.

Analytic dissection of operators and causal relations is an important aspect of understanding. We partition novel operators and causal relations into components and relations until we feel that we know how the transmutation of one event into another occurs—how one event "produces" another. In everyday life we typically analyze until we reach the level of familiar, commonly accepted relationships. Even scientific analyses rarely continue beyond the point at which further partitioning of an operator would require treatment as a statistical aggregate of minute structures implementing relations that are the focus of another discipline; for example, theoretically we could determine how force applied to a steel ball causes directional motion by dropping to the molecular level and analyzing the effects of force on individual molecules and their effect on one another within the constraints imposed by the structure of the material involved. The motion of the ball is then seen as an aggregate effect defined in terms of millions of parallel and similar events at the lower level. This, however, is far more detail than is typically wanted and we do not ordinarily maintain much interest in such a microscopic analysis. Similarly, sociological explanation usually stops short of neurological analyses of individuals, psychological interpretation usually stops short of biochemical analyses of separate cells, and biochemical studies do not often proceed to structural analyses of atoms.

A set of components alone is not enough to create an operator. The operator emerges only when the components are properly related to one another. In fact, it is possible to think of an operator as a peculiar and transient configuration—itself a kind of event—produced jointly by the existence of the set of parts in conjunction with an organizing connecting process. Operators may evolve or they may be constructed, as indicated in **1.3**.

1.3   The parts of an operator, O, can be viewed as a set of things, S, that is sufficient to create O when an appropriate organizing (or linking) process, L, is operative. Thus the set of parts implies the generation of an operator in the presence of an appropriate organizing process.

$$S \quad \boxed{\text{implies}} \!\!\!\searrow \quad O, \text{ given } L$$

One interpretation of this formulation is that availability of parts causes construction of an operator if an organizing process inevitably occurs. This formulation provides a "constructive" perspective on operator formation. When organizing processes are predetermined (say in the form of genetic mechanisms or a skilled, motivated craftsman), then assembling required materials is sufficient for the production of particular structures.

Alternatively, an "evolutionary" perspective results when the set of components is viewed as preexisting and the organizing process occurs by chance.

$$L \quad \boxed{\text{implies}} \!\!\!\searrow \quad O, \text{ given } S$$

that is, in the presence of a pool of components, randomly occurring linkages generate structures that may serve as operators for new causal relationships.

An operator forms only from compatible components. A component responds to only specific kinds of events, and if the component is to work and contribute to the action of a larger operator, it must receive the right kind of inputs from components that precede it in the system. Often the compatibility condition is fulfilled in a simple way, the causal event for one component being identical to the outcome event of another. Compatibility however, may also be achieved when one component is responsive to a configuration of outcomes from other components; for example, the outcome of a first component may be needed to "set" a second before it can produce an event that serves as an input for a third (a piston in a car engine can do no work unless there is a fuel mixture in the cylinder and a spark to ignite the fuel). A component may be sensitive to a threshold number of parallel events produced by prior components (e.g., a neuron fires only when the stimulation from other neurons cumulates to a critical level). The study of component compatibility involves a determination of the responsiveness of one entity to events produced by another (or combinations of others). This is a kind of substantive analysis that must be done anew in each different area of inquiry.

Frequently operators can be classified in terms of taxonomies and typologies, reducing diversity by treating some operators as equivalent though differing in detail. A variety of methods is available for creating these classifications: internal compositional analysis; comparisons of patterns of growth or construction; assessment of parallelism and complementarity in distribution; clustering in terms of the effects produced by different operators; and grouping in terms of functional similarity according to parallel positioning within larger systems. Indeed, an ideal goal is to define an overall classification that corresponds to all bases simultaneously, thus allowing information of one type to be translated readily into other meanings. Such inquiries are substantive in the sense that they, too, must be done anew for each class of phenomena being studied.

Fields An effect is the occurrence of a particular state or configuration of states in an operator. Consequently an effect has a specific locus in space and time. Any second operator that is to be linked to the first to form a higher order operator must be compatible; that is, it must respond to the effect produced by the first. In addition, it must be properly coordinated in space and time to be in the domain of the preceding event. In mechanical devices this is essentially a demand for contiguity. Two components must be "touching" for events to be transmitted. A more general formulation is needed, however, to cover other phenomena.

For heuristic purposes events can be conceived as fields originating at the operator that produces them but extending in space and time away from their initial spatial-temporal location. In general, the greater the distance from the origin, the lower the intensity of the field and its ability to generate action in a compatible operator. Thus one component is connected to another only if it is within the effective event field of the other. Construction of an operator requires, at minimum, the positioning of components so that some exist in the event fields of others.

A causal relation can exist between two events only if some operator effects the transformation. Now we see that an operator must be compatible and coordinated with a causal event if it is to generate an effect. Consequently we can say that a first event is the cause of a second only if the first is coordinated with some operator that responds to it and has the capacity to effect the second.

Thus a particular type of event by itself is never a universal cause of another. It has the potential for being a cause only if suitably located in relation to a responsive operator. An event that formerly produced no effect might begin doing so if a suitable operator is brought within its field. An event that has acted as a cause in the past would cease to do so if all relevant operators were removed from its field.

The general principle here is vital in everyday living—soup does not heat unless the pan is placed over fire and hunger is not sated unless food is swallowed. The principle motivates constructive activities in which two or more operators are brought together to create a larger operator with a specific function and provides a means of controlling unwanted happenings; for example by isolating certain people from the means of implementing their ideas or passions.

An event field might permeate space in a relatively simple physical way. For example, the field of a magnetic or radiant-heat event has uniform intensity in all directions but the intensity gradient declines rapidly with distance, and a responsive structure would have to be close to the event's origin to be influenced by the event. Of course, contiguity is relative. Mechanical event fields have such a rapid spatial gradient that the components must be "touching" to influence one another. Electromagnetic events have a lesser gradient, thus allowing for a more relaxed perspective on contiguity.

Event fields, however, both physical and social, can also be directed, extended, or stored by a variety of means; for example, a person's voice ordinarily provides a simple circular field for communicating events, but with the help of special devices the field can be directed (by a bullhorn or a megaphone), extended (by a telephone or transmission through dense material), or stored (by a tape recorder). When special media or devices distort event fields, the notion of contiguity with respect to a single locus in ordinary space and time no longer helps us to understand how operators influence one another. Either we must operate in peculiar *ad hoc* spaces in which the contiguity principle retains its meaning or we must allow for the distortions of the event field in ordinary space (e.g., by postulating reproductions of the original event at various points in space and time to construct the proper field according to ordinary distance principles).

With the notion of distorted event fields the possibility of an event in one place causing an effect in some other remote place has been introduced. This is contrary to a traditional canon of causal philosophy: the prohibition against action at a distance. Certainly a rigid requirement for "no action at a distance" is too restrictive and the field approach is sensible in modifying it to "less potential for action with more distance," thereby accounting for well-known phenomena like magnetism and gravitation. It may seem that distorted fields open the possibility of no constraints whatsoever. Any two remote events could be causally connected merely by postulating that the first has a distorted field reaching to an operator for the second. What needs to be added is that operators are necessary to extend fields—amplifiers to increase their range, memory devices for storage until later times. Consequently a field distortion must itself be causally accountable.

In general, a field is subject to a causal analysis of more microscopic operators acting aggregatively; for example, we might speak of the development of authoritarianism in one nation as an event with a field influencing other nations. Such a field, however, operates via the medium of individual persons (operators in their own right), and, if desired, we could study its statistical mechanics by surveying the actions of individuals. Because a field is generated by events at a more microscopic level, it can extend from one point to another only if there is a structural-causal basis for the extension at a lower level of analysis. In particular, distortions of event-fields are not arbitrary. They must be materialistically supported and causally interpretable in terms of more microscopic structures. (At present, a structural basis has not been postulated for electromagnetic and gravitational fields. This suggests that there may be fundamental exceptions to the notion of causal construction of fields or that distortions of such fields have not yet proved troublesome enough to motivate the identification of still another structural level.)

DEFINITION OF CAUSALITY

It was suggested at the beginning of this chapter that causality is involved when "the occurrence of one event is reason enough to expect the production of another." A more precise statement is needed to guide and restrict the application of the causality principle in theory construction and the design of research.

I.1   *An event C, causes another event, E, if and only if*

   (a)   *an operator exists which generates E, which responds to C, and which is organized so that the connection between C and E can be analyzed into a sequence of compatible components with overlapping event fields;*

   (b)   *occurrences of event C are coordinated with the presence of such an operator—such an operator exists within the field of C;*

   (c)   *when conditions (a) and (b) are met, when the operator is isolated from the fields of events other than C, and neither C nor E is present to begin with, then occurrences of C invariably start before the beginning of an occurrence of E.*

   (d)   *when conditions (a) and (b) are met, C implies E; that is, during some time interval occurrences of C are always accompanied by occurrences of E, though E may be present without C or both events may be absent.*

Condition (a) reflects the fact that highly structured circumstances must be present before there is a possibility of a particular causal relation existing. Condition (b) emphasizes that events must be coordinated with such circumstances before they can have effects. Together these conditions define the physical basis of causality. Causes are related to effects by specifiable structures with determinate locations in space and time.

Temporal directionality is defined in condition (c). Condition (d) states the requirement for logical implication from cause to effect. Contemporary methods of social research are elaborated largely with respect to the last two criteria. Temporal priorities are manipulated in formal experiments and complex statistical analyses are used to examine logical dependencies in situations confused by many processes.

CAUSAL INFERENCE

The preceding discussion has focused on specifying the meaning of causality, pointing out the conditions that characterize the kind of relationship between events that is called causal. Now the perspective is reversed. Definition I.1 gives the conditions that must be met in order for events to be causally related. Consequently these conditions can serve as criteria in deciding whether a causal relation exists between two kinds of event.

Causal inference begins with the assumption that any event might be a cause of any other event. We then proceed to eliminate relations that are impossible or implausible in particular circumstances. This eliminating approach is dictated by the premise that deterministic relations pervade the physical and social universe and that they may exist even though humans are unaware of them. If we were to construct our models of deterministic relations in terms of those that we know exist, the models might be seriously deficient; that is, they might ignore important processes and encourage spurious conclusions. Instead models are developed by eliminating the relations we are confident do *not* exist and retaining those that we are not sure about as well as those that are known to be operative.

I.2 *One event does not directly cause another if no effective operator is available to support the relationship.*

Sometimes it is possible to state with some confidence the kind of operator that would be needed to support a given causal relation and to conclude that no such operator is present; for example, on this basis we can conclude that the death rate in a technological society does not affect air pollution levels. This principle is used commonly in social research, often without explicit theoretical discussion, it being assumed that the lack of a particular operator is common knowledge. For this reason the major fallibility of the approach needs to be emphasized. This principle requires the conclusion that there is no operator at all for a given relationship, not simply that an obvious operator is missing. Thus we must always consider the possibility that different kinds of operator might support the relationship and discard these possibilities one by one, using all available knowledge on the topic.

Sometimes it can be concluded, with just one or two possible exceptions, that no operator exists for a given relationship. In such a case it may still be possible to achieve an interesting level of causal inference by elaborating the analysis so that it can be concluded that no *direct* relation exists between events of interest while allowing that there might be an *indirect* effect by way of other events; for example, suppose that we conclude that there are no operators that would permit normal variations in a company's productivity to affect the marital adjustment of a worker, except, perhaps, for psychological mechanisms involving morale. By including morale explicitly in the analysis we can conclude that changes in company productivity do not directly cause changes in a worker's marital adjustment, though they may cause changes in morale, which in turn may cause changes in adjustment. This statement is substantially stronger than saying merely that productivity may or may not affect a worker's marital adjustment. Increasing definiteness in this way is a common motivation for elaborating theories beyond a few events of central interest.

An operator for a given relationship may exist but may be disconnected or otherwise ineffective in a particular situation and can be treated as effectively absent; for example, a broadcast reporting a foreign invasion might cause panic at 6 P.M. when millions of radios and TV's are turned on but would not do so at 3 A.M. when most receivers are dormant. Similarly, a bureaucracy that ordinarily transforms certain inputs into corresponding outcomes may cease to operate if disorganized by a disaster. Thus special situations can sometimes be identified, or created, in which certain causal inferences are possible, even though the same inferences are not possible in more general circumstances.

I.3 *An event cannot cause another if the first event is not coordinated with existing operators.*

This principle is crucial in the design of classic experiments in which an operator is removed from the influence of all events but one in order that a particular causal relation may be studied. This may involve removing or immobilizing a required set of intervening operators to truncate an event's influence—the notion of insulation—or imposing a special operator that diverts or absorbs activity—the notion of shielding—or generating counterevents canceling those that are unwanted—the notion of homeostatic control.

Principle I.3. can also be employed in nonexperimental research to make circumstantial inferences about the absence of certain relations; for example, cultural developments in one community have no consequences in another if there is no social or material interaction between the two. Similarly, historical events do not influence individuals who are physically, socially, and communicationally removed from them (e.g., isolated prisoners, patients, and monks). Events have no certain consequences if the required operators are unavailable in a particular situation; for example, ghetto street crimes typically go unpunished unless a lawman is near purely by chance and in these circumstances criminal behavior does not cause legal sanctions. Surreptitious activities by intent do not stimulate certain operators and successful secrecy eliminates causal dependencies between events that otherwise might pertain. Moreover, people sometimes create entire settings (e.g., churches and offices) in which they are shielded from the influence of distracting events so that some ordinary determinancies may be presumed absent in these circumstances.

I.4 *An event is not caused by other events that occur after it.*

In experiments a particular event is generated to determine whether it influences subsequent events without having to wonder whether the other events could have caused the manipulation. In nonexperimental research events that have occurred earlier and whose influence remains constant (e.g., sexual or racial classification of individuals) are selected, whereupon the impact of these events can be assessed without worrying that later events may have influenced them. Indeed, such early events may be of considerable interest for analytic reasons, even if they are not especially interesting theoretically, because they can serve as instruments for dissecting complex patterns of reciprocal causation among other events (these techniques are discussed in Chapter 5).

Elimination of a causal relation in terms of temporal ordering is a matter of historical study in particular circumstances and does not preclude the possibility that causality may exist in other circumstances; for example, once a person has a college degree, no increase in wealth, motivation, or knowledge will cause the person to become a college graduate—it has already been done —but some combination of these factors may cause that outcome for another person with no degree. Similarly, in experiments it need not be claimed that the manipulated event is never caused by the experimental outcomes—only that the timing has been arranged so that this is not true in the particular circumstances.

Sometimes it may seem that the timing principle is violated in that later events determine earlier happenings; for example, because a person must have an education in order to become a physician, it may seem that the later state of being a physician causes the education. This, however, is a developmental relationship. Being a physician implies an education but does not cause it. At most, the education is caused by an aspiration to be a physician that exists before and during the educational process.

I.5 *If an event A occurs without subsequent occurrence of event B, then A does not cause B in the given circumstances.*

This principle of causal inference is based on the logical implication involved in causality. In strictly logical terms a single instance of A without B is enough evidence to conclude that A does not cause B. In fact, though, it is routine to move to a statistical perspective and discount a few instances of A-without-B if A *usually* implies B. One reason is that occurrences of events cannot always be observed without ambiguity. One event may mask another and a few instances of A-without-B may be due to observational errors. Another reason develops from the phrase "in the given circumstances" in statement I.5. If A occurs without B (and it is assumed heuristically that B was not masked), it means one of the following.

1. In the particular setting there is no operator for converting A to B.

2. Such an operator may exist but was not within the field of event A at the time of A's occurrence.

3. Such an operator existed within the field of A but was disassembled, unset, or otherwise inoperative at the time of the occurrence of A.

Generally, when we conclude that A does not cause B, we want to mean that (1) is true so that there is some generalizability to the conclusion, at least as long as the physical setting remains the same. However, if just (2) or (3) is true, then A may cause B in the same setting at another time. Therefore it cannot be concluded that A does not cause B, except at the particular time that the negative instance occurred.

Psychological learning experiments indicate that both animals and humans treat an occasional causal relation as being real enough to depend on. This psychological disposition is conservative in that it eliminates fewer causal relations than logic permits, and, as stated above, such a conservative bias is in the interest of generalizing beyond transient circumstances at the moment of observation. In effect, this tolerance for occasional failures of causality means that organisms in general take a statistical rather than a strictly logical orientation toward the implication relation in causality. Psychological learning experiments also show that humans (and other animals) are adept at discovering cues that signal when an operator is effective. Such discrimination corresponds to techniques of elaboration and specification in science by which we state the exact special conditions under which a causal relation holds and thereby refine statistical inferences in favor of stricter statements of determinism. Thus statistical orientation, combined with continuing efforts at defining the precise conditions for the existence of a causal relation, serves strategically as a funnel, bringing awareness and understanding of causal relations that are difficult to observe and even those that are in effect only on occasion.

The statistical perspective may seem to undermine a foundation stone of science—the critical observation in which absence of effect proves the absence of a relationship. Critical observations are valid only if we are focusing on a particular operator that is known to be in working order and properly coordinated with an event A. Only then does a single instance of A-without-B lead to the generalizable conclusion that the operator does not support the relation "A causes B." Thus a critical observation is a means of determining whether a *specified* operator supports a particular relationship and not whether a particular relationship is supported by some unspecified operator.

Much of the development in social science methodology has been devoted to creating sophisticated statistical techniques for discerning correspondence between events even when it is rare or when it is masked by occurrences of irrelevant events. Because of the conservativeness of the statistical approach (in terms of being able to reject relatively few hypothesized relations), special effort has gone into developing methods of identifying particular circumstances in which an apparent correlation between events disappears, thus indicating that events actually are not causally related at all. This technology is a major concern in this book, especially in Chapters 3, 4, and 5.

FLOWS

Analytic power in causal analysis can be gained by adding further assertions about the nature of reality and/or by analyzing only those parts of reality that meet certain restrictions. Several different lines of development are possible, and the one presented here has been chosen because the basic ideas are ubiquitous in contemporary social research, because the analytic principles have been elaborated extensively by applied mathematicians and statisticians, and because so many phenomena can be represented at least approximately within the perspective.

Henceforth we shall view events as homogeneous flows, subject to augmentation and diminishment. By this interpretation any event of interest is a composition of lower level events occurring repeatedly at a given rate as long as conditions remain the same. An operator producing a flow is a structure that repeatedly generates the same events and operates continuously (at least in aggregate) because of a constant influx of stimulating events. Not all events can actually be characterized in terms of flows, but the notion is adaptable, and even destructive or constructive events can often be characterized as flows within the framework of a larger structure—the rate of explosions on a battlefield or the rate of assemblies at a factory. Moreover, many social and cultural variables that seem purely categorical can be conceived in process terms amenable to a flow interpretation; for example, a person's sexual identity can be viewed processually as an ongoing presentation of certain kinds of cues in interaction. In this sense sexual identity is a lifelong flow of events, anchored in biology and augmented by early socialization.

The principles of causality apply to homogeneous flows; that is, if A and B are now conceived to be two different kinds of flow, then A causes B if A (i.e., a kind of ongoing process occurring at a given rate) implies B (i.e., a specified amount of the other kind of process), if the A flow was attained simultaneously with or before the B flow was established, and if the A flow is coordinated with an effective, analyzable operator generating B. Similarly the principles of causal inference apply. A is not the cause of B if there is no effective operator available, if A is uncoordinated with any such operator, if the level of the B process has been set before the A process begins, or if variations in the A process do not show up as variations in the B process even when other factors are controlled.

Analyses henceforth are limited to *homogeneous* flows; otherwise the above principles may not hold. A flow is homogeneous if it has the same effect regardless of how it is constituted. Thus, in dealing with homogeneous flows, we do not need to consider how a causal flow developed historically. We need to know only the value of the flow and the relations between the flow and subsequent operators in order to conduct causal analyses. It should be noted that what is a homogeneous flow in one analysis may not be in another; for example, the output of a distillery that sometimes waters its product is homogeneous with respect to shipments to distributors (the problems of transportation and storage are the same regardless of how the product is constituted). This flow, however, is not homogeneous over time with respect to the degree of intoxication produced among consumers.

Additivity

One way that the analysis of flows differs from ordinary causal analysis may be illuminated by considering an example in which A and B are two distinct causes of E. If A, B, and E were ordinary events, then the presence of A or B or both would imply the occurrence of E. In particular, the presence of both would produce the same E as either A or B alone. On the other hand, suppose that A, B, and E are flows. Now A or B alone implies E, but the presence of A and B together does *not* imply the same E. Rather, another flow, E', is implied. This new flow is an augmented version of E. With flows the operation of multiple causes produces cumulation of effects.

What is referred to as flow E really is a multitude of different flows, $E(1)$, $E(2)$, $E(3)$, and so on, ordered so that when two are implied simultaneously the result is another "higher level" flow from the same set. In particular, it is presumed that E has an indefinite number of flow levels, that the levels are ordered quantitatively, and, indeed, that these levels are associated with ordinary numbers in such a way that numerical algebra defines how values cumulate. Suppose, for example, that A produces a value of E that we identify as $E(2)$ and B produces a value called $E(3)$. Now it is presumed that the values of E have been defined so that when both A and B are present the $E(5)$ value is produced. The composite outcome is simply the sum of the separate effects. Thus we have an "addition rule" for causally analyzing the composition of flows.

Proportionality of Effect

A further complication develops when we remember that causes are also flows and that the values of a causal flow producing a given effect could be identified more precisely; for instance, a precise specification of the relations in the example cited above might be the following: $A(4)$ causes $E(2)$, $B(9)$ causes $E(3)$, and the effect of $A(4)$ and $B(9)$ together is defined by the addition rule $E(2) + E(3) = E(5)$. Now, for different values of A and B we would have to make additional statements about the relationships with E; for example, $A(2)$ causes $E(1)$, $B(6)$ causes $E(2)$, and so on. Obviously this could become unwieldy with a multitude of values for both A and B. What is needed is another simplifying principle comparable to the addition rule which allows the implication relations between all values of two flows to be stated economically.

Relations between the values of flows, from cause to effect, are described by using a multiplication rule that defines the value of an effect as proportional to the value of the cause; for instance, in the example above it was specified that $A(4)$ causes $E(2)$ and $A(2)$ causes $E(1)$. These specifications are now generalized and the relation between A and E is described for all values by the formulation "$A(i)$ causes $E(i/2)$" or simply $E = A/2$. Similarly, the specifications that $B(6)$ causes $E(2)$ and $B(9)$ causes $E(3)$ are generalized to $B(j)$ causes $E(j/3)$ or simply $E = B/3$. Thus the basic idea involved in the multiplication rule is that the value of an effect can be ascertained from the value of the cause by the following translation process. Identify the numerical value of the cause; multiply this value by a constant (like 1/2 or 1/3), and the result is the corresponding numerical value for the effect. The larger the value of a causal flow, the larger the value of the effect flow. Indeed, a strict proportionality exists between the two.

Actually, by including one minor complication the principle can be extended in usefulness. We allow that translation by multipliers alone may always be "off" by a certain amount. Hence we may have to add another constant number after carrying out the multiplication; for example, if we have relations like "$C(4)$ causes $E(2)$ and $C(8)$ causes $E(3)$," then the appropriate translating formula will be "$C(k)$ causes $E(1 + k/4)$ or $E = C/4 + 1$." In general, the formula for translating from the numerical value of a causal flow to the numerical value of an effect flow is $E = a + bC$, where **b** is the constant used as a multiplier and **a** is the number used to adjust results by a constant amount.

When more than one source is available for an effect, the addition rule and the proportionality principle together define outcomes. Again, though, it is allowed that the translation may always be "off" by a constant amount. Suppose, for example, that flow E is produced by both flow A and flow B. Then the complete equation for predicting the value of E, given information on the values of A and B, could be an equation like $E = 4 + A/2 + B/4$. If E had three sources instead of two, the formula could be the sum of a constant and three terms referring to flows. If there were four sources, it could be the sum of a constant and four other terms, and so on.

Negative Multipliers

Equations of the form $E = a + bC$ provide a flexible and general way of describing the effect of a flow C on another flow E. Indeed, such equations allow for possibilities that have not been considered, since either of the parameters in the equation (i.e., either **a** or **b**) could have a negative value. Actually, a minus sign attached to the adjustment constant **a** does not complicate matters much. It simply means that transformation of a causal flow into an effect flow must be adjusted by subtracting rather than adding a constant. However, a negative value for the multiplier constant **b** indicates a special kind of causal relationship between two flows. This is illustrated by the example in **1.4**.

1.4 Suppose that the causal relationship between two flows is described by the equation

$$E = 10 - \frac{C}{2}$$

In this case the adjustment constant is $(+10)$ and the multiplier constant is $(-\frac{1}{2})$. This equation specifies a special kind of relation between the flows as indicated by the following examples:

If C is	then E is
2	9
4	8
6	7
8	6
10	5

Thus the higher the level of C, the lower the level of E. Flow E is *inversely* related to flow C.

Negative multipliers represent inverse, or negative, relations. The higher the value of the causal flow, the lower the value of the effect flow.

A negative relation would seem to require that the causal flow interfere with or suppress the activity underlying the effect flow. Moreover, it would seem that negative relations can exist only when the effect flow has an ongoing base level of activity independent of the suppressor flow. Otherwise there is nothing to suppress. These notions do apply in certain instances of negative relations. Suppose, for example, that C is the population of foxes on an island and E is the population of rabbits (such quantities are flows because they represent the aggregated occurrences of fox and rabbit lives).

There is a negative relation here—the more foxes, the fewer rabbits, and it exists because foxes interfere with rabbit lives. In addition, the relation can exist only if the population of rabbits is maintained, by reproductive and subsistence processes, at a sufficiently high level. Were there not an adequate supply of rabbits, the foxes would eat them all, and the relation between foxes and rabbits on the island would cease to exist.

On the other hand, conceptualizations of flows sometimes can be elaborated to include negative as well as positive levels, in which case negative relations might exist without having the effect flow sustained by other factors. An important example arises when two mutually inhibiting flows are combined into a single flow—call it Z. When dominance by one component flow occurs, levels of Z are positive. When dominance by the other component flow occurs, levels of Z are negative. The attitude construct appears to be such a variable. Emotional reactions to a stimulus can involve feelings of pleasantness or feelings of unpleasantness, and these two kinds of response tend to be mutually inhibitory. An attitude is the net response—positive if pleasant feelings predominate, negative if unpleasant feelings predominate. Once such a bipolar flow is defined it is possible to define unconstrained negative relations: the higher the C flow, the lower the E flow, with the relationship continuing even into negative values of E.

It will be seen in later chapters that flows are frequently measured by arbitrary scales with a zero point placed at the average level found within a set of observations, a procedure that routinely gives negative values for some observed cases. This procedure, however, is simply an analytic convenience that eliminates adjustment constants from causal equations (see the discussion following **2.12**). The calculated zero is not necessarily a true zero that represents the absence of flow, and negative values are not necessarily true negatives that imply the inhibition of positive flow.

Terminology Conventions

At this point it is desirable to adjust terminology to correspond with other writings on causal analysis. Henceforth a specific type of flow will be called a variable unless we want to emphasize its composition from lower level events. An equation that describes the causal relation between two variables, for example, $E = a + bC$, is called a "structural equation." The adjustment constant **a** is simply the "constant." The multiplier **b** is a "coefficient" or "structural coefficient." The constant and coefficient together are "parameters" of the equation.

LINEARITY

Attention has now been directed to flows of events occurring continuously at a microscopic level. In addition, it has been required that a flow can be measured in such a way that values due to different causes cumulate additively and also that the values of a source relate proportionately to the values of an effect (after possibly making a constant additive correction). Together these restrictions of focus delimit a special realm for causal analysis—the analysis of *linear* relations. Indeed, linear causal relations involve simply this: that events can be assessed in terms of magnitudes, that effects due to different sources combine additively, and that levels of effect are proportional to levels of cause after allowing for a constant correction.

Focusing on linear relations, as we have done in this book, leaves many possible topics in causal analysis untouched because not all causal phenomena can be described in such restricted terms. The justifications for dealing just with linear relations are that they have been studied in depth, that powerful analytic methods are available for dealing with them, and that many systems of interest operate almost linearly as long as the operating conditions remain fairly stable. Moreover, focusing on linear relations allows many subtle and useful ideas in causal analysis to be developed at an introductory level.

A linear formulation of a causal relation permits a surprising and valuable translation from the language of interrelated states that we have used until now into a language of interrelated changes-in-states that will be useful in discussions to follow. The basic ideas involved in such a translation are illustrated in **1.5**.

1.5 Suppose that a linear causal relation from C to E is described by the equation:

$$E = \frac{C}{2}$$

This implies that the levels of E produced by levels of C are exactly half the numerical value of the corresponding C level; for example, $C(6)$ produces $E(3)$. The question now is, what would happen if we introduced a *change* in the level of C, say, of 4 units. Continuing the example, this would give a C level of $C(6 + 4) = C(10)$ and, using the above equation, we would obtain a new level of E as follows:

$$E = \tfrac{1}{2}(10) = 5$$

The new level of E is two units higher than the original; thus a four-unit change in C produced a two-unit change in E.

It might be thought that the amount of change in E depends on the initial values of C and E before introducing a change in C. This is not the case, however, in a linear relation, as illustrated in the table.

If C is	and E is	and C is increased 4 units to	then E becomes	which is a change of
2	1.0	6	3.0	2 units
3	1.5	7	3.5	2 units
4	2.0	8	4.0	2 units
5	2.5	9	4.5	2 units

In other words, a four-unit change in C always produces a two-unit change in E in a linear relation. Additional examples could be presented to show that a two-unit increase in C always produces a one-unit increase in E, a six-unit increase in C produces a three-unit increase in E, and so on. Moreover, if we decrease C by two units, E will decrease one unit, which can be interpreted by saying that a change of minus two units in C produces a change of minus one unit in E. Similarly a change of minus four in C gives a change of minus two in E; a change of minus six in C gives a change of minus three in E, and so on.

These examples illustrate the point that an equation that describes a linear causal relation between the levels of two flows also describes the relation between *changes* in the flows. To be precise, let Δ (delta) represent the numerical value of a change in levels. Then, from $E = C/2$, which related levels of C and E, we can surmise that

$$\Delta E = \frac{\Delta C}{2}$$

Suppose now that we have a flow F that is determined by a flow A and a flow B as follows:

$$F = \frac{A}{4} + \frac{B}{3}$$

Readers may wish to try various numerical values to illustrate that here, too, the formula that specifies relations between levels can be translated directly to a change formula; that is,

$$\Delta F = \Delta A/4 + \Delta B/3$$

The points illustrated in **1.5** can be stated as a general principle.

I.6 *If causal relations between flows are linear in form, the structural equations that describe the relations between the values of variables can be translated directly to a form that describes relations between changes-in-values. Coefficients are the same in both forms but the constant is deleted from the change equation.*

This principle is not generally applicable when the relations between flows are other than linear.

If we were given only a change-equation to begin with, we could not completely produce the structural equation because we would not know the value of the constant. On the other hand, the change-equation does provide information concerning the structural equation. The numerical values of all the coefficients are the same, and, more generally, if we know that a change in flow A causes a change in flow B, it is clear that the structural equation for B should include a term for A. This point is used frequently in translating verbal theories that express relations among changes into mathematical or graphical formulations that concern relations among states (see Chapter 2).

The translatability between state and change formulations of linear relations is especially valuable in verbal discourse because it is generally easier and more familiar to talk of changes causing changes rather than of states causing states. (Also, of course, the change perspective eliminates the need to be dealing continually with adjustment constants.) Once the causal relations of a system have been specified in change terms a structural formulation can be set up by using the procedures in Chapter 2 to provide a basis for identifying the numerical values of the coefficients (Chapter 5). Finally, once numerical values for coefficients are available, interpretations can be phrased again in terms of changes producing changes.

Interpreting Structural Coefficients

The multiplier coefficient in a linear structural equation like $E = a + b \cdot C$ is a quantity of critical importance. Indeed, the later chapters in this book are devoted mainly to various kinds of analysis involving such structural coefficients. Their significance lies in the way in which they can be interpreted theoretically from several different perspectives.

First, as shown in Chapter 5, it is possible to estimate the value of a structural coefficient from empirical observations on variables. If a structural coefficient is zero in value, this suggests that no effective operator relates two variables. Inferring the absence of causality when a coefficient is zero is the predominant way of implementing causal inference principle I.5.

Second, a structural coefficient provides evidence of the strength of an existing causal relation between variables. Suppose, for example, that two different operators support the relation C-causes-E and that $E = C/4$ describes the consequences of one, $E = C/2$, the other. The causal relation supported by the second operator is stronger because for a certain change in C it produces a larger change in E (e.g., if C changes four units, then E changes two units using the second operator but only one unit using the first). The difference in strength here is reflected in the structural coefficients: $\frac{1}{2}$ is larger than $\frac{1}{4}$. In general, if several different kinds of operator support the same causal relation, the strongest is associated with the largest structural coefficient (disregarding plus and minus signs). The strength of a relation is frequently a matter of concern in designing systems to accomplish certain objectives. Such information can also be valuable in determining how different outcomes can be produced by systems with the same pattern of relations but different components.

Third, the sign of a coefficient reveals whether the corresponding operator supports a positive relation between flows (increases causing increases) or a negative, inverted relation (increases causing decreases). Such information becomes interesting in dealing with interconnected operators in which a change introduced into one variable cascades through the network of relationships, sometimes causing increases in other variables and sometimes decreases. Techniques for tracing the consequences in such cases are provided in Chapter 2.

Finally, a structural coefficient always relates to some operator. The coefficient can be viewed as a highly succinct description of an operator, which emphasizes its consequences in relating flows rather than its internal structure and mechanisms. Occasionally it is discovered that operators supporting a relation between two flows can be systematically described in terms of some property whose magnitude corresponds to the structural coefficient for each; for example, rigid bodies are operators that transmute forces F applied to the body into accelerations A of the body; the mass of the body M identifies the proper coefficient according to an elementary law of physics: $A = (1/M)F$. Conceivably there are comparable laws in social science.

CAUSAL SYSTEMS

Especially in the social sciences, few phenomena of interest depend on just a single cause and effect. Social science phenomena usually involve many different kinds of event, determined by a number of different things, each affecting a number of other things. Networks of causal relationships, in which many different variables are linked with one another, are called systems.

The elaboration of causal relationships into systems, or networks of causation, makes causality difficult to study. At the same time it is a feature that makes causality more fascinating. The difficulties appear because complex data and analysis are needed to examine a causal relationship embedded in a network of other causal relationships. The added interest comes from the fact that causal networks produce a wide diversity of phenomena—oscillation, growth, decay, control, and amplification.

A cliché states that a system is more than the sum of its parts. This is misleading to the extent that it implies that a system defies comprehension and rational analysis, but it is correct in suggesting that the implications of systems of causal relations are far greater than we would suppose, looking at each causal relationship in isolation. To capture the complexity of real phenomena causal analysis necessarily has to be expanded into system analysis.

Multiple Causes

A given effect may be produced by any one of several causes. Such multiple causation introduces complications into analyses, especially when we are interested in inferring linear causal relations among variables. The basic problem is that an effect can be composed in many different ways when there are multiple causes. Thus it becomes difficult to determine the correspondence between an effect and another variable that might be a cause. The problem is illustrated in **1.6**.

1.6

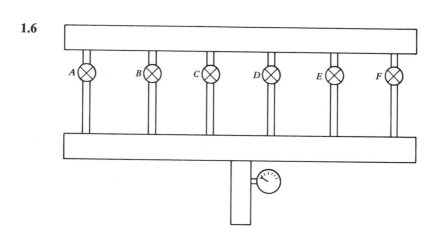

This system consists of six water taps coming off a high-pressure source. Each tap is fitted with a faucet of unknown capacity and all the taps flow together into a single outlet pipe. The output is measured by a meter reading pints-per-minute. Not represented in the figure is a scientist with control over faucet A and five monkeys who control faucets B, C, D, E, and F; the monkeys have been trained to get food by turning their respective faucets in either direction. The scientist at faucet A wants to determine its effect on the total outflow. The obvious thing to do is to turn his faucet on to see how much it will increase the flow. He does so, but at the same time Monkey B turns his faucet down, Monkey C turns his up a bit, Monkey D is sleeping, Monkey E lets his faucet run full force, and Monkey F turns his off all the way. The net effect is perhaps no change or even a decrease in flow. Certainly the scientist's faucet has a causal impact on the total flow. By turning on his faucet he has reason enough to expect an increase in flow. Yet because of all the other events it does not necessarily happen. The effect of a specific cause may be masked by the effects of other causes.

Multiple causation complicates causal analysis because it creates a situation in which the value of an effect is not determined solely by the cause of focal interest but by other causes as well. When trying to study the relation between a specific cause and effect, all the other causes act as disturbing factors that confound and frustrate analysis. To study the relationship of interest the disturbing factors somehow must be controlled. Three different strategies are available.

One approach, associated mainly with classical experimentation in the physical sciences, involves isolation of the relationship of interest. Any disturbance depends on a causal relationship, so disturbances occur because of the existence of some operator coordinated with some source event. Therefore, if the operator for a disturbance can be disconnected, made inoperative, or insulated from its stimulus events, this cause–effect relationship no longer exerts its influence. Moreover, if the causal relations for all disturbing factors are disrupted, the relation between the remaining cause and effect can be analyzed without worrying about disturbances. Use of this approach in the example in **1.6** would require removing the monkeys, welding their faucets closed, or sealing them off from the water source. Employment of this strategy is not always so simple as it may seem. It takes considerable skill and knowledge to disrupt every conceivable operator or to control all unwanted events. Indeed the strategy may be applicable only in problems in which a great deal of scientific knowledge already exists to guide experimental design.

A second method of dealing with the problem of disturbances is to establish a kind of passive control over the disturbing factors by observing them in detail to determine when one or another is creating an unwanted effect so that it can be discounted or otherwise adjusted. In its simplest form this would mean restricting analysis to periods in which disturbing factors are not creating disturbances. (Applied to the problem in **1.6**, this strategy would lead the scientist to test his faucet only when all the monkeys were asleep or otherwise distracted.)

Third, the problem of disturbing factors can be approached from a statistical perspective. It is accepted that any single observation is hopelessly confounded by disturbing factors, but if enough instances are observed in which the presumed source operates at certain levels it should be possible to determine whether the source has the proposed effect on the *average*. In averaging over many cases, the effects of the disturbing factors hopefully will cancel one another. Applied to the problem in **1.6**, this strategy would require the scientist to turn his own faucet on and off 200 or so times and to arrive at an average effect on the output. In taking an average, he would allow the chance happenings of one trial to cancel the chance happenings of another.

A key requirement here is that the disturbing factors must be unrelated to the causal event of interest. If this were not true—if one disturbing event always tended to occur with the causal event of interest—then the effect of that disturbance would not disappear with averaging. Furthermore, it is always necessary to obtain observations with the presumed cause both present and absent, or set at various levels, in order to ascertain whether the presumed source makes any difference.

The statistical averaging idea has been elaborated in two different directions. The most rigorous procedure (but frequently impractical in social situations) is the statistical experiment in which a lack of coordination between disturbing factors and the presumed cause of interest is guaranteed by randomly assigning cases for observation into two different sets and then providing the hypothesized causal event for just one of them. Then, because the presumed cause is uncoordinated with any of the possible disturbing factors, its effect can be assessed by finding the average magnitude of the outcome when the presumed cause is present and comparing it with the average magnitude when the presumed cause is absent.

In the second approach observations of disturbing factors are used to define groups of measurements in which each disturbance has a constant value. Then the value of the effect variable in each group is reset arithmetically to the magnitude it would have if disturbances had not been present, whereupon the relation of interest can be examined to see whether there is correspondence between the hypothesized cause and the adjusted effect indicating causality. In actual applications the adjustment approach really amounts to studying several causal relationships simultaneously. The procedure for adjusting for the impact of a second cause while studying a first requires making an adjustment for cause one in order to determine how much to adjust for cause two. At first, this sounds hopelessly circular and complex. In fact, procedures exist for making this separation, given numerous observations on all relevant variables (the principles are discussed in Chapters 3 and 5).

Multiple Effects

A causal variable may be a determinant of several different effects. One important consequence of such patterning is spurious correlation in which the effects tend to change up and down together because of their mutual dependence on the single cause. Spurious correlation may be viewed as a problem when we want to analyze the correspondence between variables. On the other hand, spurious correlations are the base of a systems phenomenon of intrinsic interest.

When a large number of similar effects are dependent on one or a few sources, a new higher level variable may be created. The value of the source influences the values of all the effects, thereby creating coordination in their magnitudes. Then, if the source begins a pattern of repeated change, it sets up a pattern of repeated and coordinated effects that may be identified in aggregate as another higher level flow. This new flow may serve as an element in causal analyses at another level of abstraction or it may be incorporated as a simplifying device into the original analysis; for example, the original source can be conceived as determining the composite flow while simply ignoring the individual effects.

Moreover, we may view the elementary effects as dependent on the higher level variable, which itself is seen as dependent on the source. This artificial conceptualization may suffice in some analyses if most of the elementary effects have parallel relations with other variables in the system of interest and if the composite value of a large number of elementary effects is almost independent of the unique value of any one of them. Such "causal approximations" are not uncommon in scientific and everyday thinking, and the notion often occurs in social science. When individual actions have the same causes, the concert of action can be identified as a distinct phenomenon, and this phenomenon may even "explain" the individual actions, if that is analytically useful.

Mutual Causation

Mutual causality exists whenever two variables are related to each other by two causal transformations—one in each direction. Such a double relationship is a feedback loop. In a feedback loop a change in A causes a change in B, and this change in turn is fed back to cause another change in A, which then causes another change in B, and so on. Thus the initial change in A causes a whole series of further changes in both A and B—an increment for each cycle—and because of the additivity principle the changes within each variable cumulate. Loops are the essential element in three important systems phenomena (see Chapter 6 on the dynamics of loops).

Amplification   If a change in *A* causes a similar change in *B* (e.g., an increase causes an increase) and a change in *B* causes a similar change in *A*, the arrangement amounts to an amplifying system that takes small changes and cumulatively builds them up into larger ones. The relation between sales and advertising provides a simple example. An increase in advertising produces more sales, more sales lead to more advertising, the extra advertising leads to still more sales, and so on.

Control   Suppose that a change in *A* causes a similar change in *B* but a change in *B* causes a reverse change in *A*. Then, if the value of *A* goes up, *B* goes up, but because *B* goes up *A* now goes down. *A* going down causes *B* to go down, but because *B* goes down *A* now goes up. This arrangement is at the core of many control mechanisms, including social control. The classic example in engineering is a thermostat. When the temperature in a room is too high, the source of heat is turned down or shut off; this allows the temperature to go down, and later the heat is turned up; this way the temperature in the room stays within a limited range—it is controlled. Social control mechanisms may operate in a similar way; for example, increases in a particular crime may lead to more vigilant law enforcement, which reduces the incidence of the crime, which reduces vigilence, so, theoretically the crime rate stays within a limited range.

Instability   If increments of change become larger and larger with each cycle through a feedback loop and continue to cumulate on each cycle, ultimately the values of the variables may reach levels so extreme that the operators supporting the processes will be endangered; for example, a microphone placed near a loudspeaker sets up an unstable loop and produces a howl of increasing volume that ultimately can ruin the components of the system. The relations between population and technology may constitute a social science example (assuming that, directly or indirectly, increases in population cause increases in technology and higher technology generates larger populations). At least in modern times both population and technology are increasing explosively, though we still do not seem to be convinced that the supporting social structures are endangered. These instances refer to unstable amplification in which changes on a variable continue unabatedly in a single direction until breakdown. Control loops also can be unstable. In this case the magnitudes of variables oscillate up and down, going to greater and greater extremes until disruption of one or both of the causal relationships occurs.

Not all loops are unstable. Indeed, our concern in later chapters is only with systems in which loops are stable.

SOURCES AND ADDITIONAL READINGS

Causality is one of the traditional concerns in the philosophy of science, and numerous philosophical essays are available on the topic. A recent and influential work is Mario Bunge, *Causality: The Place of the Causal Principle in Modern Science* (Cambridge, Mass.; Harvard University Press, 1959).

Among the writings on the epistemology of science are those that stress the essentially objective nature of science; for example, Karl R. Popper, *The Logic of Scientific Discovery* (New York: Harper & Row, 1968; first published 1934), and Carl G. Hempel, *Fundamentals of Concept Formation in Empirical Science* (Chicago: University of Chicago Press, 1952). Others stress the relativism and basic subjectivity of scientific knowledge such as Thomas S. Kuhn, *The Structure of Scientific Revolutions* (Chicago: University of Chicago Press; 2nd ed. enlarged, 1970), Norwood R. Hanson, *Patterns of Discovery: An Inquiry into the Conceptual Foundations of Science* (London: Cambridge University Press, 1958), and Roger Poole, *Towards Deep Subjectivity* (New York: Harper & Row, 1972). Some social scientists have recently shown an aroused interest in epistemology and the psychology of knowledge as reflected, for example, in Jean Piaget, *Psychology and Epistemology: Towards a Theory of Knowledge* (New York: Viking Press, 1971, translated by Arnold Rosin), Donald T. Campbell, "Natural Selection as an Epistemological Model," Chapter 3 in Raoul Naroll and R. Cohen, Eds., *A Handbook of Method in Cultural Anthropology* (Garden City, N.Y.: Doubleday—Natural History Press, 1970), Oswald Werner and Joann Fenton, "Method and Theory in Ethnoscience or Ethnoepistemology," Chapter 29 in Naroll and Cohen, *ibid.*, Edward E. Jones et al., *Attribution: Perceiving the Causes of Behavior* (Morristown, N.J.: General Learning Press, 1972), and Harold H. Kelley, "The Processes of Causal Attribution," *American Psychologist*, **28** (1973), 107–128.

Social scientists in particular have been concerned with methodologies for causal inference in situations in which classic experimentation is impossible. Two seminal works are Hubert M. Blalock, Jr., *Causal Inferences in Non-experimental Research* (Chapel Hill, N.C.: University of North Carolina Press, 1961), and Donald T. Campbell and Julian C. Stanley, *Experimental and Quasi-Experimental Designs for Research* (Chicago: Rand McNally, 1963).

The recent growth of a general theory of systems has greatly extended and vitalized causal analysis by injecting the notion of operators and emphasizing the analysis of networks of causality. Essays that sketch the general domain of systems analysis and some of its implications are provided by W. R. Ashby, *Introduction to Cybernetics* (New York: Wiley, 1963), and Ludwig von Bertalanffy, *General System Theory: Foundations, Development, Applications* (New York: George Braziller, 1968). A readable introduction to methods is available in Van Court Hare, Jr., *Systems Analysis: A Diagnostic Approach* (New York: Harcourt, Brace & World, 1967). Readings of interest to social scientists have been collected by Walter Buckley, Ed., *Modern Systems Research for the Behavioral Scientist: A Sourcebook* (Chicago: Aldine, 1968). His book, *Sociology and Modern Systems Theory* (Englewood Cliffs, N.J.: Prentice-Hall, 1967) focuses on implications of modern systems analysis for social theory.

The analysis of flows can be formalized largely within the framework of traditional mathematics, as illustrated in the rest of this book. However, a rigorous formal logic suitable for the analysis of operator structures has been developed only recently by mathematicians in the form of the algebra of categories. Categorial algebra provides a means of analyzing the structure of general systems: J. A. Goguen, "Mathematical Representation of Hierarchically Organized Systems," pp. 112–128 in E. O. Attinger, Ed., *Global Systems Dynamics* (New York: Wiley, 1970), and I. Băianu, "Organismic Supercategories and Qualitative Dynamics of Systems," *Bulletin of Mathematical Biophysics*, **33** (1971), 339–354. It has also been applied more specifically to social structures: Francois Lorrain and Harrison White, "Structural Equivalence of Individuals in Social Networks," *Journal of Mathematical Sociology*, **1** (1971), 49–80. The study of categories requires mathematical training, but a helpful introduction for those with the required background is Saunders MacLane and G. Birkhoff, *Algebra* (New York: Macmillan, 1967). MacLane's *Categories for the Working Mathematician* (New York: Springer-Verlag, 1971) provides a more advanced treatment.

Principles for constructing verbal theories have been a recurrent interest among social scientists. Some recent treatments of the topic are Arthur L. Stinchcombe, *Constructing Social Theories* (New York: Harcourt, Brace and World, 1968), Hubert M. Blalock, Jr., *Theory Construction: From Verbal to Mathematical Formulations* (Englewood Cliffs, N.J.: Prentice-Hall, 1969),

Jerald Hage, *Techniques and Problems of Theory Construction in Sociology* (New York: Wiley, 1972), and Abraham Kaplan, *The Conduct of Inquiry*, (San Francisco: Chandler, 1964). An example of theory construction for behavioral science within the systems perspective is provided by William T. Powers, *Behavior: The Control of Perception* (Chicago: Aldine, 1973).

EXERCISES

1. Suppose that nearly all heroin users in our society had experience with marihuana before they took the harder drug. Does it follow that marihuana usage causes heroin usage? (Which experience implies the other? Which precedes the other?)

2. A person's status may be conceived as the rate of privileged acts that that person emits or, alternatively, as the rate of deferring acts that the presence of that person evokes from others. Who is the status-producing operator in each of these conceptions? Illustrate how the different perspectives may lead to different tactics for increasing a person's status.

3. Intergenerational mobility is frequently studied by examining the education and occupational status of a father along with the education and occupational status of his son. What causal relations among these four variables can be eliminated by using the rules of causal inference?

4. Empirical studies of intergenerational mobility in modern America have indicated that the correspondence between fathers' occupational statuses and sons' occupational statuses is small for sons with the same amount of education. In other words, knowing that a father has a prestigious occupation does not allow us to predict much about the status of the son's occupation in relation to the occupations of other sons with the same education. How does this empirical information modify the model developed in exercise 3?

5. How could a nation's jet-fighter force be viewed as a flow? Is it reasonable to suppose that such a flow is linearly related to its sources? Suppose that the force is composed of both Swedish and American planes. Indicate some circumstances in which the force could be considered homogeneous and some in which it would have to be treated as nonhomogeneous.

6. If unemployment falls to about 5 percent, a government is likely to set policy as if there were no unemployment at all—as if the figure actually were zero. If unemployment drops below 5 percent, a government may even begin eliminating jobs, acting as if some sort of negative unemployment were present. Presumably, this is because 5 percent unemployment is the normative level and the norm defines the practical zero point for this variable. What is the difference between a normatively defined zero point and a true zero?

7.   Suppose that increasing persons' incomes makes them more proestablishment and increasing their educations makes them more antiestablishment. Suppose also that orientation toward the establishment can be measured as a single attitude variable with positive and negative values corresponding to pro and anti. Describe the probable stances of persons with the following kinds of status inconsistency: a high level of education but low income; a weak education combined with a lavish income. What is to be expected of a person with consistent statuses—that is, income corresponding appropriately to level of education? Is there any basic difference in the attitude of a poor illiterate person and a wealthy educated person?

8.   During a period of local economic boom Mr. and Mrs. Smith find that their material satisfactions and leisure time are far greater than they had ever hoped. One consequence is that they stop using contraceptives, try to reproduce, and even seek medical help for this purpose. As a result, Mrs. Smith has two births the following year. About five years later the Smith's burgeoning family is one contributing factor that forces the city school superintendent to increase the number of first-grade teachers.

   (a) Show how parallel events are occurring in all the city's families by using multiple chains of arrows like the following.

City's level of local commerce in year one → Smith surpluses in year 2 → Smith babies in year 3 → City's five-year-olds in year 8 → City's teachers in year 9

   (b) Use the "causal approximation" with the second and third variables in the chain (standards of living and birth rates) to obtain a simplified representation at the macrosociological level. What are the advantages and disadvantages of this representation?

9.   Describe the intervening processes by which a family's surpluses, or standard of living, might determine reproduction rate. In particular, consider what a family with unanticipated economic surpluses might do to increase births and what a family might do to suppress births when its living standards are less than desired. Assuming that all of these activities do constitute a single operator, how is it different from a physical operator like an automobile

that responds continuously to increased fuel with increased speed? In what sense is it similar?

10. Consider a biracial community with P persons of one race and R persons of another. The P's inherently control the town's real estate, commerce, and legislative council by which means they are able to suppress the size of R. The extent of P-power however, depends directly on the size of P, and consequently the suppression of R also depends on the size of P at a given time. Moreover, it happens that P's are frightened by R's to the extent that the mere presence of an R in a neighborhood terrorizes the P's. Indeed, each R taking up residence in the town typically causes several P's to move out entirely. Thus an increase in R's causes a proportional decrease in P's.

(a) Use arrows (as in exercise 8) to show the causal relations in this system. Use letters **c** and **d** to label the two arrows.

(b) Think of **c** and **d** as the structural coefficients for the two relations. What are the signs of these numbers? Do the two relations together constitute a control system?

(c) Suppose that the absolute values of **c** and **d** are greater than 1.0 and that a sudden migration produces a substantial increase in R. What will the ultimate consequence of the R migration be on the town's composition?

2 CAUSAL DIAGRAMS AND FLOWGRAPH ANALYSIS

Verbal statements of social theory have the advantage of being widely comprehensible. They have the disadvantage of being unwieldy for logical manipulations. Thus at some point it is desirable to develop mathematized formulations that will facilitate deduction of the nonintuitive implications of a theory. In addition, mathematical formulations are typically useful in confronting a theory with adequate reality tests using statistical procedures.

Social theorists are often more talented with words than with mathematics, and for such persons formulas may connote meaninglessness rather than a gain in logical power. In the hope of minimizing this kind of alienation from mathematics, the emphasis here is on constructing theoretical models based on a special kind of mathematical formulation—the flowgraph—which represents equations in iconic form. By following a few interpretive rules it is possible to obtain mathematical derivations merely by inspecting and redrawing such diagrams. Flowgraphs also provide a bridge between verbal theories and more abstract representations of theories in terms of equations.

DIAGRAMMING CAUSAL RELATIONSHIPS

The construction of a flowgraph to represent a theoretical model begins with the assignment of symbols to the variables to be considered.

II.1 *Each variable is represented in a diagram by a brief acronym or symbol.*

If socioeconomic status were a salient theoretical variable in the system being examined, the diagram could be started with the label *SES*, or perhaps just X. Brief labels have no mathematical significance. It is just that longer labels tend to obscure the graphic configuration as the diagram grows larger.

Conventionally, the letters V, W, X, Y, and Z (capitalized) are reserved for labeling variables. Sometimes the same letter is used repeatedly, distinguished by the use of subscripts (e.g., X_1, X_2). Subscripts may be avoided in small systems because they make things appear to be more technical than they really are, but when dealing with relations among many variables the use of subscripts actually simplifies notation.

When using abstract symbols, such as X, Y, and Z, it is desirable to reserve a part of the diagram as a glossary to show what each symbol signifies and to make the diagram interpretable without additional references.

The actual process of constructing a flowgraph involves focusing on one variable at a time and examining its causal relations with each of the other variables in the system. The diagramming process, outlined in the next steps, is applied only to *direct* causal relationships. A causal relationship is direct if a change in one variable leads to a change in another without necessarily changing a specified third in between; for example, if a theory states that X has an impact on Z, but only by first affecting variable Y, then the relation between X and Z is indirect, though direct causation from X to Y and Y to Z is indicated.

II.2 *A solid* (*preferably straight*) *line between the symbols for two variables indicates a direct causal connection. An arrowhead, pointing toward the influenced variable shows the direction of causality.*

2.1 $X \rightarrow Y$ means "X causes Y"

Generally it is desirable to show the cause on the left, or above, and the effect on the right, or below. This convention has no mathematical basis and it is not necessary to follow it rigidly. It does, however, assist in the orderly construction of a diagram and it enhances interpretability by positioning the system inputs toward the left or top of the diagram and the system outcomes toward the bottom or right.

II.3 *Each causal path is labeled with a unique identifying symbol.*

The path symbol carries two interpretations. First, it provides explicit recognition that an operator is needed to establish the particular cause–effect relationship and provides a means of specifying this operator in discussion.

Second, the symbol stands for the quantitative specifications of the operator—how it transforms change in one variable into change in another. As a quantitative specification the symbol could stand for a specification sheet (like that included with a high fidelity amplifier), a complex formula, or a single number. In merely diagramming a theory, no restriction exists on the complexity of the specification. In this text, however, we deal only with linear transformations that can be specified by a single number, in which case the path symbol represents the structural coefficient for that particular causal relationship.

As in labeling variables, there are conventions in symbolizing structural coefficients. Standard symbols are **a**, **c**, **d**, **e**, **f**, **g**, **p**, and **q** (**b** is reserved for other purposes). In systems that have many relationships the use of distinct letters becomes infeasible, and subscripts must be added. *A subscripted structural coefficient always receives two subscripts: the first is the symbol for the dependent or outcome variable in the relationship and the second is the symbol for the independent or source variable*; for example, if X causes Y and the letter **a** is the symbol for the structural coefficient, it is subscripted $\mathbf{a}_{YX}$. When the variables themselves are subscripted, only their subscripts define the structural coefficient; for example, if X_1 causes X_2 and the coefficient is symbolized **d**, then it is subscripted $\mathbf{d}_{21}$.

2.2 $X \xrightarrow{\ a\ } Y$ means X causes Y and **a** signifies the kind of operation that transforms change in X into change in Y. In this book it is assumed that the transformation is linear, in which case **a** is also the structural coefficient that describes the linear transformation.

$X \xrightarrow{\ a_{YX}\ } Y$ means the same as above, but here the structural coefficient is subscripted to identify it more specifically.

$Z_1 \xrightarrow{\ a_{21}\ } Z_2$ means Z_1 causes Z_2; once again $\mathbf{a}_{21}$ is the structural coefficient that describes how values of Z_1 transform into values of Z_2.

When the numerical value of a structural coefficient is unknown but its sign is known, the available information can be shown in the diagram glossary; for example, if a theory specifies a positive relation (increases in X cause increases in Y), the glossary would contain an entry like $\mathbf{a}_{YX}(+)$. If the theory specifies a negative relation, such as increases in Y produce decreases in Z, the entry would be $a_{ZY}(-)$. When the full quantitative value of a coefficient is known (e.g., $a_{YX} = .53$), we ordinarily enter this number directly on the appropriate flowgraph arrow instead of using a symbol.

COMPLEXITIES IN DIAGRAMS

The graphical representation of a system is built up piecemeal by taking the variables two at a time and applying the above principles over and over again, adding more variables and more arrows to the diagram, until all necessary aspects of the theoretical model have been considered. A flowgraph built up in this simplified fashion in the end represents the system as a whole. However, some possible points of confusion may develop as a flowgraph is constructed.

Branches

A system would be uninteresting if it consisted only of relations among separate pairs of variables with no relations connecting different pairs. Hence, in practice, some variables will be related not just to one other variable but to several others, and so a number of arrows must impinge on the same variable and/or branch from it. When several different arrows enter a variable, it means that the dependent variable has multiple causes. When several arrows emanate from the same variable, it means that the variable is a source with multiple consequences.

The drafting problem becomes more difficult when multiple causes and effects must be represented; for example, if X has two dependent variables, Y and Z, how should they be diagrammed? By convention, both should be to the right or below X, but should Y be above and to the left of Z or vice versa? It is typically not possible to decide until all the relations of Y and of Z have been examined; for instance, it may be found later that Z has a causal impact on Y, and, in this case, Z would be plotted above or to the left of Y, as shown in **2.3**.

2.3 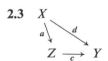   means X directly causes both Z and Y; in addition, Z directly causes Y.

We rarely are able to position all points conventionally and minimize curved lines and crossing arrows in a first drawing. Yet, because so much that comes later depends on visual inspection of the diagram, it is imperative to keep the diagram as transparent as possible. This usually means redrawing the diagram once or twice and positioning points so that the arrows seem to flow mainly from one side to another and crisscrossing and curved lines are absent or at least minimal.

Loops

A causal loop exists whenever some variable is not just passively dependent on its causes, but, in turn, it influences one or more of its own determinants. If a pair of variables forms a loop, the variables are connected by two arrows pointing in opposite directions, each labeled with a different symbol. Causal loops defy diagramming in the conventional up-down, left-right fashion. No matter what adjustments are made, an arrow points in an upward or a leftward direction.

Sometimes feedback loops are indirect and may not even be explicitly cited in a verbal theory, though they are implicit in the statement of other relations. The first inkling of a loop may appear when the arrows in a completed diagram display the unconventional directionality. The third example in **2.4** illustrates the kind of situation in which this could occur.

2.4   EXAMPLES OF FEEDBACK LOOPS

$X \xrightleftharpoons[c]{a} Y$ means that X causes Y and Y causes X

An indirect feedback loop. Y is dependent on X, Z is dependent on Y, and X is dependent on Z.

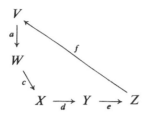

An indirect loop that might go unnoticed in verbal theory becomes evident when the diagram is drawn.

Self-Loops

A variable may be involved in a feedback loop even though additional variables in the loop are unspecified. The diagramming convention is a circular arrow that leaves and enters the same variable. The direction of the arrow is immaterial.

2.5 Self-loop. The three representations are equivalent.

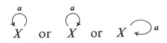

The symbol **a** stands for the operation or set of operations that converts an initial change in X into an additional subsequent change in X.

Missing Arrows

The fact that mutual causality between two variables is represented by a pair of arrows, whereas one-way causation is represented by a single arrow, highlights an important feature of flowgraphs. *The absence of an arrow conveys a definite piece of information: one conceivable causal effect is not present in the system;* for example, the lack of an arrow from variable Y to variable X in a diagram indicates that Y has *no* direct causal effect on X, and a change in Y either has no impact at all on X or at most an indirect effect moderated by changes in other specified variables. Absence of causal operators, a crucial feature of a system, gives it structure and character. As much consideration should be concentrated on the idea of not drawing an arrow between two variables as on the idea of drawing one.

A diagram with fewer arrows is generally more interesting than one with causal links connecting nearly everything in both directions. The sparer theoretical structure has the edge in parsimony, and it is usually easier to evaluate a parsimonius theory with empirical research. Indeed, a structure in which all variables are linked in both directions provides little basis for deriving any tests at all. Nevertheless, simplicity gained by assuming that causal effects are absent when they really may be present has worse repercussions. An oversimplified theoretical structure can lead to false inferences and erroneous interpretations of research findings. Hence the following rule:

II.4 *An arrow should be included rather than left out whenever there is reason to doubt the absence of a causal effect.*

Any flowgraph, including a diagrammatic translation of an existing verbal theory, cannot be considered really complete until the plausilibity of each missing arrow has been studied. A conceivable arrow between two variables should be left out only when a definite plausible argument can be made to justify the assumption of no effect. *Such arguments depend on the principles of causal inference stated in Chapter 1.*

The systematic consideration of every missing relationship can easily become confusing in large systems. It may help to make up a relational table with all variables listed in rows and columns. The cells of the table represent all possible causal relations in the system, and working with the individual cells provides a systematic routine that guarantees separate consideration of every possible pair relation.

Disturbances

Most social theories are qualified with phrases like "generally," "usually," "on the average," "other things equal," and "partial explanation." The reason is that a natural social system rarely operates in isolation. Social systems operate within the environment of other systems, and the various systems barrage one another with disturbances. These disturbances typically have no overall pattern. Sometimes they force a variable to change in one direction, sometimes in another; sometimes they effect a large change, sometimes a small one. In diagramming, the disturbances are considered in terms of their net effect on the variable of interest; that is, they are treated in aggregate as if they were a single outside source variable with an unknown value.

II.5 *Disturbances in a variable are represented by a distinct symbol near the affected variable, with an arrow leading from the disturbance symbol to the variable symbol.*

2.6 DIAGRAMMING EXTERNAL DISTURBANCES

U_Y

$\downarrow$ means that X influences Y but Y also is determined by other unspecified factors, represented jointly as U_Y.

$X \xrightarrow{a} Y$

Most social system variables are subject to disturbances. Disturbance terms, however, are not provided for the system inputs because the values of these variables are affected by nothing within the system. They are entirely a function of outside forces, and it would be redundant to represent an outside source for them in the diagram.

Disturbance terms ordinarily are symbolized by a subscripted U. The subscript refers to the variable affected by the particular disturbance, as in the example in **2.6**, in which the disturbance term for variable Y is symbolized by U_Y.

Two alternative conventions are available for labeling the arrow from the disturbance to the dependent variable. On the one hand, the hypothetical disturbance factor can be viewed as having intrinsic characteristics of its own—a value measurable on some special scale. Then it is comparable to other source variables in the system, and the arrow must be labeled to indicate how change in the disturbance "variable" is transformed to change in the dependent variable. The arrow is labeled with a letter, such as **a, c, p, q**, subscripted first with the symbol for the dependent variable and second with the letter U to indicate that a disturbance factor is involved; for example, the arrow from U to Y could be labeled $\mathbf{a}_{YU}$.

Alternatively, a disturbance factor can be defined on the same scale as the variable it affects, in which case a change in the disturbance "variable" is always the same as its effect on the dependent variable. If all sources of disturbance cause a dependent variable to change by one unit, the change in the hypothetical disturbance term is presumed to have been one unit. Here it is not necessary to label the disturbance arrow at all because it always represents the same transformation: the dependent variable is changed by the same amount as the disturbance. *This is an identity transformation involving a structural coefficient of 1.0, and by convention the lack of a label on an arrow signifies it.* Because it eliminates extra symbols, this second convention is employed here until some positive gains are to be achieved with the alternate convention.

Although disturbances probably affect almost all social variables, symbols for disturbances are not included in all flowgraphs in this book. The deletions are for the sake of simplicity in analyses and discussions. When, however, the presence of disturbances influences general conclusions, the disturbances are represented explicitly on the relevant diagram.

Nonlinear Relations

The assumption of linear relations was implicit in the procedures described for diagramming. In particular, it has been assumed that the operation signified by an arrow in no way depends on the value of the source variable or any other variable in the system. Examples can be given in which this is not the case: entertainment expenditure may be determined as a constant proportion of income but only after income has passed a certain point so that basic subsistence needs are covered.

A special diagramming convention is available to signal a situation in which a transformation takes effect only above a certain value of the source variable. The usual arrow is drawn and labeled with the symbol for the transformation; but to indicate the limitation the arrow is crossed with a short perpendicular, which in turn is labeled to show at what value of the source variable the causal operation takes effect; for instance, the diagram

---

2.7   Example of a limiter.

$$X \ \xrightarrow[\ 5\ ]{\ a\ } \ Y$$

---

in **2.7** is read as follows: X determines Y via the transformation **a**. However, the transformation takes effect only when X has a value of 5 or more. By convention, it is understood that if X is less than 5 changes in X have no effect on Y.

Complex patterns of transformation can be represented by using combinations of limiters. The possibilities are not explored here but they are covered in references listed at the end of this chapter.

Limiters in a diagram indicate nonlinearity and preclude the use of the simple and elegant methods of graph analysis discussed in this book. A single limiter, however, can be eliminated easily by elaborating a diagram into two others—one applicable below the limit value, the other above it, as illustrated in **2.8**.

2.8

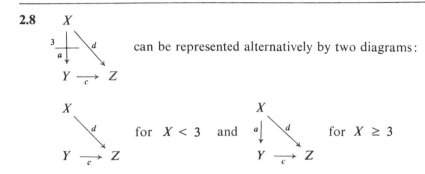

can be represented alternatively by two diagrams:

for $X < 3$ and for $X \geq 3$

Sometimes the form of a relation between two variables depends on the value of some other variable in the system; for example, both income and education probably are determinants of the consumption of "high culture" (books, classical records, theater attendance, and so on); but the strength of this relation probably increases with the level of education. Thus income and education *interact* in their determination of high-culture consumption.

Another diagramming convention is available to represent such interactions. Arrows from the interacting variables are drawn to terminate at a circle that is labeled externally with the symbol for the dependent variable and internally with a symbol (usually **f** or **g**) that stands for the special transformation for converting values of the source variables into a value for the dependent variable.

2.9   An example showing graphical representation of an interaction.

where **f** stands for the expression $Z = X \cdot Y$.

Interactions are closely related to limiters, and interactions, like limiters, preclude straightforward flowgraph analyses. Sometimes, as with limiters, a diagram can be elaborated into several restricted diagrams in which the interaction effect is eliminated or minimized; for example, the diagram in **2.9** could be elaborated into two different ones to correspond to, say, high and low values of Y. Alternatively, it may be possible to treat one of the variables as a parameter that must be set for each entity before analysis. The example in **2.9** is represented this way in **2.10**.

2.10   An alternative method of diagramming the multiplicative interaction in **2.9**.

$$X \xrightarrow{\ Y\ } Z$$

Sometimes interactions can be eliminated from a diagram by changing the scales on which variables are measured. The relation in **2.9** would become conventional if X, Y, and Z were measured in terms of the logarithms of their original scale values because multiplicative relations become additive in logarithmic transformation. Other more general techniques for dealing with interactions in flowgraphs require a higher level of mathematics than we use in this book, and the interested reader must consult the chapter references.

FLOWGRAPH ANALYSIS

Linear flowgraphs can be "read" to define the net effect from one variable to another even when the variables are connected indirectly and complex connections involve multiple chains of causation and intervening feedback loops. These analyses allow us to trace the reverberations of inputs; they indicate the kinds of diversity that will exist among cases affected by the system; they suggest how system variables will be correlated in empirical data and give a basis for further causal inference; and they provide insights into how a system would have to be modified to change its outcomes.

   The principles outlined in this chapter apply only to linear systems of certain kinds. First, the rules apply to systems in which the causal relationships are *stationary* over time. A change in X leads to the expectation of a certain amount of change in Y, no matter when the X change occurs. Second, the focus in this chapter is on the terminal effects of an input change, not on the intermediate dynamics by which variables reach their final state. On the one hand, this means that concern is limited to *stable* systems that achieve steady states, excluding those whose very nature leads to endless oscillations or infinite growth. On the other hand, the assumption requires that the values of all variables have stabilized at unchanging or *static* values at the time of observation. (System dynamics is taken up briefly in Chapter 6.)

In addition, it might be emphasized that the restriction to linear relations implicitly requires measurements of variables on interval scales so that the additivity and proportionality principles hold. Actually what is required is a reasonable approximation to interval measurement, not perfection; for example, a mass-produced ruler is not a perfect interval scale, but it is an adequate approximation for the study of many everyday objects. Measurement technology in the social sciences is sufficiently advanced to provide reasonable approximations to interval measurement for the analysis of many causal systems.

Equation Formation

A flowgraph, in conjunction with a few rules, allows us to express the values of a dependent variable in terms of the values of its source variables.

II.6 *The value of a variable determined by only a single source is the value of the source times the structural coefficient.*

2.11 $X \xrightarrow{a} Y$ implies $Y = a \cdot X$

The equation in **2.11** may seem incomplete because even simple equations usually contain some constant correction factor; for example, $Y = a \cdot X + 5$. Here constants are not written as part of the expressions derived from a flowgraph, which means implicitly that every variable has to be measured on a scale adjusted so that the constants do not appear.

If desired, correction constants could be retained in graph analysis by modifying the diagrams slightly as shown in **2.12** (writing the equation requires the application of rule II.7).

2.12

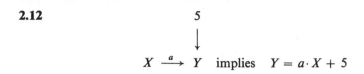

$$X \xrightarrow{a} Y \quad \text{implies} \quad Y = a \cdot X + 5$$

A constant should not be confused with a disturbance term. The constant is a special kind of source that remains the same, no matter what, whereas a disturbance is a special kind of source that symbolizes variable forces impinging from outside.

Obviously the inclusion of a constant complicates diagrams, and it is easy to show that this is unnecessary when dealing with linear systems. Taking the example in **2.12**, we create a new measurement Y' by subtracting 5 from every original measurement of Y; that is,

$$Y' = Y - 5$$

which means that

$$Y = Y' + 5$$

Now, substituting this into the equation in **2.12** gives

$$Y' + 5 = a \cdot X + 5$$

or

$$Y' = a \cdot X$$

So a slightly revised way of measuring Y produces an equation without the constant, and this simpler equation has a simpler graph, like that in **2.11**.

II.7 *The value of a variable determined by two or more sources is the sum of the source values, each multiplied by its respective structural coefficient. The order of the summation does not matter.*

2.13 X
$$\begin{array}{l} Z = a \cdot X + c \cdot Y \\ \text{implies} \quad \text{or} \\ Z = c \cdot Y + a \cdot X \end{array}$$

The summation rule applies no matter how many sources. However, it applies only to direct sources; for example, in **2.13** variables that indirectly affect Z by, say, influencing Y first are not entered into the summation. Such indirect effects are analyzed by the rules that follow.

Because most social science diagrams include a disturbance term as one of the sources for any dependent variable, it is worth considering an example to determine how the summation rule applies.

2.14 U_Y $Y = a \cdot X + 1 \cdot U_Y = a \cdot X + U_Y$

             $\downarrow$ implies   or

$X \xrightarrow{a} Y$ $Y = U_Y + a \cdot X$

Thus the summation rule applies to a disturbance term just like any other source. Moreover, as indicated in **2.12**, the summation rule would apply if one of the sources were a constant.

Structural-Equation Representations

The preceding rules allow us to write out the structural equations of a theory; that is, these rules define how verbal statements of theory are converted to a flowgraph formulation and how the flowgraph defines mathematical equations. Structural-equation formulations are particularly important in more advanced treatments of complex systems.

The structural equation for each dependent variable in a system is obtained with rule II.7, once the flowgraph has been drawn. Paths branching away from a variable are ignored in writing the equation for that variable, but every incoming arrow signals a term that must be included. A variable in a feedback loop is treated like any other variable: its equation includes a term for each of its immediate sources, whether or not the source is another loop variable. Because most dependent variables are affected by disturbances, most equations also include a disturbance term.

In order to examine a moderately elaborate example of the procedure, consider the system represented in the first flowgraph in **2.43** (ahead). There are three dependent variables—that is, three variables with arrows coming into them. Thus the mathematical formulation has three equations:

$$X = aW + eY + cZ + U_X$$
$$Y = dZ + U_Y$$
$$Z = fX + U_Z$$

This set of simultaneous equations is the static structural-equation model of the system represented in the flowgraph.

In more advanced literature dependent variables (X, Y, Z in the preceding example) frequently are called *endogenous* variables. The variables whose values are set by forces outside the system (only W in this example) are called *exogenous* variables. This book uses the term *inputs* instead of "exogenous variables."

Reduction Rules

II.8   *When one variable determines a second and the second determines a third, the value of the third variable can be expressed as the value of the first variable times the product of the structural coefficients along the chain. The same principle applies when the chain has more than two links.*

2.15 $X \xrightarrow{a} Y \xrightarrow{c} Z$ implies $Z = a \cdot c \cdot X$

This "chain rule" defines indirect effects of a source by eliminating consideration of the variables that intervene between the source and an outcome of interest.

The expression obtained from applying the chain rule in **2.15** could be rewritten as $Z = (a \cdot c)X$ and this expression would correspond to the diagram $X \xrightarrow{a \cdot c} Z$. In fact, as far as the variables X and Z are concerned, this new diagram would be completely equivalent to the original and, the chain rule defines a means for reducing a graph to a simpler form:

2.16 $X \xrightarrow{a} Y \xrightarrow{c} Z$ reduces to $X \xrightarrow{a \cdot c} Z$

This principle also holds no matter how many links there are in the chain.

II.9   *To express the value of a dependent variable in terms of multiple direct and indirect sources the separate effects along each chain are obtained first by rule II.6 or rule II.8. The summation of all effects is then obtained by rule II.7.*

2.17

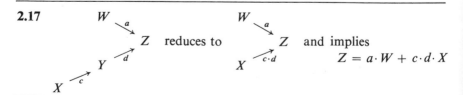

A special case of major importance occurs when several indirect sources operate through the same intervening variable. The chain from each source is defined in isolation, as if the other sources were absent.

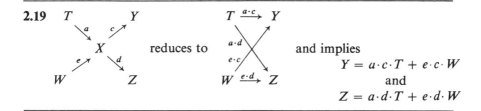

2.18 W

$\qquad Y \xrightarrow{d} Z$ reduces to W Z and implies

X X $Z = a \cdot d \cdot W + c \cdot d \cdot X$

The rule also applies when there are several outcome variables rather than just one. We simply apply the rule repeatedly to obtain a different expression for each outcome.

2.19 $T \qquad Y$ $T \xrightarrow{a \cdot c} Y$

X reduces to   and implies

$W \qquad Z$ $W \xrightarrow{e \cdot d} Z$ $Y = a \cdot c \cdot T + e \cdot c \cdot W$
                                                                                 and
                                                                                 $Z = a \cdot d \cdot T + e \cdot d \cdot W$

Another case of special interest develops when an intervening variable in a chain is affected by disturbances. The disturbance term is treated as another source and rule II.9 is applied.

2.20 U_Y U_Y

                 reduces to   and implies

$X \xrightarrow{a} Y \xrightarrow{c} Z$ $X \xrightarrow{a \cdot c} Z$ $Z = a \cdot c \cdot X + c \cdot U_Y$

It constitutes only a minor elaboration to include a disturbance term for Z as well.

2.21 $U_Y \qquad U_Z$ $U_Y \qquad U_Z$

                 reduces to   and implies

$X \xrightarrow{a} Y \xrightarrow{c} Z$ $X \xrightarrow{a \cdot c} Z$ $Z = a \cdot c \cdot X$
                                                                                 $+ c \cdot U_Y + U_Z$

II.10 *If a source and a dependent variable are linked by multiple paths, the total effect between the two is the sum of the effects along each separate path. The path effects are obtained by rules II.6 and II.8. The order of summation does not matter.*

2.22

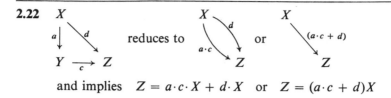

and implies $Z = a \cdot c \cdot X + d \cdot X$ or $Z = (a \cdot c + d)X$

2.23

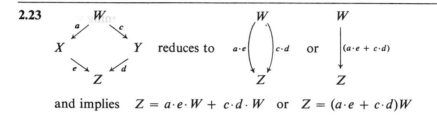

and implies $Z = a \cdot e \cdot W + c \cdot d \cdot W$ or $Z = (a \cdot e + c \cdot d)W$

A question may be asked about the procedure when the intervening variables have additional sources. We first partition the effects due to different sources, using rule II.9, then apply rule II.10.

2.24

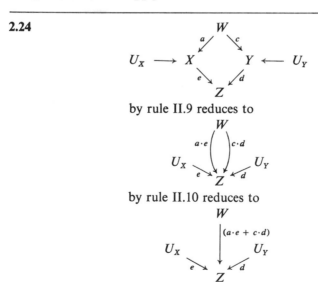

by rule II.9 reduces to

by rule II.10 reduces to

The expression defining the value of Z could now be obtained by using rule II.7.

Additional Interpretations of the Rules

Some of the rules stated above have more interesting implications than may be evident at first glance; for example, the chain rule (II.8) implies that if all the coefficients along a chain have positive signs an increase in the source will lead to an increase in the final variable and a decrease in the source will lead to a decrease in the final variable. On the other hand, a single negative sign anywhere along the chain will cause the directionality of change to be reversed from source to outcome. In general, if there are no negative coefficients or an even number of negative coefficients along a path, changes in the source will lead to changes in the dependent variable *without* reversal. If an odd number of negative coefficients occurs along a path, changes in the source will lead to changes in the final dependent variable *with* reversal of direction.

The absolute numerical values of structural coefficients in social systems are often fractions (i.e., their absolute values are less than one and greater than zero), when all variables are measured on comparable scales. Fractions multiplied together produce more fractions with still smaller values than the original terms. Thus a chain effect tends to be less in magnitude than any of the direct effects along the chain. The longer the chain, the smaller the net effect because the product of fractions becomes smaller as more of them are multiplied. This implies that long chains of causation may be of little practical significance in analyzing social systems, and theories that account for some end effect in terms of a long sequence of preceding linkages may be explaining only a minute portion of the total variations in an outcome.

Rule II.10 shows that effects from one variable to another cumulate over all the paths that connect the two variables. A situation of special interest is one in which one of the multiple paths is direct and involves a single arrow from the source to the dependent variable; the other paths (or path) are indirect and involve chains through several other variables in the system, in which case the source has an immediate effect through the direct path and an indirect effect through the other paths. The magnitudes of these two kinds of effect could be compared. If we were to manipulate the source to achieve a particular effect in the dependent variable, we would have to allow for the indirect as well as the direct effects.

Flowgraphs with Loops

II.11 *A chain of arrows that leaves, and ultimately returns, to the same variable is a "loop", provided that no reversals of direction occur along the path and that the path impinges on no variable more than once, except for the variable used as a starting point, which is impinged on just twice.*

Some typical examples of loops are given in **2.25**. Note that a source variable, not involved in the loop, is always represented. A source is necessary to enter the loop subsystem, and a loop without at least one source would be unrealistic. Note also that loops may be "hidden" in the context of a larger diagram, as illustrated in the lower half of **2.25**.

2.25

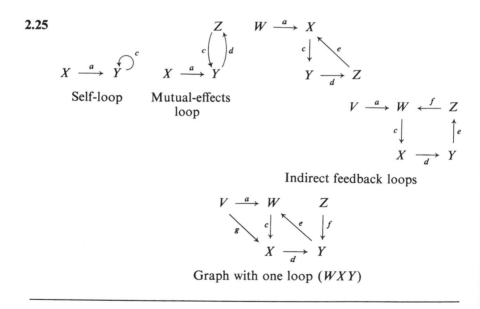

Self-loop   Mutual-effects
                        loop

Indirect feedback loops

Graph with one loop (*WXY*)

The convention used here to identify loops is to simply list sequentially the variables through which the loop passes. The starting variable is not listed twice, though it should be understood that it also is the end variable. These identifications are *not* unique because any variable along the loop may be used as a starting point. Thus in the lower example in **2.25** any of the following identifiers refer to the loop: (*WXY*), (*XYW*), (*YWX*).

The convention of drawing arrows downward or to the right helps to find loops; for example, notice how arrow e signals the loop in the lower figure of **2.25**. It is sometimes inconvenient, however, to follow the convention rigidly in drawing diagrams; arrows pointing in the "wrong" direction at best serve as clues.

The chain (VWX) in **2.25** is *not* a loop because arrow g reverses the direction of the path. Notice also that a chain like $(WXYW)$ should *not* be viewed as a loop because the path impinges more than once on W, and, presuming that it ends at X, this chain therefore would touch two variables twice.

Many systems contain multiple loops:

2.26 System with three loops: (XY), (XYZ), (Z)

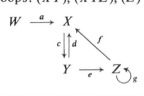

This system illustrates a nest of loops—that is, multiple loops whose paths partly overlap. *A loop in a nest should be identified as separate if there is so much as a single arrow distinguishing that loop from others*; **2.27** is another example of multiple loops:

2.27 System with two loops: $(WXYZ)$, (WYZ)

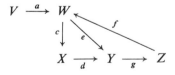

In this example there are two loops but there is only one wrong-direction arrow. This again emphasizes that the directionality principle is only an aid to finding loops. In particular, the "wrong-direction" principle may fail to signal the existence of a nest of loops that uses the same return path.

Loops that are merely adjacent do not create nests:

2.28   System with two loops: (XY), (YZ)

$$W \xrightarrow{a} X \underset{e}{\overset{c}{\rightleftarrows}} Y \underset{f}{\overset{d}{\rightleftarrows}} Z$$

The path $(XYZ\,Y)$ is not a loop because it impinges twice on the intervening variable Y.

Finding all distinct loops is a crucial step in analyzing systems with feedback and, because there is no simple routine guaranteeing loop discovery, the ability has to be cultivated as a skill.

II.12   *The "return effect" of a loop, symbolized L, is equal to the product of the coefficients along the loop chain.*

The diagrams in the top half of **2.25** are reproduced in **2.29** to provide some examples. The sets of symbols that have served as loop identifiers are now used as subscripts to identify a particular return effect:

2.29

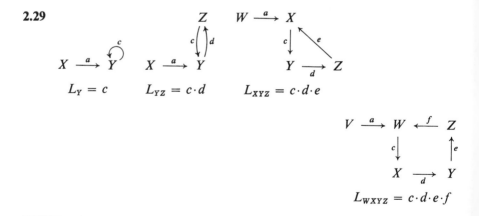

$$L_Y = c \qquad L_{YZ} = c \cdot d \qquad L_{XYZ} = c \cdot d \cdot e$$

$$L_{WXYZ} = c \cdot d \cdot e \cdot f$$

The choice of starting point does not matter; for example, in the third diagram, $L_{XYZ} = c \cdot d \cdot e = L_{ZXY} = e \cdot c \cdot d$.

The following graph offers a more complex example:

2.30 $V \xrightarrow{a} W$

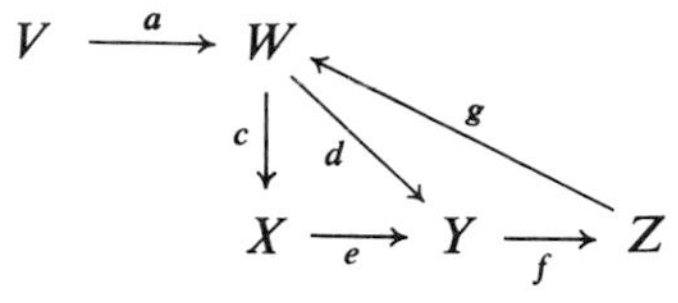

$L_{WXYZ} = c \cdot e \cdot f \cdot g$

$L_{WYZ} = d \cdot f \cdot g$

(with arrows labeled c, d, g from W; $X \xrightarrow{e} Y \xrightarrow{f} Z$)

The return effect has a meaningful interpretation. It indicates how much a variable in a loop will change after just one cycle around the loop, following an initial one-unit change. Consider, for example, the case in **2.31**.

2.31

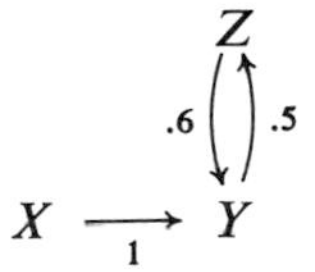

Z

$.6 \big(\big) .5$

$L_{YZ} = (.5)(.6) = .3$

$X \xrightarrow{1} Y$

Assume that X is manipulated to create an initial change of one unit in Y. This causes a change of .5 units in Z. The change in Z causes another change in Y: $(.5) \cdot (.6) = .3$ units. So after one cycle Y is incremented by the value of the return effect. Of course, this .3 unit change would move around the loop, causing still another increment in Y (.09 units), and it in turn would move around the loop, and so on, but the return effect—the increment occurring one cycle after an initial one-unit change—is a most important quantity. It is sufficient information to calculate the net effect of all the cycles following the initial change (using rule II.16 ahead).

II.13 *A chain of arrows is an "open path," provided that no reversals of direction occur along the path and that the path impinges on no variable more than once.*

A simple example of an open path is provided in **2.16**.

Open paths contrast with loops, which are "closed paths" with no real beginning or end. (Choosing a loop "starting point" is arbitrary and only a convention for identifying the loop; any variable on a loop serves equally well as a starting point.)

The notation that identifies open paths is similar to that used for loop identification; for example, (XYZ) refers to an open path starting at X, moving to Y, and terminating at Z. Of course, the chain does not return to the starting point in an open path. Also, the sequence of symbols is unique; (XYZ) is not the same as (YZX). Loop identifiers and open path identifiers are always employed as subscripts on different symbols and in practice there is little chance of confusing the two.

Open paths are basically familiar, inasmuch as rules II.6—II.10 deal exclusively with them; for example, the diagram in **2.22** shows two open paths between X and Z: (XZ) and (XYZ). They are of more general interest, however, because they can be identified across loops or within loops, as shown in **2.32**.

2.32   This system has one open path between W and Z: $(WXYZ)$. There are two open paths between Y and Z: (YZ) and (ZXY).

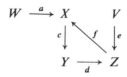

A pair of variables may be linked by no open paths at all (e.g., X and V in **2.32**), by just one open path (e.g., W and Z), or by several open paths (e.g., Y and Z). The open paths connecting Y and Z in **2.32** are opposite in directionality; this is characteristic of open paths that connect variables in the same loop.

II.14   *An "open path effect," symbolized E, is equal to the product of the coefficients along an open path chain.*

Some examples of open path effects are given in **2.33**. The sets of symbols used to identify open paths serve as subscripts to identify the open path effects.

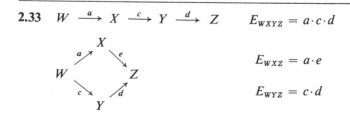

2.33 $W \xrightarrow{a} X \xrightarrow{c} Y \xrightarrow{d} Z$ $E_{WXYZ} = a \cdot c \cdot d$

$E_{WXZ} = a \cdot e$

$E_{WYZ} = c \cdot d$

$$W \xrightarrow{a} X \underset{e}{\overset{c}{\rightleftarrows}} Y \overset{f}{\circlearrowright} \underset{g}{\overset{d}{\rightleftarrows}} Z \qquad E_{WXYZ} = a \cdot c \cdot d$$

$$W \xrightarrow{a} X \qquad\qquad E_{WX} = a; \; E_{XY} = c; \; E_{YZ} = d;$$
$$\qquad\qquad\qquad\qquad E_{ZX} = e; \; E_{WXY} = a \cdot c$$

$$c \downarrow \; \nwarrow e$$

$$Y \xrightarrow{d} Z \qquad\qquad E_{WXYZ} = a \cdot c \cdot d; \; E_{XYZ} = c \cdot d;$$
$$\qquad\qquad\qquad\qquad E_{YZX} = d \cdot e; \; E_{ZXY} = e \cdot c$$

The expressions for only a few selected open path effects are given in the first three examples; all open path effects are indicated in the last example.

Touching Paths

II.15 *Two loops "touch" if their identifiers contain one or more symbols in common. A loop "touches" an open path if any symbol in the open path identifier except the first also appears in the loop identifier.*

The identifiers of loops and open paths are the lists of variables traversed by their paths; for example, in **2.32** $(WXYZ)$ is the identifier for the open path from W to Z and (XYZ) is the identifier for the loop. The two paths touch because their identifiers share three symbols. Alternatively, it may be noted that E_{WXYZ} is the open path effect and L_{XYZ} is the loop's return effect. These two effects have three subscripts in common, so by rule II.15 they are associated with touching paths.

Another important example is offered in **2.34**. The open path (WZ) is touched by neither of the loops in the system—(WX) and (XY)—because no symbol in the open path identifier *except the first* appears in the identifiers of the loops.

2.34 V

$$a \downarrow$$

$$W \underset{d}{\overset{c}{\rightleftarrows}} X \underset{f}{\overset{e}{\rightleftarrows}} Y$$

$$\downarrow g$$

$$Z$$

Loop (WX) touches open path (VWZ) but not open path (WZ). Loops (WX) and (XY) touch.

The "touching" concept allows us to define *relevant feedback* as follows:

Suppose a variable X is an input for a variable Y because X directly or indirectly causes Y but Y does not affect X either directly or indirectly. Clearly, there must be one or more open paths from X to Y. If loops are also in the system, the relevant feedback for the X–Y relation is the set of all loops touching any one of the open paths from X to Y, plus the additional loops touching any of the loops in the first set, plus any loops touching those in the second set, and so on.

As an illustration, consider again the system in **2.34**. Variable W is a legitimate input for Z, but neither of the system's loops provides relevant feedback for this relation because neither "touches" the open path (WZ). V, however, is also a legitimate input for Z, and in this case both loops provide relevant feedback—loop (WX) because it touches the open path (VWZ) and loop (XY) because it touches loop (WX).

Reduction with Loops

The basic principles of analyzing the graph of a system with loops were presented for engineering applications by Samuel Mason in 1951. The key rule is the following:

II.16 *The total effect T from an input variable to any dependent variable can be determined as follows: $E, E', E'', \ldots$, are the distinct open path effects from the input to the dependent variable; $L, L', L'', \ldots$, are the return effects for all distinct loops providing relevant feedback; then*

$$T = \left[\frac{(E + E' + E'' + \cdots)\cdot(1 - L)\cdot(1 - L')\cdot(1 - L'')\cdot\ \cdots}{(1 - L)\cdot(1 - L')\cdot(1 - L'')\cdot\ \cdots}\right]^*$$

*where * is a special operation in which the multiplications in the numerator and in the denominator are carried out before division, terms are deleted if they multiply the effects of touching paths, and division is carried out only after such terms have been deleted.*

A simple illustration is given in **2.35**.

2.35 Find the total effect from X to Z in the following diagram:

There is only one open path effect between X and Z: $E_{XYZ} = a \cdot c$; there is only one loop, with return effect $L_Y = d$. Thus

$$T_{ZX} = \left[\frac{(E_{XYZ}) \cdot (1 - L_Y)}{(1 - L_Y)}\right]^* = \left[\frac{E_{XYZ} - E_{XYZ} \cdot L_Y}{1 - L_Y}\right]^*$$

The open path from X to Z and the loop at Y are touching; hence the [ ]* operation requires deletion of the term $(E_{XYZ} \cdot L_Y)$ from the expression to give

$$T_{ZX} = \frac{E_{XYZ}}{1 - L_Y} = \frac{a \cdot c}{1 - d}$$

The simplest loop system possible is shown in **2.35**. Some of the principles involved in rule II.16 can be illustrated best in this case. Suppose that variable X is manipulated so that Y goes from a value of zero to exactly 1.0 immediately after the change in X. Assuming that X is held at its new value (as we always do in static analyses), Y will be held at its value of 1.0. However, the original change in Y now passes on through the self-loop. It is multiplied by the return effect of the loop L_Y and this increment in turn is added to Y. Because Y is already being held at 1.0, its new value is $1.0 + L_Y$. Moreover, this second increment depends indirectly on X, and as long as X is held constant the value of Y is maintained at $(1.0 + L_Y)$. At this point the secondary change in Y of L_Y units also passes on through the self-loop. Multiplied by the return effect of the loop, it adds another increment L_Y^2 to Y. Thus the value of Y becomes $1 + L_Y + L_Y^2$ and will be maintained at this level as long as X stays constant. Obviously the tertiary change in Y also passes through the loop and causes another increment L_Y^3 to be added to Y. Indeed, this process continues indefinitely, and the final value of Y must be equal to the following summation.

$$1 + L_Y + L_Y^2 + L_Y^3 + L_Y^4 + \cdots$$

This summation continues on into infinity. Nevertheless, it can be shown mathematically that Y converges on a definite final value if only L_Y is a fraction —that is, if $-1.0 < L_Y < +1.0$. (If L_Y is not a fraction, the series of summations would not converge and the loop would be unstable.) Furthermore, the value of Y will closely approach its final value after only a few cycles. This is because each of the later terms in the series is a fraction taken to a very high power and the later increments are quite small; for example, if $L_Y = (\frac{1}{2})$, then $L_Y^5 = (\frac{1}{2})^5 = (\frac{1}{32})$. The value of this summation can actually be defined exactly. In particular, it can be proved mathematically that the following is true when L_Y is a fraction:

$$\frac{1}{1 - L_Y} = 1 + L_Y + L_Y^2 + L_Y^3 + \cdots$$

This, of course, is the quantity that appears when Mason's principle is used. In more complicated systems Mason's principle similarly defines a divisor that reflects the ultimate consequence of repeated cyclings through all relevant loops.

If the value of L_Y is positive, then $(1 - L_Y)$ is a number less than 1.0 and $[1/(1 - L_Y)]$ is a number greater than 1.0. Thus effects on open paths touching the loop are exaggerated or amplified. If L_Y is negative, then $(1 - L_Y)$ is greater than 1.0 and $[1/(1 - L_Y)]$ is a fraction. Therefore open path effects passing the loop are diminished, attenuated, or controlled.

As noted above, parenthetically, the stability characteristics of a system with a single loop can also be deduced from the value of the loop's return effect. If the absolute value of the return effect is equal to or greater than 1.0 (i.e., the return effect is either 1.0 or greater or -1.0 or less), the system will be unstable. Given any input, the values of variables will increase endlessly in one direction or another. *If the value of the return effect is between -1.0 and $+1.0$, a system containing only this one loop will be stable.* A system with multiple loops may be unstable even though each loop is stable individually. Also, it is possible for some loops to be individually unstable while the system as a whole reaches equilibrium because the loops counteract one another. The net impact of multiple loops on system stability can be assessed, but the techniques require somewhat complicated mathematical analyses that give explicit recognition to system dynamics (see Chapter 6 references).

Relevant loops that do not actually touch an open path lack their full impact on that path. In general, their effects are attenuated by their remoteness from the main path, and adjustment of the numerator of the transmittance expression is required to reflect this fact. However, this adjustment is obtained routinely when rule II.16 is applied.[1]

Rule II.16 has been stated to apply even to extremely intricate networks. However, *if there is only a single loop in a diagram, its impact is simply to*

---

[1] This function of the multiplier terms obtained by Mason's rule was brought to my attention by James A. Davis.

adjust all the open paths it touches by the factor $1/(1 - L)$. One demonstration was provided in **2.35**. Other examples are given in **2.36**:

2.36

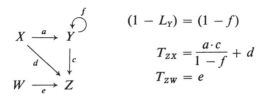

$$(1 - L_Y) = (1 - f)$$

$$T_{ZX} = \frac{a \cdot c}{1 - f} + d$$

$$T_{ZW} = e$$

Only the $(X\,YZ)$ open path is affected by the loop; hence only one open path effect is adjusted above.

$$
\begin{array}{cc}
V & W \\
\downarrow a & \downarrow f \\
X \underset{d}{\overset{c}{\rightleftharpoons}} Y \\
& \downarrow e \\
& Z
\end{array}
$$

$$(1 - L_{XY}) = (1 - cd)$$

$$T_{ZV} = \frac{a \cdot c \cdot e}{1 - c \cdot d}$$

$$T_{ZW} = \frac{f \cdot e}{1 - c \cdot d}$$

The following more complex example displays all the key aspects of rules II.15 and II.16 and also illustrates the use of numerical subscripts in dealing with larger systems.

2.37   Find the total effect from X_1 to X_5.

$$
\begin{array}{c}
X_1 \\
a_{21} \swarrow \quad \searrow a_{31} \\
X_2 \underset{a_{23}}{\overset{a_{32}}{\rightleftharpoons}} X_3 \underset{a_{34}}{\overset{a_{43}}{\rightleftharpoons}} X_4 \\
a_{52} \downarrow \\
X_5
\end{array}
$$

There are two open paths from X_1 to X_5:

$$E_{125} = a_{21} \cdot a_{52}$$
$$E_{1325} = a_{31} \cdot a_{23} \cdot a_{52}$$

There are two loops in the system:

$$L_{23} = a_{32} \cdot a_{23}$$
$$L_{34} = a_{43} \cdot a_{34}$$

Thus the total effect from X_1 to X_5 is

$$T_{51} = \left[\frac{(E_{125} + E_{1325}) \cdot (1 - L_{23}) \cdot (1 - L_{34})}{(1 - L_{23}) \cdot (1 - L_{34})}\right]^*$$

It usually saves effort to expand the bottom quantity first because it appears in both the numerator and the denominator. The result of carrying out the multiplication is

$$1 - L_{23} - L_{34} + L_{23}L_{34}$$

The two effects in the last term are associated with the paths of touching loops and that term is deleted.

$$[1 - L_{23} - L_{34} + L_{23} \cdot L_{34}]^* = (1 - L_{23} - L_{34})$$

This equation can now be used to rewrite the formula for T_{51}:

$$T_{51} = \frac{[(E_{125} + E_{1325}) \cdot (1 - L_{23} - L_{34})]^*}{(1 - L_{23} - L_{34})}$$

Working out the product in the top gives

$$E_{125} + E_{1325} - \underline{E_{125}L_{23}} - \underline{E_{1325}L_{23}} - \underline{E_{125}L_{34}} - \underline{E_{1325}L_{34}}$$

The underscored terms multiply effects associated with touching paths, and these terms are dropped from the total expression to give

$$T_{51} = \frac{E_{125} + E_{1325} - E_{125}L_{34}}{1 - L_{23} - L_{34}} = \frac{E_{125}(1 - L_{34}) + E_{1325}}{1 - L_{23} - L_{34}}$$

or, substituting the more specific expressions for each effect,

$$T_{51} = \frac{a_{21}a_{52}(1 - a_{43}a_{34}) + a_{31}a_{23}a_{52}}{1 - a_{32}a_{23} - a_{43}a_{34}}$$

These examples have shown the analysis of loops in systems without disturbances. Disturbances were not shown on the diagrams for the sake of clarity, and the same procedures apply, without modification, when disturbances are present.

Reduced Form of a System

II.17   *Once all total effects, relating every dependent variable to all the input variables, have been obtained, a reduced-form diagram can be drawn to show each dependent variable directly linked to the inputs and eliminating intervening variables.*

Two examples are given in **2.38**.

2.38

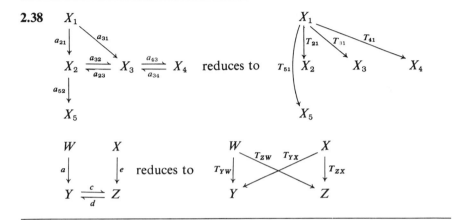

As these examples show, loops are eliminated in a reduced-form diagram.

Reduced-form diagrams are subject to the usual flowgraph rules. Thus by drawing the reduced form and applying these rules the value of any dependent variable can be expressed simply as a weighted sum of system inputs, even when the system contains complex feedback loops. The coefficients in the reduced-form diagram (the T's) consist of the expressions for the total effect between each input and each dependent variable, defined in rule II.16.

One unique benefit of flowgraph analysis is that the effect of a single input on a focal variable can be defined *without* deriving the full reduced form.[2] This is not generally true of algebraic approaches.

Semireduction

The fact that the reduced form eliminates loops is of crucial importance in causal analyses. It is frequently desirable, however, to reduce a graph only

[2] This observation was communicated to me by Doris Entwisle.

in part by eliminating the loops but leaving the rest intact. This can be done by creating additional hypothetical variables corresponding to variables in the loop and reducing the loop onto them.

II.18 *Loops can be eliminated in a graph by reducing them onto hypothetical "input" variables intervening between the loop and other parts of the graph.*

For example, if Y and Z are variables linked by a loop, two new variables Y' and Z' are created. The hypothetical Y' is entered as an intervening variable between the sources of Y (outside the loop) and Y itself. Similarly, Z' becomes an intervening variable between the outside sources of Z and Z itself. An example is given in **2.39**.

2.39

Notice that no symbols are attached to the arrows from the hypothetical sources; this implies that these arrows have coefficients of 1.0. Thus the effect to, say, Y from any of the original sources of Y is the same in the modified graph as in the original graph.

Now, using the ordinary reduction procedures defined in rule II.17, applied to the subgraph consisting of the hypothetical variables and the loop, the values of the original loop variables can be expressed in reduced form. The example is continued in **2.40**.

2.40

becomes

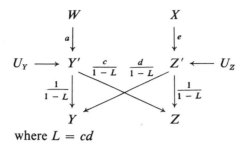

where $L = cd$

If a loop variable has only one outside source, the hypothetical variable is redundant and may be eliminated, as indicated by the examples in **2.41**:

2.41

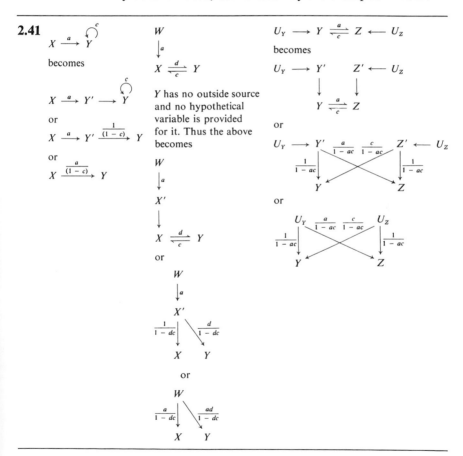

Elimination of a loop in this way maintains the correct relations between the loop variables and all the original inputs. Moreover, reduced loops maintain the proper relations among variables "above" and "below" a loop, as illustrated in **2.42**.

2.42

$$W$$

$$\downarrow a$$

$$U_X \longrightarrow X \; \underset{c}{\overset{e}{\rightleftarrows}} \; Y \longleftarrow U_Y$$

$$\downarrow d$$

$$U_Z \longrightarrow Z$$

$$T_{ZW} = \left(\frac{aed}{1-ec}\right) W \qquad \text{becomes}$$

$$W$$

$$\downarrow a$$

$$U_X \longrightarrow X' \quad \frac{e}{1-ec} \quad \frac{c}{1-ec} \quad U_Y$$

$$\frac{1}{1-ec} \qquad\qquad \frac{1}{1-ec}$$

$$X \qquad\qquad Y$$

$$\downarrow d$$

$$U_Z \longrightarrow Z$$

$$T_{ZW} = \left(\frac{aed}{1-ec}\right) W$$

Nested loops also can be semireduced as illustrated in **2.43**.

2.43

$$W \qquad\qquad U_Y \qquad\qquad\qquad W$$

$$\searrow a \qquad\qquad \downarrow \qquad\qquad\qquad \downarrow a$$

$$U_X \longrightarrow X \underset{f}{\overset{e}{\longleftarrow}} Y \quad \text{becomes} \quad U_X \longrightarrow X' \qquad U_Z \qquad U_Y$$

$$U_Z \longrightarrow Z \qquad\qquad\qquad\qquad \downarrow \qquad\quad \downarrow \qquad\quad \downarrow$$

$$X \underset{c}{\overset{f}{\rightleftarrows}} Z \overset{d}{\longrightarrow} Y$$

or

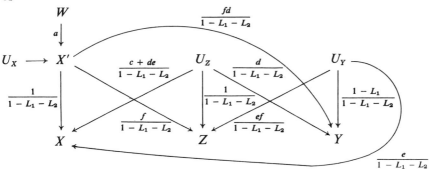

where

$$L_1 = L_{XZ} = fc \quad \text{and} \quad L_2 = L_{XZY} = fde$$

Extrication is another form of semireduction that will be useful in Chapter 5 when we study a procedure called two-stage least squares estimation.

II.19   *A selected variable may be "extricated" from loops by eliminating any feedback arrows branching away from it and representing all other dependent variables in the system in reduced form.*

2.44

$$\begin{array}{cc} W & X \\ a\downarrow & e\downarrow \\ Y \underset{d}{\overset{c}{\rightleftarrows}} Z \end{array}$$ can be drawn with Z extricated $$\begin{array}{cc} W & X \\ \frac{a}{1-cd}\downarrow \quad \frac{ed}{1-cd} & \downarrow e \\ Y \underset{c}{\longrightarrow} Z \end{array}$$

The dependency of Y on Z is obscured in the revised diagram but all total effects from the sources are accurately represented:

$$T_{YW} = \frac{a}{1-cd}; \quad T_{YX} = \frac{ed}{1-cd}; \quad T_{ZW} = \frac{ac}{1-cd}$$

$$T_{ZX} = e + \frac{edc}{1-dc} = \frac{e - edc + edc}{1-dc} = \frac{e}{1-dc}$$

$$\begin{array}{ccc} S & V & W \\ h\downarrow & f\downarrow & g\downarrow \\ X \underset{e}{\overset{a}{\rightleftarrows}} Y \underset{d}{\overset{c}{\rightleftarrows}} Z \end{array}$$

can be drawn with Y extricated:

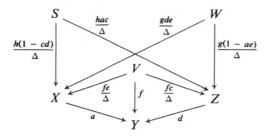

where $\Delta = 1 - ae - cd$. Again, total effects from the sources are represented accurately in the revised diagram:

$$T_{YS} = \frac{h(1 - cd)}{\Delta} \cdot a + \frac{hac}{\Delta} \cdot d = \frac{ha}{\Delta}(1 - cd + cd) = \frac{ha}{\Delta}$$

Extricating a variable constitutes an alternative way of reducing loops, and it keeps intact more of the original loop relationships than semireduction by rule II.18. Reduction by extrication, however, is not symmetric and alternative reductions are always possible, as shown in **2.45**.

2.45   The first example in **2.44** can also be drawn with Y extricated:

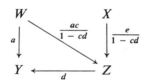

Similarly either X or Z may be extricated in the second example:

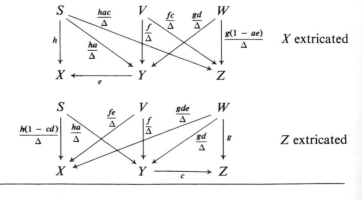

Extrication provides insight into the relation of a loop variable to external (nonloop) sources. The first extrication in **2.44** shows that Z changes e units when X changes one unit but a change in X produces a further indirect effect because of changes in Y via the loop. Extrication partitions the effect of an external source into a direct component and an indirect component due to loop dynamics and shows that these two different kinds of effect are simply summative.

Extensions of Flowgraph Analysis

Additional rules for graph analysis exist, and, in particular, there are rules for graph inversion. Roughly, this means changing the direction of arrows to correspond with the rewriting of an equation like $Y = a \cdot X$ as $X = Y/a$. The inversion rules are not presented here, but more advanced texts on flowgraph analysis listed in the references present rules for graph inversion.

The 19 rules above allow us to diagram and analyze systems with a variety of structures, including those with loops and nests of loops. It should be noted, however, that large complex systems demand such involved graphs that it is often practical to convert them to sets of structural equations and use conventional mathematics for analysis.

RESEARCH APPLICATIONS

A basic purpose of theorizing is to organize information in a way that will develop its nonobvious implications. The statement of a theory in terms of simple pairwise relationships generally does not do this. The propositions must be manipulated logically to produce deductions that give new insights. The preceding rules provide a means of sounding the deeper implications of a theory that has been represented in diagrammatic form.

Critical Cases

A causal theory implies that an observed case should have a particular configuration of outcome values once the values of the inputs have been set and the causal processes have had sufficient time to operate. Moreover, a causal theory states the sequence by which this configuration should develop—the process of adjustment should begin at the source and cascade along the arrows of a flowgraph to various dependent variables. Thus cases that can be observed during the process of reaching their final configuration may serve as critical cases for theoretical analysis.

Suppose a simple chain theory is under consideration: $X \to Y \to Z$, in which all the relationships are positive. Further, suppose that a case can be found in which X suddenly takes on a very high value, whereas both Y and Z are low. Theoretically, this configuration should not last because Y is directly dependent on X and so should increase in value; Z, which in turn depends on Y should increase also. If these hypotheses were confirmed by further study, the theory would have some degree of confirmation.

This is an approach taken by many theorists to document their theories; for example, Meggers[3] used the technique to increase the credibility of the thesis that cultural complexity is directly dependent on the cultivation potential of land occupied by a society. Mayan satellite communities, sent off from the central society to sites in the jungle, took on an extremely low value on the cultivation-potential variable, whereas the dependent variable of cultural complexity initially retained a high value. Accordingly, if the theory is correct, the extreme low cultivation potential ultimately should have produced reduced complexity as well. Through historical reconstructions, Meggers found that this indeed was the case. The satellite communities in the course of a few centuries were reduced to "primitive" cultures.

Explanation

Reduced-form expressions define the values of dependent variables in terms of the values of system inputs. In linear systems such algebraic expressions can be inverted to show that a particular value on a dependent variable implies a predetermined value on the source variable. Suppose, for example, that "crime rate" (R) is increasing and that it is known to be dependent on three sources, W, X, and Y. Suppose that W and X show no notable changes in recent history but that Y recently has taken on a new value that is now being maintained as a constant. It would be plausible to say, then, that the change in Y is what accounts for the increase in crime or that the increase is due to disturbances not considered explicitly. If we assume that disturbances are minimal, the reduced-form expression (T_{RY}) relating R to T may be of interest in assessing whether the crime-wave has reached its peak or will continue to grow. If the present level of Y multiplied by the reduced-form

[3] Betty J. Meggers. "Environmental Limitation on the Development of Culture" *American Anthropologist*, **56** (1954), 801–824.

expression yields a value close to the present crime rate, the surge would seem to be over. If it yields a value larger, further increases in crime may be expected.

The value of such analysis for explanation is that we can go far beyond simple interpretations and seek out remote and indirect causes even in complicated systems. With multiple paths and intervening loops it becomes almost impossible to state adequate verbal explanations of phenomena in terms of remote causes, but it is not impossible with analytic procedures.

Of course, the logical power gained by graph analysis does not reduce the uncertainty of explanations when uncertainty is a part of the system being analyzed (as in unspecified disturbances affecting crime rate). Also, we either have to estimate or guess the values of structural coefficients (i.e., the magnitudes of effects) before the analysis has sufficient specificity to be of value.

Prediction

The reduced-form expressions obtained from graph analysis constitute input-output equations for a system. Given a particular configuration of values among the input variables at a given time, the ultimate consequences for all dependent variables can be calculated. Thus a theory, along with numerical estimates of the structural coefficients may be used to anticipate future events that follow as repercussions from present changes. The use of graphs and reduced-form expressions provides two benefits over more informal approaches to prediction. First, a change in an input can be traced readily to all its consequences, even when multiple and convoluted pathways are involved. Second, changes in a dependent variable can be estimated from all the system inputs, thereby avoiding oversimplifications and errors of judgment.

Interdiction

Flowgraphs, and their reduced-form expressions, can guide policy decisions by indicating the source variables that can be changed to achieve a desired effect, by suggesting how much manipulation is necessary to obtain the desired change, and by revealing the additional effects that a manipulation will have besides the desired one.

In defining the source variables that may be manipulated to achieve a desired effect, the flowgraph analysis serves to emphasize that undesirable outcomes need not be undone directly; that is, an outcome Z may have an unwanted value because of its dependence on, say, input X, and one way to eliminate the unwanted value of Z is to undo it by changing X; but if the dependent variable has another source, Y, then the unwanted value of Z may be eliminated by manipulating Y instead. Recognition of multiple sources provides increased flexibility in policy in terms of practicality, costs, and ethics.

With numerical estimates of the coefficients in reduced-form expressions it becomes possible to define the amount of change in a source that is needed to achieve a desired change in an outcome. This kind of quantification lends itself readily to objective analyses of the best way to proceed. It may be true, for example, that one source has a large effect on a dependent variable of interest but that costs or ethical factors prohibit manipulation of this sort. Then a less efficient manipulation on another source, or a combination of manipulations on several sources, may be preferred and relatively exact costs-benefits analysis can be carried out by using the reduced form expressions.

Once a particular source or set of sources has been chosen, the consequences of the manipulation can be traced not only to the outcome of interest but to other outcomes in the system as well by using the reduced-form expressions for the other variables. Thus by analytically simulating the process before it is implemented we may conclude that the overall configuration of effects produced by the manipulation is not so desirable as we first thought. In such a case, of course, it is possible to continue the analysis by seeking a source or set of sources to manipulate that gives optimal benefits and at the same time incurs minimal damage.

SOURCES AND ADDITIONAL READINGS

Another introduction to elementary flowgraph analysis, oriented for social scientists, is provided by Arthur L. Stinchcombe, *Constructing Social Theories* (New York: Harcourt, Brace & World, 1968). In addition, many textbooks on systems analysis devote a section or a chapter to flowgraph analysis; for example, Arthur D. Hall, *A Methodology for Systems Engineering* (Princeton, N.J.: Van Nostrand, 1962). A highly readable survey of more advanced flowgraph techniques is made in W. H. Huggins and Doris R. Entwisle, *Introductory Systems and Design* (Waltham, Mass.: Blaisdell, 1968). This source provides numerous examples and problems with solutions. Charles S. Lorens, *Flowgraphs for the Modeling and Analysis of Linear Systems* (New York: McGraw-Hill, 1964), presents the techniques in a more mathematical format and shows how applications can be extended to a number of technical problems of general interest.

EXERCISES

1. A structural coefficient has units of measurement attached to it, even though the units are rarely shown on flowgraphs; for example, suppose a structural coefficient from variable X to variable Y is .4. This means that the causal operator generates .4 units of Y per unit of X, and thus the complete coefficient is

$$\left[.4 \ \frac{\text{unit of } Y}{\text{unit of } X} \right]$$

Suppose occupational status is measured on a scale of rated social standing (such as that developed by the National Opinion Research Center): we can call each unit on the scale a NORC for convenience. Also, let education be measured in terms of years of schooling, or "schoolyears." Finally, suppose the following has been discovered: if man A has an occupation 20 NORCS above that of man B, then A's sons typically have three schoolyears more education than B's sons. Given this "finding," what is the complete coefficient, with units, relating father's occupation to son's education?

2. Suppose a man's occupational status is assessed as 60 NORCS. Use the result from problem 1 to determine the expected education of his sons. In particular, show how the units of measurement attached to the father's status cancel those in the structural coefficient to yield the result.

3. Suppose that some misfortune causes a man to drop 10 NORCS in occupational status during his early adult life. Using the result from problem 1, determine the expected impact of this on the education of his sons. In particular, show how the units of measurement attached to his drop in status cancel units attached to the structural coefficient to yield the result.

4. Suppose that the structural coefficient relating a son's education to his ultimate occupational status is

$$\left(5.0 \, \frac{\text{son-NORCS}}{\text{son-schoolyear}}\right)$$

Use this and the result in exercise 1 to predict the occupational standing of the sons of a man with an 80-NORC occupation. Show how units of measurement cancel in the calculations.

5. Suppose we are studying a society in which the relations defined in problems 1 and 4 hold and in which fathers typically use the contacts and influence associated with their statuses to improve their sons' standings directly. Assume that the structural coefficient from father's status direct to son's status is

$$\left(.25 \, \frac{\text{son-NORC}}{\text{father-NORC}}\right)$$

(a) Provide a flowgraph for this hypothetical system of intergenerational mobility that shows the structural coefficients with their units attached. (Ignore the possibility of disturbances.)

(b) Use graph reduction rules to write the equation relating a father's occupational level to his son's. Carrry units of measurement through the reduction process.

(c) In this system what is the expected occupational level of a man's son when the man has an 80-NORC occupation?

6. It possibly is true that

- increasing the proportion of poverty-level people in a city increases the crime rate;
- a high crime rate generates demands for more police;
- a greater density of police in a city deters crime.

Let the variables be defined as follows:

$$I \text{ (proportion impoverished) is } \frac{\text{number of impoverished in city}}{\text{number of dwellers in city}}$$

$$C \text{ (crime rate) } \qquad \text{is } \frac{\text{number of crimes in city}}{\text{number of dwellers in city}}$$

$$P \text{ (police-to-citizen ratio) } \qquad \text{is } \frac{\text{number of police in city}}{\text{number of dwellers in city}}$$

Also let the numerical values of the structural coefficients for each of these relations be represented by **d**, **e**, and **f**, respectively.

What are the signs of each coefficient? What are the units of each coefficient? Draw a flowgraph for the system and include the units associated with each coefficient.

7. What units are attached to the return effect of the loop in problem 6? How would the return effect be affected if the crime rate had a different base—say, crimes per 1000 dwellers rather than crimes per dweller?

8. Interpret the meaning of the following interdictions in terms of the system defined in exercise 6 and indicate the effects on crime rate and the police ratio.

(a) A minimum-income program is instituted to lift almost all persons out of poverty.

(b) Without changing actual incomes, increased effort is given to a welfare program in which the impoverished are provided with basic material needs and are insulated from stresses and debasements that might lead them to criminal acts.

(c) Police are given improved technology to increase their power and efficiency, and the mass media are encouraged to publicize it.

(d) Federal funds are allocated to all cities to increase their police forces by one officer per 10,000 dwellers.

9. The causal connection from crime rate to police ratio in exercise 6 may arise because of politicalization of law enforcement; that is, demands for more (or fewer) police are made by politicians and the mass media depending on changes in the crime rate. Can we expect crime to be permanently eradicated once this political operator enters into a law enforcement system? Why?

10. Again we continue with the assumptions presented in exercise 6. This time the problem is to weigh the impact of adding an additional control loop to the system by means of a federally sponsored program. In one plan the variable, federal support of local police, is linked to the system so that a high level of support leads to an increased police ratio and a high police ratio leads to reduced federal support.

$$ I \xrightarrow{d(+)} C \underset{f(-)}{\overset{e(+)}{\rightleftarrows}} P \underset{g(+)}{\overset{j(-)}{\rightleftarrows}} F $$

A second plan links national police (such as FBI or Treasury agents) directly

to a city's crime rate. The higher the crime rate, the more agents assigned to
that city, and the more agents assigned, the lower the crime rate.

$$I \xrightarrow{d(+)} C \begin{array}{l} \nearrow N \\ k(+) \\ l(-) \\ e(+) \\ f(-) \searrow P \end{array}$$

Assume that the programs are designed so that the power of the control
loops is the same in both cases; that is, $j \times g = k \times l = L$. Which program
will lead to the greatest overall reduction in crime? Explain this result in
words.

11. Let the strength of the military establishments in the United States,
the USSR, and the Peoples' Republic of China be symbolized by A, R, and
C, respectively. A single scale of measurement presumably applies to all
three variables. Suppose that the military strength of any one nation is
determined by the following:

- The size of the territory being defended by the nation (T). A larger area
  generates a larger defensive force, with the nation's military-adminis-
  trative branch acting as operator (**a**).
- The nation's level of achievement in basic science (S). Scientific advances
  of all kinds have been converted repeatedly to advances in military
  technology, with the military-industrial complex serving as operator
  (**d**). On the other hand, military research and development programs
  seem to have little impact on pure science (as distinguished from technology), and the causal direction can be treated as one-way.
- The military strengths of the other two superpowers. Americans are
  familiar with the routine of investing more in the military as a response
  to increased strength of another superpower. We may assume that the
  same process occurs in the other nations as well. In each case the operator
  responding to foreign moves (**f**) is a complex assembled from a nation's
  intelligence, political, and military-industrial sectors.

(a) Draw the flowgraph representing this system, using subscripts whenever
necessary to distinguish between variables and operators. Also write out the
structural equations.

(b) How many loops are in the system? Which are amplifying loops and
which are control loops?

(c) Find the total effect (T) from the US level of scientific advancement

(S_A) to US military strength (A). In ordinary language describe how each loop in the system contributes to this total effect.

12. We continue with the system in exercise 11. Assume now that increased military strength in one nation generates a constant amount of increase in the other two nations and that the relations are the same, regardless of which nation is the source. In other words, all **f**'s are positive and all **f**'s are equal. In addition, assume that the time required for a response is the same, regardless of the nations involved. Under these circumstances the system will be stable only if the value of **f** is less than .5. (This was determined by analyzing the system dynamics.) Interpret the meaning of **f** coefficients with values less than .5 and on the basis of your interpretation estimate whether this international system would be stable or unstable.

13. (a) Extricate the US military strength from the system introduced in exercise 11. For simplicity assume again, as in exercise 12, that the **f**'s are all equal.

(b) Perhaps a certain kind of person actually perceives the system in its extricated form. If so, operators (or accountings) for the new arrows that are introduced must be provided. What kind of operators could explain these paths? How would such a person explain the changes in military forces occurring after a new advance in American science? After a new advance in Russian science? What are the strengths and weaknesses of perceiving the system in extricated form, assuming that the original feedback system is a more accurate model?

3 STATISTICAL CONCEPTS

A flowgraph describes the causal processes impinging on a particular instance of a social system (e.g., a family, firm, or ecological setting) and the same structural description may not be apropos for any other cases. This, however, is not the usual goal of social research. More often a model is sought that generalizes to a class of cases—for example, all father-absent families, all banks, all frontier towns—such that the same system description can be used to understand the outcomes of any case in terms of the common causal structure and that case's unique inputs. Then, given any case, something is known about its mode of operation, some of its history can be inferred from its present state, and predictions can be made about how it would respond to new inputs.

Considering a whole class of cases at once moves us into a different realm of causal analysis than the one we have considered so far. We are no longer dealing with a single system, considering how it might respond to this or that input. Rather we are now attending to a population of equivalent systems and considering the distribution of outcomes produced by each case responding to its own inputs.

This expansion yields new power in theoretical analyses and in empirical research aimed at causal inference and the quantitative description of systems, as discussed in Chapters 4 and 5. To develop these benefits we must have a language for describing populations, particularly for describing their distributions on variables, and how their distributions on different variables are related. This is a focus of statistics and some elementary statistical concepts are outlined in this chapter.

DISTRIBUTIONS

A structural equation defines the algebraic relation existing between values of cause and effect variables when the cause is being maintained at a constant value and all causal operations have been completed in producing the outcome; for example, in the simple system, $X \xrightarrow{\frac{1}{2}} Y$, the value of Y is determined completely by X, and if X is set at a value and held there then (sooner or later) Y must have the value of $X/2$. If X is set at 1, then Y should be $\frac{1}{2}$; if X is set at 5, Y should equal 2.5.

Suppose that a case is observed in which X somehow has taken on the value of $+1.0$; another is found in which X is -3.0, another in which $X = -1.0$, and still another in which $X = 3.0$. From the equation $Y = X/2$ it is to be expected that Y has the respective values of $+.5$, -1.5, $-.5$, and $+1.5$. The table in **3.1** has been set up to display all this information in concise form:

3.1 Distributions on two variables, X and Y

Case	X Value	Y Value
1	$+1.0$	$+.5$
2	-3.0	-1.5
3	-1.0	$-.5$
4	$+3.0$	$+1.5$

The columns in **3.1** display the variables X and Y in something of a new light. A variable takes on different values as we proceed down the columns— the value varies depending on the case observed. Certainly X (or Y) still represents a variable causally related to the other variable in the system, but the multiple values within each column emphasize that X (or Y) also has a *distribution* in this particular cross section of cases. Because distributions are the basic focus in all that follows, it is useful to conceptualize a distribution graphically and to provide concepts for characterizing it as a whole.

Graphs of Distributions

The distribution of X values in **3.1** can be represented graphically by showing the scale of X measurement as a horizontal axis and representing the number of cases at each measurement point in the vertical dimension; for example, the X (and Y) distribution in **3.1** would be graphed as follows:

3.2 Graphs of the distributions in **3.1**.

Distributions typically involve more cases than this—hundreds or thousands —and the graph of a distribution takes on a shape as more cases are added; for example, in 25 cases the distribution of X may take the form shown in **3.3**.

3.3 Possible distribution of 25 cases on a variable X.

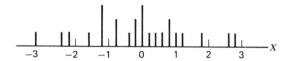

As the number of cases gets larger still, the top of the distribution looks more and more like a smooth curve, as illustrated in **3.4**.

3.4 Possible distribution with a large number of cases.

As shown in **3.4**, the distribution of a variable need not be symmetric. The validity of the analyses that follow does not depend on symmetry. In particular, none of the following analytic procedures depends on the assumption that a distribution has a "normal" shape:

3.5 Normal curve.

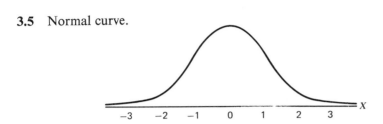

Normal distributions are of major importance in probability theory, so they are of interest when a probabilistic inference about all cases in a population is attempted, given information on only a few. However, *normal curves need not be assumed to characterize distributions when work is being done at a purely analytic level of systems analysis* because the analytic procedures are developed in reference to the population of all existing cases; hence no probabilistic inferences are made. Only when we are estimating the values of structural coefficients from sample data does the assumption of normality become a consideration, at which time the normality assumption is involved in developing a judgment of confidence in the results of estimation. (However a pattern in which the distributions on some variables is asymmetric and others are approximately normal may suggest that the underlying system is not strictly linear; see exercise 2.)

The statistical study of static systems does involve another assumption about the distribution of variables. It is assumed that the diversity on any variable is finite, meaning that the probability of a case existing above some high value on the measurement scale or below some low value on the scale is extremely small. The prior restriction of analyses to stable linear systems ensures this; therefore no new assumption needs to be made at this point.

The Mean

The mean is the center of gravity of a distribution—the point on the measurement scale at which a cutout of the distribution would just balance if placed on a fulcrum. A mean is calculated by adding up the values of all cases and dividing by their number.

The mean has such important mathematical characteristics that it is applied over and over, almost whenever a distribution of any kind turns up. Accordingly, it is useful to develop some special rules for working with means in populations.

3.6   ALGEBRA OF EXPECTATIONS

The "expected value" of a variable is its mean, computed in the population of all possible cases. The expected value is symbolized by an $\mathscr{E}$ preceding the variable name given in parenthesis; for example, $\mathscr{E}(X)$ is the mean of X over all cases in a population. If a variable is defined in terms of an algebraic expression, the expected value of the variable can be defined in terms of the algebraic expression by using the following rules.

1.   The expected value of a constant times a variable equals the constant times the expected value of the variable.

$$\mathscr{E}(a \cdot X) = a \cdot \mathscr{E}(X)$$

2.   The expected value of the sum of two variables equals the sum of the expected values.

$$\mathscr{E}(X + Y) = \mathscr{E}(X) + \mathscr{E}(Y)$$

3.   The expected value of a variable times itself or times another variable cannot be decomposed:

$$\left.\begin{array}{l}\mathscr{E}(X \cdot Y) \\ \mathscr{E}(X^2)\end{array}\right\} \text{ cannot be reduced further}$$

EXAMPLE

Suppose Z is defined by the equation

$$Z = (a \cdot X) + (b \cdot Y) + (c \cdot X \cdot Y)$$

Then the expected value of Z is

$$\begin{aligned}\mathscr{E}(Z) &= \mathscr{E}(a \cdot X + b \cdot Y + c \cdot X \cdot Y) \\ &= \mathscr{E}(a \cdot X) + \mathscr{E}(b \cdot Y) + \mathscr{E}(c \cdot X \cdot Y) \\ &= a \cdot \mathscr{E}(X) + b \cdot \mathscr{E}(Y) + c \cdot \mathscr{E}(X \cdot Y)\end{aligned}$$

Despite the fundamental importance of means, they will not appear here in expressions concerning distributions of variables because henceforth *it is assumed that variables are measured on scales adjusted so that the zero point of the scale is at the mean of the distribution*; that is, variables are assumed to be measured in terms of deviation-from-mean scores or just *deviation scores*. As noted in Chapter 2, flowgraphs, and the expressions obtained from flowgraphs, can be simplified if measurement scales are adjusted so that constant terms drop out. That is exactly what is being done here. The use of deviation scores eliminates constants from diagrams as well as from derived expressions and this convention simplifies statistical analyses. As pointed out in Chapter 2, adding or subtracting constants to adjust measurement scales to more convenient forms does not constitute a restrictive assumption in static analyses. Deviation scores are simply measurements that have been adjusted by subtracting a constant—the expected value of the variable—from every original value.

No change in symbols is introduced to signal the fact that measurements are now presumed to be in terms of deviation scores. Rather the convention can be viewed as retroactive to preceding discussions.

Variance

The distributions generated by the relationship $X \xrightarrow{1} Y$, shown in **3.2** have the same mean (.0) but there is an obvious difference in how they are spread out: the X distribution has a greater range than the Y distribution. Put differently, the X values, on the average, are further from the center of their distribution than the Y values are from the center of theirs. The X values show more diversity.

The most useful measure of diversity—the *variance*—is the average squared-distance of individual cases from the mean of the distribution. With the convention of measuring all variables in terms of deviation scores, variances can be obtained merely by squaring observed values and taking their mean. Thus the variance, represented by σ^2, is the expected value of the squared deviation scores.

3.7   DEFINITION OF VARIANCE

$$\sigma_X^2 = \mathscr{E}(X^2)$$

when the measurement scale for X is calibrated in terms of deviation scores.

EXAMPLE.

The variance of the X distribution in **3.1** is

$$\sigma_X^2 = [(1.0)^2 + (-3.0)^2 + (-1.0)^2 + (3.0)^2]/4$$
$$= [1 + 9 + 1 + 9]/4$$
$$= 20/4$$
$$= 5.0$$

The variance of the Y distribution is

$$\sigma_Y^2 = [(.5)^2 + (-1.5)^2 + (-.5)^2 + (1.5)^2]/4$$
$$= [.25 + 2.25 + .25 + 2.25]/4$$
$$= 5/4$$
$$= 1.25$$

JOINT DISTRIBUTIONS

A causal relation between two variables coordinates their values; for example, in **3.1** the positive values of X are associated with positive values of Y and negative values of X are associated with negative values of Y. To study the coordination of two variables it is necessary to consider their joint distribution.

Graphs of Joint Distributions

A graph, or scattergram, of a joint distribution is made up by representing the measurement scale of one variable on the horizontal axis and the measurement scale of the other on the vertical axis. Cases with a particular combination of values on the two variables are shown as points on the graph. (If more than one case falls at a particular location, it can be indicated by writing the number of cases at that location.)

From one standpoint a scattergram is simply a somewhat refined version of a cross-tabulated table, revealed by comparing the chart in **3.9** with the graph in **3.8**.

3.8 Scattergram showing a joint distribution of 10 cases on variables Y and Z.

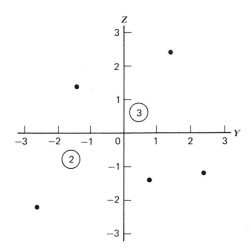

3.9 The joint distribution of Y and Z represented in tabular form.

		Y					
		−3 to −2.1	−2 to −1.1	−1 to −0.1	0 to 0.9	1 to 1.9	2 to 2.9
Z	2 to 2.9					1	
	1 to 1.9		1				
	0 to 0.9				3		
	−1 to −0.1		2				
	−2 to −1.1				1		1
	−3 to −2.1	1					

From another standpoint a scattergram represents a three-dimensional graph viewed from the top. Each point indicates a short one-unit line rising vertically from the paper and indicating that one case occurs at that location; a number on the graph means that a longer line rises vertically from that position (e.g., the number 2 in the graph of **3.8** indicates that a line two units long rises from that location). When a small number of cases is being considered, the surface produced by the tops of these vertical lines is irregular. As the number of cases grows very large, however, the surface smooths out, typically taking on something like a bell shape.

3.10 A possible smooth surface produced by the joint distribution of two variables when a large number of cases is considered. Such surfaces are typically bellshaped, though the bell may be distorted in various ways.

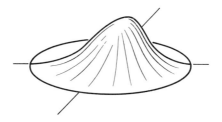

When dealing with only a few hundred cases, the vertical dimension in scattergrams can be largely ignored in favor of attending to the pattern formed by points on the two-dimensional representation. If the values of two variables are coordinated to some degree, their joint distribution displays some characteristic pattern in a scattergram.

3.11a Scattergram for two variables with uncoordinated values.

3.11b Scattergram for two variables whose values are coordinated to a considerable degree. The straight line passing through the points could be used to predict the expected value of Z, given a particular value of X.

3.11a

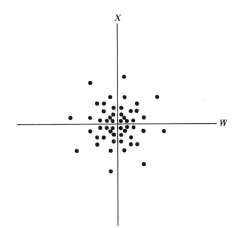

3.11b

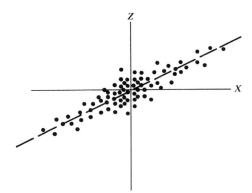

3.11c

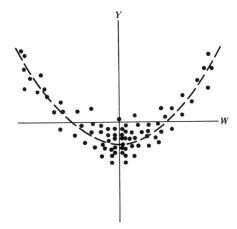

3.11c   Scattergram for two variables whose values are coordinated to a considerable degree. The curved line running through the points could be used to predict the expected value of Y, given a particular value of W.

Graph 3.11a indicates no coordination; the two variables are uncorrelated with one another. Graph 3.11b shows two variables whose values are related. The fact that the points seem to cluster around a straight line means that the relationship can be described as *linear. Such linear relations are presumed in many statistical analyses and in all of the analyses in this book*.

Graph 3.11c shows coordinated variables, but the relationship is nonlinear. Special procedures would have to be adopted in causal analysis of the variables in this graph; for example, two approximately linear analyses may be carried out: one for values of W greater or equal to zero, another for values of W less than zero.

Additional examples of *linear relationships* are given in **3.12**, in which ellipses represent the outlines of distributions:

3.12

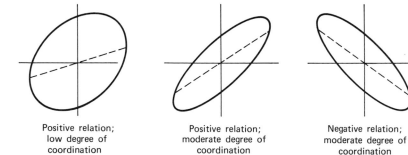

| Positive relation; low degree of coordination | Positive relation; moderate degree of coordination | Negative relation; moderate degree of coordination |

Scattergrams are constructed typically from tables of observed values; for example, returning to the example introduced in **3.1**, we get the graph in **3.13**.

3.13 Case X Y

Case	X	Y
1	$+1.0$	$+.5$
2	-3.0	-1.5
3	-1.0	$-.5$
4	$+3.0$	$+1.5$

gives the scattergram

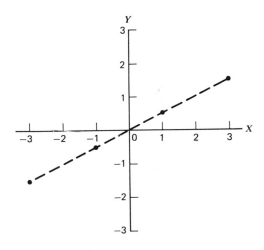

This example is interesting because the cases plot exactly along a straight line and suggest *perfect* linear coordination between X and Y. In fact, this is the case because the values of Y were generated from the values of X and the relationship $X \xrightarrow{\frac{1}{2}} Y$. Because nothing but X determines Y, the coordination of their values must be perfect. It is instructive, however, to consider what would happen were a slightly more complicated causal pattern involved.

3.14 W

$$X \xrightarrow{\frac{1}{2}} Y \quad \text{implies} \quad Y = \tfrac{1}{2}X + \tfrac{1}{4}W$$

If cases exist with the following values

Case	X	W	Y
1	−3.0	−1.0	−1.75
2	−1.0	+3.0	+.25
3	+1.0	−3.0	−.25
4	+3.0	+1.0	+1.75

then the X, Y scattergram is

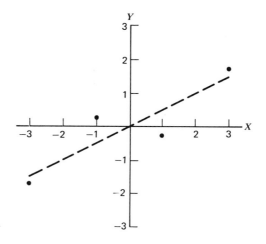

Clearly, adding another determinant for Y caused the net degree of linear coordination between X and Y to decline. The points in the X, Y scattergram no longer fall exactly on the straight line, and it is no longer possible to make an exact prediction of the value of Y for a new case, given just its value on X. This illustrates the manner in which disturbances confound expectations. They *add on* variations that cannot be accounted for in terms of the variables that have been observed.

Another thing to notice in **3.14** is that predictability went down, even though the causal relationship between X and Y remained the same as in **3.13** (the effects of X on Y are exactly the same in the two examples). This is because in the second example Y has additional variations induced by W and so X determines a smaller *proportion* of Y's total variance. More specifically, Y has a larger variance in the second example (1.56) than in the first example (in which the variance is 1.25). Because the variable X contributes the same amount of variance to Y in both instances, it necessarily contributes *proportionately* less to the variance of Y in the second example, thereby becoming a poorer predicter than it was in the simpler situation.

Covariance

Scattergrams are useful for determining whether coordination exists between two variables and what form it takes, but a more exact approach is needed to assess the degree of coordination. The most useful measure is the *covariance*. This index of coordination is analogous to the variance, but it characterizes the joint distribution of a pair of variables rather than the distributions of a single variable. The variance was obtained by multiplying the deviation scores by themselves and averaging. Similarly, the covariance is obtained by multiplying the deviation scores of one variable by the corresponding deviation scores on the second variable, and averaging the products. A covariance is represented by σ subscripted with the symbols of the two variables used to compute it. The order of subscripts does not matter: for example, $\sigma_{XY} = \sigma_{YX}$.

3.15 DEFINITION OF COVARIANCE

$\sigma_{XY} = \mathscr{E}(X \cdot Y)$, when both X and Y are measured as deviation scores.

Calculating covariances—example from **3.1**,

Case	X	Y	$X \cdot Y$
1	+1.0	+.5	+.5
2	−3.0	−1.5	+4.5
3	−1.0	−.5	+.5
4	+3.0	+1.5	+4.5
		Sum =	10.0

$\sigma_{XY} = \dfrac{10}{4} = 2.5$

If a covariance equals zero, it indicates that values of the two variables are completely uncoordinated (as in **3.11a**) or perhaps that the relationship is nonlinear (as in **3.11c**). Nonzero values of a covariance reflect the magnitude of a linear relationship like that shown in the first or second figure in **3.12**. A negative value signals a relationship like that in the third figure in **3.12**.

The covariance of a dependent variable and a source variable does not change if the system is modified by adding additional sources that are un-related to the original source; for example, the covariance between X and Y is the same in both diagrams in **3.16**.

3.16   The covariance σ_{XY} is the same in both cases, providing σ_X^2 is constant and X and W are uncoordinated.

$$W$$
$$\downarrow^{\frac{1}{2}}$$
$$X \xrightarrow{\frac{1}{2}} Y \quad X \xrightarrow{\frac{1}{2}} Y$$

The constancy of a covariance in situations like that in **3.16** is useful some-times, but, on the other hand, it means that the covariance obviously does not reflect the loss in predictability that occurs when disturbances are added. Another index is needed to indicate degree of predictability.

The Correlation Coefficient

A correlation coefficient measures the degree to which variations on one variable can be predicted from information on another. One of the most important correlation coefficients is the Pearson product-moment correla-tion, ρ (rho), which is the ratio of the actual covariance between two variables to the maximum possible covariance. If the observed covariance is zero, ρ is zero, and this value thus signifies that there is no linear coordination at all between variables. If the actual covariance is equal to the maximum covariance, ρ equals 1.0, and this means that the values of one variable can be predicted perfectly from values of the other. The observed covariance may be negative, indicating that high values of one variable correspond to low values of the other; ρ also is negative in such a case, thereby reflecting the fact of inverted coordination.

The maximum possible covariance is defined in terms of the product of two average deviation scores, one for each variable. The required quantities for this computation are the *standard deviations*, or the square roots of the variances of the two variables. Variances, of course, are the mean squared deviations, and so the square root of a variance represents an average deviation score.

Thus the formula defining the product moment correlation is

3.17 DEFINITION OF PEARSON'S PRODUCT-MOMENT CORRELATION COEFFICIENT

$$\rho_{XY} = \frac{\sigma_{XY}}{\sqrt{\sigma_X^2}\sqrt{\sigma_Y^2}} = \frac{\sigma_{XY}}{\sigma_X \sigma_Y}$$

The creation of deviation scores by subtracting the mean of the overall distribution from original measurements has been a useful strategy for simplifying formulas, and standard deviations can be used in a somewhat similar way to obtain certain additional simplifications in the definition of ρ.

Standard scores are deviation scores divided by the standard deviation of the distribution. The distinction between standard scores and ordinary deviation scores is reflected in the symbols for variables—*lower case letters are used for standard scores.*

3.18 DEFINITION OF A STANDARD SCORE. It is understood that X is already a deviation score.

$$x = \frac{X}{\sigma_X}$$

Variables measured in terms of standard scores always have a mean of zero (they are still deviation scores) and a variance of 1.0. This unique value of the variance is demonstrated in **3.19.**

3.19 The variance of a standardized variable is 1.0.

$$\sigma_x^2 = \mathscr{E}(x^2) = \mathscr{E}\left(\left[\frac{X}{\sigma_X}\right]^2\right) = \mathscr{E}\left(\frac{X^2}{\sigma_X^2}\right) = \mathscr{E}\left(\left[\frac{1}{\sigma_X^2}\right] \cdot X^2\right)$$

Now the value of $1/\sigma_X^2$ is constant because it is the same regardless of the particular observation of X being considered at the moment. Because it is a constant, it can be taken outside the expected-value term to give

$$\sigma_x^2 = \frac{1}{\sigma_X^2}\cdot\mathscr{E}(X^2) = \frac{1}{\sigma_X^2}\cdot\sigma_X^2 = 1.0$$

Moreover the correlation between two variables expressed in standard scores is exactly equal to their covariance:

3.20 The correlation of two standardized variables is the same as their covariance.

$$\rho_{xy} = \sigma_{xy}$$

because

$$\rho_{xy} = \frac{\sigma_{xy}}{\sqrt{\sigma_x^2}\sqrt{\sigma_y^2}} = \frac{\sigma_{xy}}{\sqrt{1}\sqrt{1}}$$

$$= \sigma_{xy}.$$

By following a procedure like that in **3.19** it can also be shown that the correlation between two variables in standardized form is equal to the correlation of the variables in unstandardized form; that is, $\rho_{XY} = \rho_{xy}$. However, the *covariance* of two variables measured in terms of regular deviation scores is not generally the same as their covariance when measured in standard scores. There are no numerical limits for covariances in general, but the covariances of standard scores must fall within the range -1.0 to $+1.0$ because they are equivalent to correlation coefficients.

LINEAR REGRESSION

Coordination between two variables makes it possible to transform information concerning one variable into information about the other; for example, referring again to **3.11b**, it can be seen that the value of X has implications concerning the value of Z—a positive X value is usually associated with positive Z, a negative X value generally implies negative Z. Actually, the line drawn through the points suggests that a particular X value can be transformed into the precise value of Z to be expected with that X, as demonstrated in **3.21**:

3.21

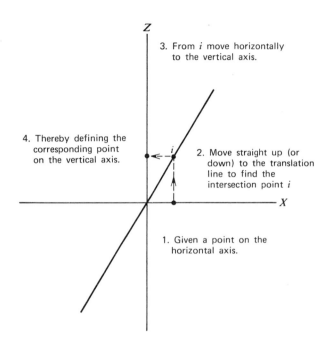

3. From i move horizontally to the vertical axis.

4. Thereby defining the corresponding point on the vertical axis.

2. Move straight up (or down) to the translation line to find the intersection point i

1. Given a point on the horizontal axis.

Of course, the expected value of Z generated from the value of X is rarely exactly the same as the observed value of Z. Such exact correspondence holds true only for those cases that fall right on the translation line. Nevertheless, the predicted values provide better guesses about the values of Z than, say, just guessing that every case has a Z value equal to the mean value of Z over the whole distribution.

   Lines for translating values of one variable into expected values on another are called *regression lines*. If X is a causal determinant of Z, the word "regression" can be interpreted as follows: the line shows the value of Z to which all cases with a given X would "regress" if disturbances in Z were removed. Regression lines may be linear **(3.11b)** or curvilinear **(3.11c)**, but here only linear regression lines are considered in accordance with the decision to restrict attention to linear systems. The linear assumption is restrictive: it implies that certain relationships (like **3.11c**) either cannot be dealt with or must be approximated, in one way or another, by linear relations.

A regression line ideally defines a precise expectation about the value of a predicted variable, given information on a predictor variable, and such precision cannot be obtained just by eyeballing a line through a set of points. Some objective procedure is needed to define the single best translation line.

The best line is the one that comes closest to predicting the vertical positioning of every point on the scattergram, and it is desirable to measure "closeness" in terms of squared distances. Moreover, it is presumed that extreme points on the scattergram are more crucial for positioning the line than those close to the center; therefore the importance of each case is also weighted by its squared deviation score on the predictor variable. The best line thus is identified as one that produces the smallest sum of weighted squared distances between the line and all points on the scattergram. Finding such a line is a problem that can be solved mathematically by calculus. Only the results of the mathematical analysis are considered here, however.

The desired line always passes through the origin of the scattergram when variables are measured in terms of deviation scores. In addition, the mathematical analysis defines a *regression coefficient*, or slope, that equals the expected value of the predicted variable when the predictor variable equals $+1.0$. Thus we know two points through which the optimal regression line passes, and thereby the regression line can be plotted exactly.

Having defined closeness-of-fit in terms of squared deviations weighted by other squared deviations, it is not too surprising to find that the mathematical solution for the regression coefficient is defined in terms of a variance and a covariance.

3.22   A regression coefficient is defined as the slope of a regression line for predicting Z from values of X. The order of subscripts on the regression coefficient is significant: the first is the predicted variable, the second is the predictor.

$$b_{ZX} = \frac{\sigma_{ZX}}{\sigma_X^2}$$

A subscripted letter b is conventional for symbolizing a regression coefficient. *This is why subscripted b's are avoided as symbols for structural coefficients: the letter b is reserved as a symbol for regression coefficients.*

The regression coefficient can be used in an algebraic formula to predict one variable from another, thereby eliminating the need to draw a graph.

3.23 Use of the regression coefficient in a prediction formula. $\hat{Z}$ is the expected value of Z, given a value of the predictor X, when X and Z are measured in terms of deviation scores

$$\hat{Z} = b_{ZX} \cdot X$$

There is no statistical basis for deciding which variable should be the predictor and which the predicted, and indeed two regressions that will result in two prediction formulas can always be run. In general, the regression coefficients in the two formulas are not the same; that is, $b_{ZX} \neq b_{XZ}$. In causal analyses a selection is made between the two coefficients on the basis of theoretical information. Attention is usually focused on the coefficient for predicting an outcome variable from values of a source variable.

Residual Variance

Suppose we calculated the average squared difference between observed values and the predicted values obtained from a regression formula. The resulting quantity is a variance—a mean squared difference between observed and expected values—that can be interpreted from three somewhat different perspectives. First, it is a measure of the scattering of points around the regression line; that is, this new variance equals zero if all points fall exactly on the regression line and it becomes larger than zero as the average distance between points and the regression line increases. Second, it is a measure of the residual variations left in the predicted variable after predictions have been made. Thus it measures the extent to which variations in the dependent variable cannot be predicted. For the third interpretation suppose that the errors in prediction were caused by adding the values of a variable e to the predicted values. The new variance is the variance of this variable e, or σ_e^2. The variable e may be considered as a composite variable representing all factors that cause errors in prediction.

3.24 DEFINITION OF RESIDUAL OR ERROR VARIANCE

$$\sigma_e^2 = \mathscr{E}([Z - \hat{Z}]^2)$$

Because the regression line was mathematically derived to take account of every bit of linear coordination between the predictor and the predicted variable, the residuals, or errors in prediction, are themselves uncorrelated with the values of the predictor; for example, in a linear relation the prediction errors cannot all be positive when the predictor X is positive because such a situation would have forced the regression line to twist upward to take advantage of the extra predictability available from the residuals. This independence between predictions and errors permits a basic principle to be stated.

The total variance in the predicted variable is equal to the variance of the predicted values plus the variance of the residuals.

3.25 The variance of a variable can be partitioned into the component that is predictable from a linear regression plus the variance of the residuals that are left when the predicted values are subtracted from the observed values.

$$\sigma_Z^2 = \sigma_{\hat{Z}}^2 + \sigma_e^2$$

A more convenient formula for calculating residual variance can be obtained by defining a *coefficient of determination:*

3.26 The coefficient of determination for a linear regression is the variance of the predicted values divided by the variance of the observed values. The ratio is symbolized by a subscripted R^2.

$$R_{Z \cdot X}^2 = \frac{\sigma_{\hat{Z}}^2}{\sigma_Z^2}$$

When Z is predicted from just *one* other variable, the coefficient of determination is identical to the squared correlation coefficient:

$$R_{Z \cdot X}^2 = \rho_{ZX}^2$$

Given the formulas in **3.25** and **3.26**, the value of the error variance can be defined as follows:

3.27   This alternate formula defines the residual variance

$$\sigma_e^2 = \sigma_Z^2(1 - R_{Z \cdot X}^2)$$

If only one variable (X) is used to predict Z, this is equivalent to

$$\sigma_e^2 = \sigma_Z^2(1 - \rho_{XZ}^2)$$

MULTIPLE REGRESSION

Predictions usually can be improved by using several predictor variables rather than just one—by moving from a bivariate to a multivariate analysis; for example, if the predicted variable is Z and it is coordinated with a variable Y as well as with the original predictor X, then perhaps Y can be used to predict some of the residual variations that are left after Z is regressed on X. If so, it actually should be possible to develop a single prediction formula to show the expected value of Z, given measurements on both X and Y. The variance of the residuals left after applying this new formula should be less than the residual variance after predicting from X alone.

The basic rationale of *multiple regression* is to attempt to predict the residuals left from one regression by carrying out still another thereby building up a more accurate prediction based on multiple predictors. This essentially simple notion, however, is complicated by the requirement that the regression coefficients must fit together into a single prediction formula. This would not be a problem if predictor variables were always uncorrelated with one another, for then predictions from one variable would have no coordination with predictions from other variables, and the results of different predictions could be added together. But typically, predictors *are* correlated; so their predictions are coordinated to some degree, and the redundancy in predictions will create a bias if they are just added one to another.

So the problem actually is defined as follows: obtain a single formula for predicting the value of one variable (Z) from the values of other variables $(X, Y, \text{etc.})$. Take into account any correlations among the predictors so that each regression coefficient reflects only the differing predictions that would be made from variations in one variable when all the other predictors have a constant value.

In effect, the mathematical solution of this problem calls for a multitude of different regressions; for example, the coefficient for predicting Z from X, controlling for Y, is obtained by first regressing Z on Y to obtain the residuals from that prediction. Then, in case there is any correlation among the predictors, X is also regressed on Y to obtain a set of residual X values that are uncorrelated with Y. Finally, the Z residuals are regressed on the X residuals to obtain the regression coefficient with the desired properties. The same steps are repeated to obtain the regression coefficient for predicting Z from Y, controlling for X.

Thus the coefficients in a multiple regression problem represent the slopes of regression lines that predict the values of one set of residuals from the values of another. These slopes, or *partial regression coefficients*, are also symbolized by a b, but now with dot subscripts; for example, $b_{ZX \cdot Y}$ is the coefficient for predicting Z residuals from X residuals when both have been regressed on Y; $b_{ZY \cdot X}$ is the coefficient for predicting Z residuals from Y residuals when both have been regressed on X.

Partial regression coefficients are not inflated by coordinated predictions because each coefficient depends only on the coordination between a predictor and predicted variable left after other predictions have been made and after the correlations among predictors have been statistically removed. Put together in a single formula they are nonredundant and provide a single unbiased prediction.

3.28   This example of a prediction formula is based on multiple regression:

$$\hat{Z} = b_{ZX \cdot Y}X + b_{ZY \cdot X}Y$$

where X, Y, and Z are measured as deviation scores.

Fortunately a multitude of different regressions need not be carried out to obtain partial regression coefficients. When there are just two predictors, the formula in **3.29**, obtained by mathematical analysis, accomplishes the same result.

3.29 Calculating formula for a partial regression coefficient:

$$b_{ZY \cdot X} = \frac{\sigma_X^2 \sigma_{ZY} - \sigma_{ZX}\sigma_{YX}}{\sigma_Y^2 \sigma_X^2 - (\sigma_{YX})^2}$$

When there are more than two predictors, the calculating formulas become complex and it is generally impractical to calculate coefficients by hand. Electronic computers are economical in such cases, and most computer libraries contain a multiple-regression program that will calculate partial regression coefficients from the variances and covariances of variables or from original observations on them.

In the multivariate case, just as in the bivariate, the residuals can be obtained by subtracting predicted scores ($\hat{Z}$) from original scores (Z). Again *the nature of the mathematical solution guarantees that the residuals are uncorrelated with any of the predictor variables.*

The variance of the residuals from multivariate prediction can be obtained easily by using the multivariate definition of the coefficient of determination. This is provided by the formula in **3.30** in the case of two predictors.

3.30 Coefficient of determination for two predictor variables:

$$R_{Z \cdot XY}^2 = b_{ZY \cdot X}^2 \left(\frac{\sigma_Y^2}{\sigma_Z^2}\right) + b_{ZX \cdot Y}^2 \left(\frac{\sigma_X^2}{\sigma_Z^2}\right) + 2b_{ZY \cdot X}b_{ZX \cdot Y}\left(\frac{\sigma_{XY}}{\sigma_Z^2}\right)$$

With more than two predictors the formula becomes complex. Computer programs ordinarily calculate the *multiple regression coefficient*, or *R*, and the coefficient of determination is simply the square of *R*. So the squared multiple correlation coefficient can be used in the top formula of **3.27** to define the residual variance in a multiple regression problem.

STANDARDIZED COEFFICIENTS

Regressions can be carried out with variables that have been standardized. The slopes of regression lines are generally changed by changing measurement scales to standardized form, and this is reflected in the use of a different symbol for the *standardized regression coefficients*—a subscripted β instead of a subscripted b. The values of the standardized coefficients can be obtained without actually rescaling the original measurements and rerunning the regression as shown by the formula in **3.31**.

3.31 Standardized regression coefficients can be calculated from the statistics for unstandardized data:

$$\beta_{zx} = b_{zx}\frac{\sigma_x}{\sigma_z}$$

In the bivariate case (one predictor variable) a standardized regression coefficient is identical to the correlation coefficient (ρ); the coefficient obtained when the original predictor and predicted variables are reversed also equals ρ.

3.32 If there is just one predictor variable, then

$$\beta_{XY} = \beta_{YX} = \rho_{XY}$$

These equalities do not hold generally in the multivariate case. In fact, then a β may even be outside the -1 to $+1$ range of the correlation coefficient.

Partialed β's may be obtained in the multivariate case directly from the correlations among variables. The formula, when there are just two predictors, is given in **3.33**.

3.33 Computing formula for a standardized partial regression coefficient:

$$\beta_{zx\cdot y} = \frac{\rho_{zx} - \rho_{zy}\cdot\rho_{xy}}{1 - \rho_{xy}^2}$$

Most computer programs for regression analysis calculate the standardized coefficients as well as the unstandardized coefficients; problems involving more than two predictors are rarely calculated by hand.

The formulas for coefficients of determination given in **3.26** and **3.30** can be rewritten in different forms by using standardized regression coefficients.

3.34   When there is just *one* predictor variable,

$$R^2_{y \cdot x} = \beta^2_{yx} = \beta^2_{xy}$$

When there are *two* predictor variables,

$$R^2_{z \cdot yx} = \beta^2_{zy \cdot x} + \beta^2_{zx \cdot y} + 2\beta_{zy \cdot x} \cdot \beta_{zx \cdot y} \cdot \rho_{xy}$$

The second formula can easily be extended to the general multivariate case or computer calculations can be depended on when there are more than two predictors.

The formula in **3.27** can still be used to define the variance of the residuals left after subtracting predicted values from original values, but because measurement scales are now standardized the original variance of the predicted variable must be 1.0 and therefore the variance of the residuals is simply 1.0 minus the coefficient of determination.

REGRESSION AND CAUSAL INFERENCE

A regression equation is only a means of translating one kind of information into another. Causal processes may be the reason why such a translation is possible, but this does not mean that a regression equation will reveal those processes in any simple way. For example, the system $Y \xleftarrow{a} X \xrightarrow{c} Z$ leads to coordination between the values of X and Y, allowing us to predict Y from information on X. The regression equation $Y = b_{YX}X$ has some correspondence with the structural equation that specifies the causal linkage between X and Y, and in this simple case b_{YX} is an estimator of **a**. However, one could use the same empirical coordination to predict values of X from values of Y, and the coefficient b_{XY} would not be a direct estimator of **a**. Further, the system will coordinate Y and Z (because of their mutual dependence on X), allowing prediction from one to the other, even though these two variables have no direct causal linkage at all. In this case the regression coefficient will correspond to no single structural coefficient.

Moreover, coordination between variables can be produced by selection mechanisms that are unrelated to causal linkages between the variables; for example, suppose that cases occur in a population only if the sum of two attributes, X and Y is above a criterion value. Then, within that population, X and Y will be coordinated to some degree (low values on one variable must be associated with high values on the other), and perhaps a regression equation could be used to translate information on one variable into information on the other. The regression equation has no value at all, however, for inferring a causal linkage between X and Y because the coordination was not generated by causal relations between these variables but rather was imposed by a "gating" mechanism.

It will be seen later that regressions are useful in causal analyses, but *regression equations cannot be viewed routinely as structural equations directly representing causal processes.*

SOURCES AND ADDITIONAL READINGS

Numerous serviceable texts on statistics are available—too many to list. The titles given here are mentioned because they are oriented explicitly toward the use of statistics in causal analysis and model building. An elementary presentation is provided by Hubert M. Blalock, Jr., *Social Statistics* (New York: McGraw-Hill, 1960); on regression techniques see F. Kerlinger and E. Pedhazur, *Multiple Regression in Behavioral Research* (New York: Holt, Rinehart & Winston, 1973). Arthur S. Goldberger, *Econometric Theory* (New York: Wiley, 1964), provides a mathematical treatment of regression analysis and maintains a high level of clarity and relevance throughout. John P. Van de Geer, *Introduction to Multivariate Analysis for the Social Sciences* (San Francisco: Freeman, 1971), describes a wide variety of statistical procedures and uses flowgraphs to show how different analytic techniques —regression analysis, canonical analysis, and factor analysis—relate to various causal models.

All advanced treatments of multiple regression and other multivariate techniques depend to some degree on the use of matrix algebra. An entertaining introduction to this topic is available in Philip J. Davis, *The Mathematics of Matrices: A First Book of Matrix Theory and Linear Algebra* (New York: Blaisdell, 1965). The Van de Geer and Goldberger texts provide additional instruction.

EXERCISES

1. A President of the United States might be treated as an operator who produces certain relationships. Is it possible to study a given presidency statistically within a static framework?

2. The distribution of families on income is typically skewed—most of the families have relatively low incomes, whereas a few are worth millions. Assume that such a skewed income distribution occurs in a specially defined population in which the size of family dwellings is approximately normally distributed. Also assume that in this population the rich have larger dwellings.

(a) Make a graph for plotting the joint distribution of income and dwelling size and roughly outline the shape that the distribution would require.

(b) Could such a distribution be generated by a linear causal system involving a relation from income to dwelling size? Could the distribution be evidence of a developmental process as opposed to a causal process (see Chapter 1)?

(c) Suppose another population were examined in which the distribution of dwelling size was also skewed, most families having relatively small dwellings. Could there be a linear relation between income and dwelling size in this case?

3. All buses have one driver. Suppose another driver with equal control of the vehicle were added beside the first but with a wall between them and their control actions summated before being transmitted to the vehicle. Would these buses be safer with two drivers determining the variations in speed and direction?

4. What can be said in the following instances:

(a) A researcher finds a product-moment correlation of $+1.08$ between I.Q. and grade point average (GPA).

(b) The unstandardized regression coefficient for predicting I.Q. from GPA is $+10.00$.

5. Convert the following expression to a more elementary form by using the algebra of expectations and the definition of the mean:

$$\mathscr{E}[(X - \bar{X})^2]$$

(These X's indicate original measurements, not deviation scores. Note, however, that the quantity in parenthesis represents a deviation score, and in fact the whole expression is the definition of the variance of X.)

6. Reduce the following expression, as in problem 5.

$$\mathscr{E}[(X - \bar{X})(Y - \bar{Y})]$$

(Note that the expression defines the covariance of X and Y.)

7. Reduce the following expression.

$$\mathscr{E}[(\hat{X} + e)^2]$$

Here, however, presume that both $\hat{X}$ and e are measured as deviation scores. From your results specify exactly what must be true if the variance of a variable is exactly equal to the variance of predicted values plus the variance of errors from predictions.

8. Suppose that $\beta_{SF\cdot E} = .015$, where S stands for a son's occupational status, E stands for a son's education, and F stands for a father's occupational status. Interpret the "finding" from a purely statistical standpoint.

9. In Bizarreville USA, the correlations among the variables in problem 8 are

$$\rho_{FE} = -.60, \qquad \rho_{ES} = .30, \qquad \rho_{FS} = .50$$

Calculate the standardized partial regression coefficient $\beta_{SF\cdot E}$ by using the formula in **3.33**. Interpret the meaning of the answer.

4 PATH ANALYSIS

Most causal analyses in the social sciences are conducted within the framework of *cross-sectional statics*. It is presumed that a single basic causal structure is operative for numerous separate cases and that each case is observed after its inputs have been set and held constant long enough for all causal consequences to be realized. Thus, for example, the socioeconomic achievement of individuals might be studied from this perspective, presuming that essentially the same system of personal, social, and cultural operators applies for all persons studied, that key inputs are set at some point early in an individual's life, and that observations of the individuals are delayed until they have actualized the full consequences of their inputs.

Such an orientation is static because observations are made after the causal consequences of the predetermined variables are realized, when both inputs and outputs are being maintained in steady states. Of course, this is the same condition that applied in Chapter 2. The approach is cross-sectional in that it does not focus on a single example of a causal system (as in Chapter 2) but on a multitude of cases with equivalent causal structures, all observed at more or less the same time.

Within this framework knowledge of a system's causal structure can be used to transform a statistical description of inputs into a statistical description of outcomes. The techniques are the topic of this chapter. On the other hand, given statistical descriptions of inputs and outcomes, it is possible to make some inferences about the causal structure that transformed one to the other. This is the topic of Chapter 5.

All analyses in cross-sectional statics are based on the premise that the causal systems operating in different cases are equivalent: they have the same organization and structural parameters and the causal operators are in working order for each. In this and the following chapter it is assumed that these

111

requirements are met by careful definition of the set of cases to be considered, excluding those that have deviant structures or nonworking operators.

FLOWGRAPH MODIFICATIONS

Expressions for the variances, covariances, and correlations generated by a system can be read directly from a causal diagram that has been modified properly. The basic principles, called *path analysis*, were developed in the 1910s and 1920s by biologist Sewall Wright. The sections that follow describe how to modify a diagram so it is subject to path analysis and then rules are stated for expressing covariances, variances, and correlations as products and sums of diagram quantities. The conventions and rules of path analysis presented in this chapter differ somewhat from traditional presentations by Wright and others. The adjustments have been made to emphasize the basic simplicity of the procedures, to demonstrate that the procedures are applicable to studying covariances as well as correlations, and to extend routine path analytic procedures to the study of systems with loops.

Loop Reduction

As originally developed, path analysis applied only to systems without feedback loops of any kind. From one perspective this restriction still holds, and the theory of flowgraphs extends path analysis only by showing how loops can be removed from a diagram so that the ordinary path analysis rules apply. Because of its conceptual simplicity, this is the perspective adopted here.

IV.1 *Path analysis of systems with loops requires redrawing the system diagram with each loop or loop complex in semireduced form* (see rule II.18).

Actually, it would be possible to state special rules of path analysis for analyzing loops in their original form, but such rules would add to the conceptual complexity of path analysis. For an introductory treatment it may be preferable to make the diagrams complex (by reducing all loops) but leaving the ideas simple.

Input Covariances

The statistical outcomes of system operations depend on the system's structural coefficients and the statistical characteristics of inputs. In turning from flowgraph analysis of individual cases to path analysis of a cross section of cases, modifications must be made in diagrams to summarize certain statistical characteristics of inputs. In particular, an explicit representation must be provided for the coordination of inputs *before* the system operates.

IV.2 *The covariances of sources must be represented on a system flowgraph before the diagram can be interpreted statistically. A covariance is represented graphically as a source for its two variables, and is linked to them by dotted- rather than solid-line arrows.*

4.1 Elaboration of a diagram representing covariances among input variables.

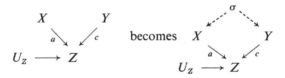

The dotted-line arrows are used because *the covariance terms are not compatible with ordinary flowgraph analyses; they represent distributional quantities and are applicable only in deriving distributional statistics.*

In traditional biological and sociological path analyses correlations among inputs have been represented by curved double-headed arrows labeled with a symbol for the correlation coefficient. The convention adopted here provides a more distinctive signal for these special kinds of path (which is desirable when complex systems with loops are considered), and the treatment of covariances as "pseudo-sources" helps to simplify the statement of path analytic rules. For the sake of continuity, however, the old convention is retained when path analysis of standardized variables, the original concern, is discussed.

Disturbance Covariances

Disturbance terms represent unspecified sources for each dependent variable in the system; therefore the statistical characteristics of disturbances must be considered in any study of the system's statistical consequences. The covariances of disturbances with each other and with explicit inputs must also be added to the diagram as shown in **4.2**.

4.2

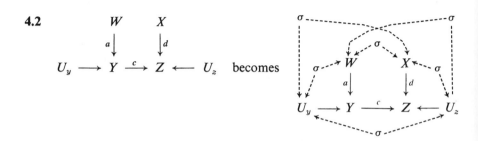

Clearly, disturbance covariances will complicate a diagram considerably. It will be seen later that if the covariance of two inputs is zero in value, that covariance contributes nothing to distributional statistics. Thus such a term can be deleted from a diagram without loss and will simplify appearance. In the following sections it is generally presumed that disturbance terms are not correlated with specified inputs or with one another; hence their covariances need not be added to the diagram. Path analysis rules are not restricted by this assumption. It is adopted only heuristically to keep diagrams simple. On the other hand, it is shown in Chapter 5 that uncorrelated disturbances are frequently required when identifying system operators in empirical data.

ANALYZING STATISTICAL COORDINATION

Coordinating Paths

Causal relations can create coordination among system variables in three different ways.

1. Two variables may have coordinated values because they are dependent on the same system sources (e.g., $Y \leftarrow X \rightarrow Z$, where Y and Z are mutually dependent on X). Changes in the source are transmitted to both dependent variables, causing their values to be coordinated to some degree.

2. Two variables may also be coordinated because of preexisting coordination on source variables. This coordination causes outcome variables to be more aligned than would otherwise be expected; for example, if W and X are source variables and the system transforms values of W to get values of Y and values of X to get values of Z, then any preexisting coordination between W and X will tend to be passed on to Y and Z.

3. If one variable causally determines another, either directly or through intervening variables, the values of the two variables are coordinated by the causal transformation of source values into values on the dependent variable.

Coordinations produced by the first two mechanisms are referred to as spurious correlations in that they do not originate in direct causal linkages. However, in statistical analysis coordination is important whatever its source. Therefore the following rule, which defines the kinds of path in causal diagrams that generate coordination, makes no special distinction between the three mechanisms; it incorporates all three into the concept of a coordinating path.

IV.3 *A "coordinating path" between two variables consists of a sequence of arrows that fulfills the following conditions:*

(a) *The two variables of interest are the end points of the path.*
(b) *The path consists of two subchains, each branching away from a variable or a covariance term on the graph and proceeding unidirectionally toward the end points. The variable or covariance term where the subchains begin is the path's "origin." The subchains point away from the origin toward the end points.*
(c) *The path impinges on any variable or covariance term only once.*
(d) *The origin of a path may be one of the end points, in which case one of the two subchains is not distinguishable and the entire coordinating path consists of a single subchain.*

Despite the lengthiness of this rule, coordinating paths are easy to identify. Essentially we begin at one variable, trace back along arrows to an origin, then forward until the other variable is reached. *A coordinating path is identified symbolically by the variables on which it impinges. The origin is identified by script or by a covariance symbol.*

4.3

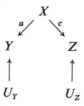

A single coordinating path exists between Y and Z: it is ($Y\mathscr{X}Z$) or ($Z\mathscr{X}Y$). The two identifiers are equivalent—they represent a single coordinating path.

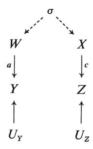

The only coordinating path for Y and Z is ($YW\sigma XZ$). The σ in a path identifier always represents the covariance of the variables on either side of it.

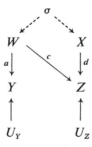

Here Y and Z have two coordinating paths: ($Y\mathscr{W}Z$) and ($YW\sigma XZ$).

$$W \xrightarrow{a} X \longleftarrow U_X$$
$$d \downarrow$$
$$U_Y \longrightarrow Y \xrightarrow{c} Z \longleftarrow U_Z$$

$(X\mathscr{W}\,YZ)$ is the only coordinating path between X and Z. $(X\mathscr{W}\,Y)$ is the only coordinating path between X and Y.

The procedure of tracing back from one end point, then forward to the other, must be adhered to rigorously. We cannot trace forward, then backward, or backward, forward, backward. In general, once we have begun tracing forward along arrows, the path cannot be extended by changing direction.

4.4

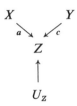

No coordinating path exists between X and Y in this diagram. In particular, $(X\mathscr{Z}\,Y)$ is *not a coordinating path* because the arrows do not lead *from* the origin *to* the end points.

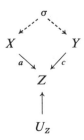

Here $(X\sigma Y)$ is the only coordinating path between X and Y.

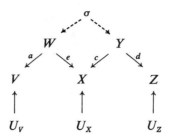

V and Z are coordinated by $(VW\sigma YZ)$ only. $(VW\mathcal{X}YZ)$ is *not* a coordinating path because it involves changing direction more than once.

Part (c) of the rule, which states that a path cannot impinge on the same variable twice, further limits the possible definitions of coordinating paths in some cases, as illustrated in **4.5**.

4.5

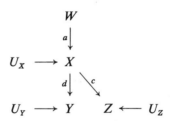

Y and Z have only one coordinating path $(Y\mathcal{X}Z)$. In particular, $(YX\mathcal{W}XZ)$ is not treated as a coordinating path because it passes through X twice.

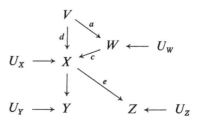

Again, only $(Y\mathcal{X}Z)$ is a coordinating path for Y and Z. $(YX\mathcal{V}WXZ)$ passes through X twice.

Part (d) of the rule extends the definition to the important special case in which the origin is identical to one of the end points. Its application is illustrated in **4.6**.

4.6 $$X \xrightarrow{a} Y \longleftarrow U_Y$$

X and Y are coordinated by the path $(\mathcal{X} Y)$.

$$
\begin{array}{c}
X \\
a \downarrow \quad \searrow d \\
U_Y \longrightarrow Y \xrightarrow{c} Z \longleftarrow U_Z
\end{array}
$$

X and Y are coordinated by $(\mathcal{X} Y)$.
Y and Z are coordinated by $(Y\mathcal{X}Z)$ and $(\mathcal{Y}Z)$,
X and Z are coordinated by $(\mathcal{X} YZ)$ and $(\mathcal{X}Z)$.

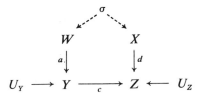

W and Y are coordinated by $(\mathcal{W} Y)$. W and Z are coordinated by $(\mathcal{W}\sigma XZ)$ and $(\mathcal{W} YZ)$. Y and Z are coordinated by $(YW\sigma XZ)$ and $(\mathcal{Y}Z)$. X and Y are coordinated by $(X\sigma WY)$. Additional coordinating paths exist between X and Z.

The identification of coordinating paths in diagrams with loops presents no special problems, provided that the diagrams are appropriately redrawn with loops in semireduced form.

4.7

$$
\begin{array}{c}
X \xrightarrow{a} Y \overset{\circlearrowright d}{\longleftarrow} U_Y \\
\downarrow c \\
Z \longleftarrow U_Z
\end{array}
\quad \text{is redrawn} \quad
\begin{array}{c}
U_Y \\
\downarrow \\
X \xrightarrow{a} Y' \xrightarrow[\frac{1}{1-d}]{} Y \\
\qquad\qquad\quad \downarrow c \\
\qquad\qquad\quad Z \longleftarrow U_Z
\end{array}
$$

X and Y have one coordinating path, $(\mathcal{X} Y'Y)$; X and Z have one coordinating path, $(\mathcal{X} Y' YZ)$; Y and Z have one coordinating path $(\mathcal{Y}Z)$.

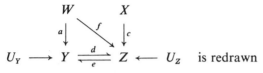

X and Y have one coordinating path: $(\mathscr{X}\,Y'\,Y)$; X and Z have one coordinating path $(\mathscr{X}\,Y'Z)$.

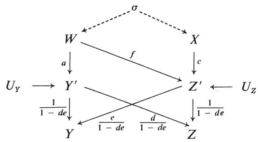

Coordinating paths between W and Z $(W\sigma XZ'Z)$, $(\mathscr{W}\,Z'Z)$, $(\mathscr{W}\,Y'Z)$. There are six coordinating paths between Y and Z: $(YY'\mathscr{W}\,Z'Z)$, $(Y\mathscr{Y}'Z)$, $(YZ'\mathscr{W}\,Y'Z)$, $(Y\mathscr{Z}'Z)$, and two others.

Covariance Analysis

IV.4   *A "coordinating-path effect" is the product of the structural coefficients along the path times the variance of the origin variable. If the origin is a covariance term, the effect is the product of the structural coefficients times that covariance term.*

A coordinating-path effect is symbolized by a C, subscripted with the path identifier. Examples are provided in **4.8**.

4.8

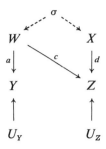

There are two coordinating paths between Y and Z. Their effects are

$$C_{YW\sigma XZ} = a \cdot 1 \cdot 1 \cdot d \cdot \sigma_{WX} = a \cdot d \cdot \sigma_{WX}$$
$$C_{YWZ} = a \cdot c \cdot \sigma_W^2$$

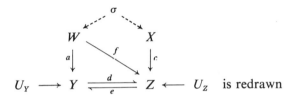 is redrawn

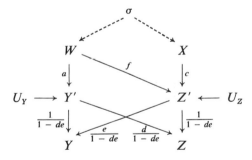

For the coordinating paths between W and Z

$$C_{W\sigma XZ'Z} = \frac{c}{1 -\!- de}\sigma_{WX}$$

$$C_{WZ'Z} = \frac{f}{1 - de}\sigma_W^2$$

$$C_{WY'Z} = \frac{ad}{1 - de}\sigma_W^2$$

For the six coordinating paths between Y and Z

$$C_{YY'\mathscr{W}Z'Z} = \frac{a}{1-de} \cdot \frac{f}{1-de}\sigma_W^2 = \frac{a \cdot f}{(1-de)^2}\sigma_W^2$$

$$C_{Y\mathscr{Y}'Z} \quad = \frac{d}{(1-de)^2}\sigma_{Y'}^2$$

$$C_{YZ'\mathscr{W}Y'Z} = \frac{e \cdot f \cdot a \cdot d}{(1-de)^2}\sigma_W^2$$

$$C_{Y\mathscr{X}'Z} \quad = \frac{e}{(1-de)^2}\sigma_{Z'}^2$$

$$C_{YY'W\sigma XZ'Z} = \frac{ac}{(1-de)^2}\sigma_{WX}$$

$$C_{YZ'X\sigma WY'Z} = \frac{e \cdot c \cdot a \cdot d}{(1-de)^2}\sigma_{WX}$$

Coordinating paths traced in reverse directions are not distinguished if they impinge on the same points. The effect is the same regardless of the end point used to start tracing the path.

4.9

$C_{Y\mathscr{X}Z} = a \cdot c \cdot \sigma_X^2$; $C_{Z\mathscr{X}Y} = c \cdot a \cdot \sigma_X^2$. Thus $C_{Y\mathscr{X}Z} = C_{Z\mathscr{X}Y}$.

A coordinating path effect defines the covariance between two variables resulting from a particular chain of causal linkages; for example, with $X \xrightarrow{a} Y$ we have $C_{\mathscr{X}Y} = a \cdot \sigma_X^2$, the correct expression for the covariance of X and Y. (It is not proved here, but **4.17** illustrates how any path analysis result can be confirmed algebraically.) In more complicated problems, with multiple coordinating paths between variables, covariances are defined by rule IV.5.

IV.5 *The covariance of two variables is the sum of the effects along all distinct coordinating paths between the variables.*

In other words, each coordinating path generates a certain amount of co-variation between two variables—the amount indicated by the coordinating path effect. The total covariation is the sum of the covariations produced by all the different coordinating paths. The examples in **4.10** illustrate sundry ways in which covariation between two variables can accumulate.

4.10 $X \xrightarrow{a} Y \longleftarrow U_Y$
$\qquad\qquad\qquad\qquad\qquad\qquad\qquad \sigma_{XY} = C_{\mathscr{X}Y} = a\sigma_X^2$

$$X$$
$$a \swarrow \quad \searrow c$$
$$U_Y \longrightarrow Y \qquad Z \longleftarrow U_Z \qquad\qquad \sigma_{YZ} = C_{Y\mathscr{X}Z} = ac\sigma_X^2$$

$$\sigma$$
$$W \quad\quad X$$
$$a\downarrow \qquad \downarrow c$$
$$U_Y \longrightarrow Y \qquad Z \longleftarrow U_Z \qquad\qquad \sigma_{YZ} = C_{YW\sigma XZ} = ac\sigma_{WX}$$

$$\sigma$$
$$V \quad\quad W$$
$$a\downarrow \quad X \quad \downarrow e$$
$$\quad c\swarrow \searrow d$$
$$U_Y \longrightarrow Y \qquad Z \longleftarrow U_Z$$
$$\qquad\qquad\qquad \sigma_{YZ} = C_{Y\mathscr{X}Z} + C_{YV\sigma WZ}$$
$$\qquad\qquad\qquad\quad = cd\sigma_X^2 + ae\sigma_{VW}$$

$$W$$
$$a\downarrow \quad\backslash$$
$$U_X \longrightarrow X \quad \backslash c$$
$$f\downarrow \quad \backslash d$$
$$U_Y \longrightarrow Y \xrightarrow{e} Z \longleftarrow U_Z$$
$$\sigma_{YZ} = C_{\mathscr{Y}Z} + C_{Y\mathscr{X}Z} + C_{YX\mathscr{W}Z}$$
$$\quad = e\sigma_Y^2 + fd\sigma_X^2 + afc\sigma_W^2$$
$$\sigma_{XZ} = C_{X\mathscr{Y}Z} + C_{\mathscr{X}Z} + C_{X\mathscr{W}Z}$$
$$\quad = fe\sigma_X^2 + d\sigma_X^2 + ac\sigma_W^2$$

The coordinating-path rules apply in systems with loops, once the loops have been reduced, as in **4.11**.

4.11

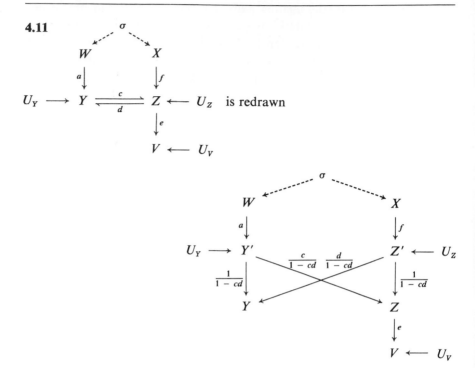

Covariances among the variables can be read from the revised diagram, as in the following examples:

$$\sigma_{WZ} = C_{W'Y'Z} + C_{W\sigma XZ'Z} = \frac{ac}{1-cd}\sigma_W^2 + \frac{f}{1-cd}\sigma_{WX}$$

$$\sigma_{WV} = C_{W'Y'ZV} + C_{W\sigma XZ'ZV} = \frac{ace}{1-cd}\sigma_W^2 + \frac{fe}{1-cd}\sigma_{WX}$$

$$\sigma_{YZ} = C_{Y'Y'Z} + C_{YZ'Y} + C_{YY'W\sigma XZ'Z} + C_{YZ'X\sigma WY'Z}$$

$$= \frac{c}{(1-cd)^2}\sigma_{Y'}^2 + \frac{d}{(1-cd)^2}\sigma_{Z'}^2 + \frac{af}{(1-cd)^2}\sigma_{WX} + \frac{afcd}{(1-cd)^2}\sigma_{WX}$$

$$\sigma_{ZV} = C_{Z'V} = e\sigma_Z^2$$

Analysis of Correlations

Because correlations are merely the covariances of standardized variables, they, too, can be read directly from a path diagram by using the above rules.

However, the structural coefficients and the input covariances have to be modified because the values of these quantities depend on the scales of measurement. All quantities in the diagram must be converted to standardized form.

The standardized values of structural coefficients are called *path coeffi-cients* and are represented as subscripted **p**'s. The standardized values of the input covariances are simply the correlations (ρ) among inputs. Thus to read correlations directly the symbols in a diagram are converted to these forms. In addition, in the standardized case correlation paths are represented as solid, double-headed arrows to maintain continuity with tradition in path analysis.

4.12

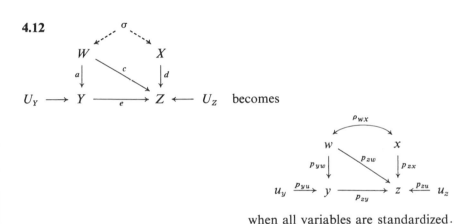

when all variables are standardized.

The disturbance terms also have been represented as standardized variables in the modified diagram. This means that a variable's disturbances have been translated into a separate hypothetical variable with a variance of 1.0—the same as every other system variable. Because a dependent vari-able is partly determined by other system variables the contribution of the disturbance term must be scaled down again before it can be summed with other sources. This is done by using new coefficients (p_{yu} and p_{zu}). It would be possible to leave the disturbances unstandardized as we have done up to now. However, coefficients like p_{yu} and p_{zu} provide an explicit indication of the degree to which a system variable is influenced by unspecified factors, and they are shown traditionally on a path diagram for standardized variables.

With both variables and system parameters in standardized form, expressions for correlations can be read directly from the diagram by using the coordinating-path rules. A significant simplification in expressions occurs as a result of standardization. *When a system diagram is defined in terms of path coefficients and used to define correlations, the variances of origins need not be shown in the defining expressions because all of these variances equal 1.0.*

4.13

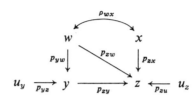

The correlation between w and z equals their covariance because all variables are in standardized form. There are three coordinating paths between w and z.

$$
\begin{aligned}
C_{wz} &= p_{zw} \cdot \sigma_w^2 = p_{zw} \cdot 1 = p_{zw} \\
C_{wyz} &= p_{yw} \cdot p_{zy} \\
C_{wpxz} &= 1 \cdot 1 \cdot p_{zx} \cdot p_{wx} = p_{zx} \cdot p_{wx}
\end{aligned}
$$

Hence $\rho_{wz} = \sigma_{wz} = p_{zw} + p_{yw} \cdot p_{zy} + p_{zx} \rho_{wx}.$

Standardized Versus Unstandardized

Path coefficients simplify expressions for the decomposition of correlations. In addition, they give some basis for comparing the strength of different operators in a system.

Any structural coefficient in a diagram indicates the units of change expected in a dependent variable, given a one-unit change in a source variable and all other variables held constant. Thus the numerical value of a structural coefficient is tied to the measurement units of both variables. If the measurement scale for either one is changed, the value of the coefficient must be changed as well, and if measurement scales are arbitrary, say that different scales are used in different studies, then the values of the coefficients are also arbitrary: their values cannot be compared meaningfully across studies. Standardizing variables and coefficients on the basis of population variances may circumvent some of these difficulties by making the units of measurement less arbitrary. Every variable is measured on a scale whose units are statistically comparable to those of other scales in the sense that the variance on all variables is the same (1.0). The units of measurement on different variables have been "equalized," and the relative strengths of different coefficients in the same system can be compared because each indicates how changes on one standardized scale are converted into changes on another. Moreover, the conversion to standardized units permits a comparison of different studies of the same population because the standardization procedure converts measurements on instruments calibrated differently to measurements in standard units that depend on the population's distribution rather than on the particular instrument used.

Yet standardization is subject to its own pitfalls which follow from the very factor that make it useful—its dependence on population distributions. *Path coefficients do not provide a valid basis for structural comparisons of systems operating on populations with different distributions.* When populations have different distributions on system variables, standardization within each population does not lead to equivalent measurement units across populations; therefore structural coefficients depending on these units are incomparable. This limitation extends to a single population studied over time if the population distributions are changing. In this case scales standardized on the basis of the variances at different times are incomparable, as are the structural coefficients based on these units. *Standardization is to be avoided in comparative studies of different populations or in longitudinal studies of a changing population.*

ANALYZING STATISTICAL DIVERSITY

A variance is a special case of covariance. It is the covariance of a variable with itself. This conceptualization allows expressions for variances to be read from system diagrams by almost the same rules already introduced.

The covariance of a variable with itself can be obtained by representing the variable twice on the same diagram, duplicating its relations with all other variables exactly, as shown in **4.14**.

4.14   DUPLICATION OF THE VARIABLE Z.

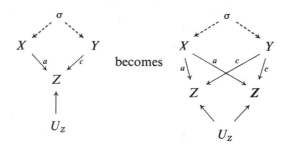

The covariance σ_{ZZ} of Z and $\mathbf{Z}$ in the second diagram can be obtained as follows:

$$C_{Z\mathscr{X}Z} = a \cdot a \cdot \sigma_X^2 = a^2\sigma_X^2$$
$$C_{Z\mathscr{Y}Z} = c \cdot c \cdot \sigma_Y^2 = c^2\sigma_Y$$
$$C_{ZX\sigma YZ} = a \cdot 1 \cdot 1 \cdot c \cdot \sigma_{XY} = ac\sigma_{XY}$$
$$C_{ZY\sigma XZ} = c \cdot 1 \cdot 1 \cdot a \cdot \sigma_{XY} = ac\sigma_{XY}$$
$$C_{Z\mathscr{U}Z} = 1 \cdot 1 \cdot \sigma_{U(Z)}^2 = \sigma_{U(Z)}^2$$

Hence $\sigma_Z^2 = \sigma_{ZZ} = a^2\sigma_X^2 + c^2\sigma_Y^2 + 2ac\sigma_{XY} + \sigma_{U(Z)}^2$

Redrawing the diagram to define each variance would become burdensome, but the need can be eliminated by modifying the coordinating-path rules slightly when defining variances.

IV.6   *The variance of a variable X is the sum of all "contributing-path effects." A contributing path effect is the same as a coordinating path effect defined under special conventions.*

(a)   *A contributing path has X at both endpoints.*
(b)   *The path may traverse a solid arrow twice, though it still may impinge on no variable (other than X) more than once. The path may traverse a dotted arrow only once.*
(c)   *Contributing paths are distinct if their subscripts are different and if the order of subscripts is different.*

4.15 $X \xrightarrow{a} Y \xrightarrow{c} Z$

There is one contributing path with Z at both end points $(Z \mathcal{Y} Z)$, here the arrow c is traversed twice. The variance of Z is

$$\sigma_Z^2 = c \cdot c \cdot \sigma_Y^2 = c^2 \cdot \sigma_Y^2$$

The path $(Z Y \mathcal{X} YZ)$ is not a contributing path because it passes through Y twice.

$$X$$
$$a \downarrow \quad \searrow d$$
$$U_Y \longrightarrow Y \xrightarrow{c} Z \longleftarrow U_Z$$

There are five contributing paths with Z at both end points:

$$C_{Z\mathcal{X}Z} = d^2\sigma_x^2$$
$$C_{Z\mathcal{Y}Z} = c^2\sigma_Y^2$$
$$C_{Z\mathcal{U}Z} = \sigma_{U(Z)}^2$$
$$C_{Z\mathcal{X}YZ} = a \cdot d \cdot c \cdot \sigma_X^2$$
$$C_{ZY\mathcal{X}Z} = a \cdot d \cdot c \cdot \sigma_X^2$$

In defining variances, the last two effects are treated as distinct because the order of subscripts is different.

The variance of Z is the sum of all five effects:

$$\sigma_Z^2 = d^2\sigma_X^2 + c^2\sigma_Y^2 + 2adc\sigma_X^2 + \sigma_{U(Z)}^2$$

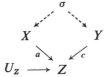

In this diagram $(ZX\sigma YZ)$ and $(ZY\sigma XZ)$ are distinct contributing paths for defining σ_Z^2 because the order of variables is different.

$$\sigma_Z^2 = a^2\sigma_X^2 + c^2\sigma_Y^2 + 2ac\sigma_{XY} + \sigma_{U(Z)}^2$$

$(X\sigma X)$ and $(Y\sigma Y)$ are *not* contributing paths for X and Y because each traverses a dotted arrow twice. Thus the variances of the inputs X and Y are basic givens that cannot be analyzed further.

The contributing-path rule also defines variances in systems with loops if
the loops are represented in semireduced form, as shown in **4.16**.

4.16

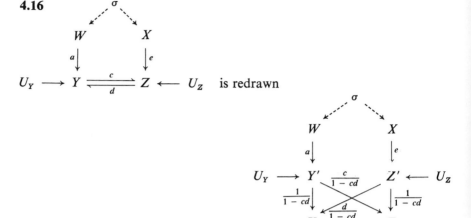

$$U_Y \longrightarrow Y \begin{smallmatrix} c \\ \rightleftharpoons \\ d \end{smallmatrix} Z \longleftarrow U_Z \quad \text{is redrawn}$$

Contributing paths for the variance of Y are

$$C_{Y\mathscr{Y}'Y} = \frac{1}{(1 - cd)^2}\sigma_{Y'}^2$$

$$C_{Y\mathscr{Z}'Y} = \frac{d^2}{(1 - cd)^2}\sigma_{Z'}^2$$

$$C_{YY'W\sigma XZ'Y} = \frac{aed}{(1 - cd)^2}\sigma_{WX}$$

$$C_{YZ'X\sigma WY'Y} = \frac{aed}{(1 - cd)^2}\sigma_{WX}$$

$$\sigma_Y^2 = \frac{1}{(1 - cd)^2}(\sigma_{Y'}^2 + d^2\sigma_{Z'}^2 + 2aed\sigma_{WX})$$

Similar procedures lead to

$$\sigma_{Y'}^2 = \sigma_{U(Y)}^2 + a^2\sigma_W^2$$
$$\sigma_{Z'}^2 = \sigma_{U(Z)}^2 + e^2\sigma_X^2$$

Substituting the last two expressions into the formula for σ_Y^2 gives

$$\sigma_Y^2 = \frac{1}{(1 - cd)^2}[a^2\sigma_W^2 + e^2d^2\sigma_X^2 + 2aed\sigma_{WX} + \sigma_{U(Y)}^2 + d^2\sigma_{U(Z)}^2]$$

PATH ANALYSIS AND ALGEBRAIC DERIVATIONS

The rules that have been presented for obtaining covariances, variances, and correlations define the same expressions that are derivable by more traditional algebra, as exemplified in **4.17**.

4.17   MATHEMATICS CORRESPONDING TO PATH ANALYSIS

A brief exercise in the algebra of expectations highlights the mathematical principles involved in the preceding rules.

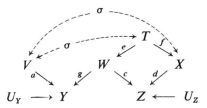

The goal is to define the covariance of Y and Z by employing algebra rather than graph analysis. First, we recall that

$$\sigma_{YZ} = \mathscr{E}(Y \cdot Z)$$

This definition might become interesting if we could define expressions for Y and Z that could be substituted into the expectation term. Of course, such expressions can be read off the graph:

$$Y = aV + gW + U_Y$$
$$Z = cW + dX + U_Z$$

Now multiplying these expressions for Y and Z is equivalent to multiplying the variables themselves; that is,

$$Y \cdot Z = acVW + gcW^2 + cWU_Y + adVX + gdWX + dXU_Y$$
$$+ aVU_Z + gWU_Z + U_YU_Z$$

The expectation of this expression defines the covariance of Y and Z according to the first formula above.

$$\sigma_{YZ} = \mathscr{E}(Y \cdot Z) = \mathscr{E}(acVW + gcW^2 + cWU_Y$$
$$+ adVX + gdWX + dXU_Y + aVU_Z + gWU_Z + U_YU_Z)$$

which reduces to

$$\sigma_{YZ} = ac\mathscr{E}(VW) + gc\mathscr{E}(W^2) + c\mathscr{E}(WU_Y) + ad\mathscr{E}(VX)$$
$$+ gd\mathscr{E}(WX) + d\mathscr{E}(XU_Y) + a\mathscr{E}(VU_Z) + g\mathscr{E}(WU_Z) + \mathscr{E}(U_Y U_Z)$$

All expectations in this formula are themselves variances or covariances and the expression can be written

$$\sigma_{YZ} = ac\sigma_{VW} + gc\sigma_W^2 + c\sigma_{WU(Y)} + ad\sigma_{VX} + gd\sigma_{WX}$$
$$+ d\sigma_{XU(Y)} + a\sigma_{VU(Z)} + g\sigma_{WU(Z)} + \sigma_{U(Y)U(Z)}$$

Many of the terms in the last expression involve the covariances of disturbances with explicit sources or among themselves. However, the original diagram indicates that all such covariances are zero and the terms involving them may be dropped from the expression.

$$\sigma_{YZ} = ac\sigma_{VW} + gc\sigma_W^2 + ad\sigma_{VX} + gd\sigma_{WX}$$

This is not quite the same expression we would obtain by path analysis because it contains terms with σ_{WX} and σ_{VW} that do not appear in the path analysis expression. If the algebra of expectations were applied again, it would be found that

$$\sigma_{WX} = ef\sigma_T^2 \quad \text{and} \quad \sigma_{VW} = e\sigma_{VT}$$

and if these terms were substituted into the preceding formula we would get

$$\sigma_{YZ} = ace\sigma_{VT} + gc\sigma_W^2 + ad\sigma_{VX} + gdef\sigma_T^2$$

which is the path analysis formula exactly. All variances and co-variances of dependent variables in a system can be defined in a similar way.

Nothing essential is lost in the graphical procedures, compared with the algebraic procedures, because the graphs themselves *are* mathematical representations of the system.

GATING MECHANISMS

In the foregoing discussions the input variances and covariances were taken as given and treated as statistical parameters that influence the variances and covariances of other system variables. Yet it is possible to move still another step back and consider what it is that determines the values of these parameters. Necessarily, the focus changes from the system of interest to the forces operating in the system's environment.

Defining the sources of diversity and coordination in a set of inputs requires specifying a prior or encompassing system in which these variables are the outcomes. In fact, the original choice of one set of inputs rather than another may have been only a matter of convenience; for example, personality traits may be inputs to the system of occupational behavior, but personality traits are outcomes with respect to the socialization system and presumably the system definition could be extended by incorporating socialization variables. If consideration were extended to the sources of personality, we might have to include dozens of socialization variables and genetic factors as well. For the sake of simplicity we stop with personality, but the extension to socialization variables could be made.

The issue is not always uncomplicated, however, because some social systems do not process all the cases that were processed by a prior system. A variety of *gating mechanisms*, ranging from self-selection to specific procedures of recruitment, selection, and rejection at the boundaries of the system, may intervene. Gating mechanisms act to reduce the diversity of entities admitted to the system when the gate consists of entering only those above (or below) some cutoff value on a selection variable. (Gates could also be designed to increase input variabilities, for example, by accepting only entities with extreme values.) Gating that restricts the range of variables affects covariances as well as variances, and it tends to reduce correlations among system variables. The essential idea here is described in **4.18**.

Gating on a number of different inputs simultaneously affects their statistical characteristics. Consequently the statistical characteristics of outcomes are influenced as well; for example, conjunctive gating (no admittance unless the entity meets cutoff criteria on several variables) can reduce both the diversity and the correlations among system inputs. Thus conjunctive gating may also reduce the variances and the correlations among outcomes. Disjunctive gating (admittance if any one criterion is met) would increase input variances while usually reducing their covariances, and the net effects on outcomes would depend on the system at hand.

A gating mechanism partitions a population into two sets: one whose cases are subject to a particular subsystem of operations and the other whose members are unaffected. Alternatively, it might be said that the subsystem

4.18   REDUCED CORRELATION DUE TO RESTRICTION OF RANGE

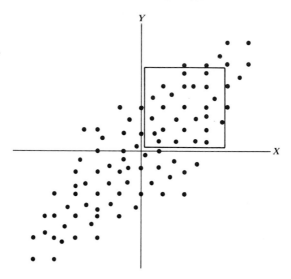

X and *Y* show a moderate degree of correlation when their full ranges are considered and almost no correlation when the range of both variables is restricted to values between 0 and +2.0.

applies to all members of the population, but the gating mechanism "turns off" the system's operators for a selected subpopulation. This, in turn, is somewhat akin to the notion of a limiter—if a case is less than (or more than) a particular value on a variable, the subsequent structural coefficients have a value of zero. A gate nullifies *all* subsequent operations in the subsystem rather than just one following the gated variable, however.

Both gates and limiters have pernicious consequences for path analyses. We cannot apply the model for the subsystem to the whole population because a gate (or a limiter) on an input causes the subsystem effects to be added to outcomes for only selected cases. Worse, the effects when they do occur are biased because inputs for the treated cases deviate systematically from values in the rest of the population. Thus the causal effects of these inputs are systematically deviant. Such biases can create extra variance and covariance among outcomes when the whole population is considered. These inflated statistics would be quite uninterpretable from a formulation of linear effects in the subsystem.

Gates therefore are convincing points at which to bound a system. The system operating after a gate works on a different, less inclusive population than the system that operates before the gate. Thus the system after the gate is naturally distinguished from its environment. Moreover, the peculiar variances and covariances produced by gates perhaps can be embraced in a causal analysis if the gating variables are among its inputs. The statistical characteristics of inputs are among the givens for an analysis, whether or not these characteristics were generated causally.

In fact, special care is needed in extending path analyses beyond a gate, even supposing that attention is restricted properly to the subpopulation of cases that pass the gate. Such cases are affected by operators both before and after gating, but the selection process may ensure that some system disturbances are biased in ways that ordinarily would not be represented in a model; for example, if the members of an organization are selected for their conservatism, some will be included because their families raised them as conservatives. Others from liberal families will belong only because they have been subject to uniformly conservative influences in adulthood. This implies that the adult disturbances of the conservatism variable in this population will be negatively correlated with family determinants of conservatism. Analysis of paths from family socialization to the conservatism variable will be distorted unless this correlation is taken into account.

GENERAL IMPLICATIONS

Sources of Diversity

Two populations with similar distributions on source variables but different variabilities of outcomes must be subject to different systems. If a system has no negative operators, then greater variability among outcomes implies stronger system operations and/or redundant operations.

Generally speaking, the diversity of system outcomes may be increased by strengthening the effect of system operations; for example, if a society chooses to offer greater rewards to talent, greater status variability will emerge unless status differences are controlled by other mechanisms. Redundant operations have similar consequences. Suppose that economic interests

4.19   ORIGINAL SYSTEMS

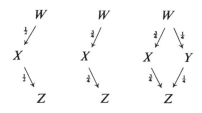

REDUCED FORMS

$$\sigma_Z^2 = \tfrac{4}{16}\sigma_W^2 \qquad \sigma_Z^2 = \tfrac{9}{16}\sigma_W^2 \qquad \sigma_Z^2 = \tfrac{10}{16}\sigma_W^2$$

If we assume that σ_W^2 is the same in all three cases, the second system produces more diversity in Z than the first because its operators are larger in magnitude. The third produces still more diversity in Z because it has an extra path or "redundant" operation.

---

are transformed to political attitudes in part by the mass media. Adding new communication media to a social system would lead to greater political diversity in the population when no control mechanism is added simultaneously.

Structural coefficients with negative values complicate these principles to the point that it is difficult to generalize. Understanding must be reached by studying the reduced-form expressions for the system at hand. Still, an important principle concerning diversity can be stated when negative operators are structured to form control mechanisms or loops with a negative return effect. Call a control mechanism "stronger" if the return effect of the corresponding loop has a larger negative value. Then diversity in a population is less to the extent that systems affecting the population have more stable and/or stronger stable controls. Adding controls to constrain deviancy is a workhorse idea in politics and lawmaking, but it is a principle of general importance in evolved as well as legislated systems.

4.20 $X \xrightarrow{a} Y \underset{d}{\overset{c}{\rightleftharpoons}} Z$

Suppose that X is talent, Y is accomplishments, Z is status, **a** represents the transformation of talent into accomplishments, **c** represents the transformation of accomplishments into status, and **d** represents administrative, social, and emotional distractions that convert high status into a reduction of accomplishments.

If **a** and **c** happen to be 1.0 and **d** $= 0$ because there are no distractions, then

$$\sigma_Z^2 = \left(\frac{ac}{1 - cd} \right)^2 \sigma_X^2 = \sigma_X^2$$

If we now add a small distractive effect, $d = -\frac{1}{4}$, we obtain

$$\sigma_Z^2 = \left(\frac{1}{1 - (-\frac{1}{4})} \right)^2 \sigma_X^2 = \frac{16}{25} \sigma_X^2$$

Thus the development of a negative feedback reduces variability in statuses.

Diversity of outcomes depends also on the statistical distributions of inputs. The more variable the inputs, the more diverse the outcomes, given a system consisting of positive operators and no coordination among the inputs; for example, assuming again that economic situations are transformed into political attitudes, we might expect that as a population increases in socioeconomic diversity it will display greater diversity in political attitudes. This same principle also applies to disturbances. The greater the variance of disturbances, the more diverse the system outcomes.

The impact of coordination among inputs is more complex. If two populations are subject to identical systems of positive operators and the variances of inputs is the same in both populations but inputs in one population are more positively coordinated, then outcomes in that population will be more diverse. Suppose, for example, that two populations are subject to a system that transforms greater academic talent (T) and higher parental status (S) into more years of education (E): $T \rightarrow E \leftarrow S$. Suppose, further, that the populations are identical in their variabilities of talent and parental statuses. Even with all these parallels one population will have greater variability in levels of education if it has a higher level of coordination between talent and parental status. (This difference might occur if one society rewarded parents on the basis of certain genetic potentials which are transmitted to children and which condition children's academic talent, whereas the other society awarded parental statuses on a different basis.) In the society with coordination there will be many instances of matching between a child's talent and status background, and the two forces will often work together to produce outcomes of high or low education. In the society without coordination the matching will be random and less frequent, the two forces will often cancel each other, and the system will produce many examples of education at about the mean level.

On the other hand, negative coordination among inputs in a system of positive operators produces even more efficient canceling of operations and yields still less output variability; for instance (continuing the above example), if a third population actually had negative coordination among inputs—the higher the parental status, the slighter the offspring's talent—the two forces would cancel each other more efficiently, thus giving still less variability in educational levels.

These points can be summarized as follows. In systems of positive operators outcome diversity can always be reduced by reducing the variability of inputs or by making the coordination among inputs less positive or more negative. When systems involve negative operators, the diversity of outcomes can be adjusted by manipulating input variances and covariances, but the necessary manipulations must be determined on an *ad hoc* basis.

Coordination of Outcomes

If two systems differ only in the strength of their operations (say, all operations in one system have twice the effect of those in the other), the system with stronger operators will produce greater coordination of outcomes, whether coordination is measured in terms of covariances or correlations. If a system consists only of positive operators, coordination of outcomes increases even if operators are strengthened by different amounts. If a system contains negative operators, then differential strengthening might cause some canceling of effects and the effects on outcome organization would have to be determined on an *ad hoc* basis.

If two identical systems with all positive coefficients operate on populations differing only in the variances of input variables, the outcomes will be more organized in the population with greater diversity on inputs. As usual, however, systems with negative structural coefficients have to be examined *ad hoc* to determine the exact impact of source variances.

Increasing the amount of disturbance in an outcome decreases that variable's correlation with other system variables that are not dependent on it—notably its source variables. At the same time, the change strengthens correlations among variables that are dependent on the one immediately affected, as illustrated in **4.21**.

4.21

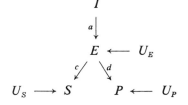

I: Intelligence
E: Educational attainment
S: Occupational status
P: Interest in political affairs

Increasing the disturbances in educational attainment reduces the correlation between it and intelligence, but this same change would *increase* the correlation between occupational status and level of political interest. For example, college scholarships for all veterans or all members of an ethnic group in a society with few college graduates will reduce the correlation between intelligence and education in the population as a whole, but ultimately the increased variance in education will lead to more systematic diversity in statuses and in levels of political interest. Thereby it will be easier to predict from one of these to the other.

A third factor affecting the correlation of system variables is the level of coordination among inputs. The greater the magnitude of correlations among the inputs, the greater the correlations among other variables in the system, at least if all the system operations are positive. If some of the input correlations and some of the system operations are negative, canceling of effects may take place, and the impact of the input correlations has to be assessed on an *ad hoc* basis.

Correlations in Loops

Variables in a loop with a positive return effect will become more highly correlated if the loop operators are strengthened or if the variances of variables inputting into the loop are increased. More powerful operators or greater input variances, however, do not uniformly produce higher correlations among the variables in a loop with negative return effect. Indeed, *correlation phenomena in control loops are highly peculiar, and misunderstandings about such phenomena easily can contribute to confusion in important scientific debates.*

To examine these phenomena a formula is needed that will specify the correlation among loop variables. The algebra complicates rapidly and therefore attention is restricted to a simple two-variable loop.

4.22

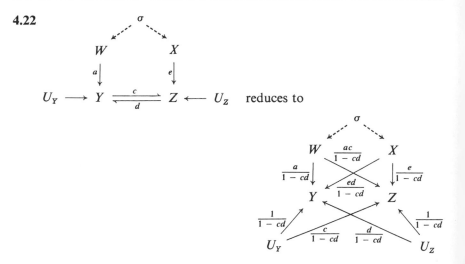

The variances of Y and Z and their covariance can be obtained by using path analysis rules. Substituting the resulting expressions into the formula for the correlation coefficient **(3.17)** gives

$$\rho_{YZ} = \frac{a^2 c \sigma_W^2 + e^2 d \sigma_X^2 + c \sigma_{U(Y)}^2 + d \sigma_{U(Z)}^{22} + ae(1 + cd)\sigma_{WX}}{\sqrt{a^2 \sigma_W^2 + e^2 d^2 \sigma_X^2 + \sigma_{U(Y)}^2 + d^2 \sigma_{U(Z)}^2 + 2aed\sigma_{WX}}}$$
$$\cdot \sqrt{(e^2 \sigma_X^2 + a^2 c^2 \sigma_W^2 + \sigma_{U(Z)}^2 + c^2 \sigma_{U(Y)}^2 + 2aec\sigma_{WX})}$$

For heuristic purposes many of the parameters can be set at convenient values:

$$a = e = 1$$
$$\sigma^2_{U(Y)} = \sigma^2_{U(Z)} = 1$$
$$\sigma_{WX} = 0$$

The formula then reduces to

$$\rho_{YZ} = \frac{c\sigma^2_W + d\sigma^2_X + c + d}{\sqrt{\sigma^2_W + d^2\sigma^2_X + 1 + d^2} \sqrt{\sigma^2_X + c^2\sigma^2_W + 1 + c^2}}$$

The loop coefficients may be given the following convenient values that define a negative return effect:

$$c = \tfrac{1}{2} \qquad d = -\tfrac{1}{2}$$

in which case the formula becomes

$$\rho_{YZ} = \frac{2(\sigma^2_W - \sigma^2_X)}{\sqrt{4\sigma^2_W + \sigma^2_X + 5} \sqrt{4\sigma^2_X + \sigma^2_W + 5}}$$

The implications of this formula can be seen by setting the variances of W and X at different levels and solving for ρ:

σ^2_W	σ^2_X	ρ_{YZ}
2.0	.0	+.42
2.0	1.0	+.16
2.0	2.0	.0
1.0	2.0	−.16
.0	2.0	−.42

Clearly the correlation among variables is peculiarly sensitive to the variances of variables feeding into the loop.

The examples in **4.22** illustrate that *by modifying levels of diversity in the source variables of a control loop the correlations among loop variables can be adjusted to positive, negative, or zero values. Accordingly, the existence of a positive, negative, or zero correlation between the variables in a control loop by itself implies nothing about the nature of their causal relations.* Considering the ubiquity of control mechanisms, this finding accents the need for caution in inferring causal structure from observed correlations.

An example illustrates how correlation phenomena in control loops might be contributing to scientific confusion. It is often argued that attitudes must not affect actual behavior because the correlation between the two is so small —nearly zero in many studies. The negligible correlation actually could be masking a substantial effect of attitudes on behavior, if we allow for social control mechanisms that convert deviant behavior toward an object (too favorable or too unfavorable) into attitude change in the opposite direction. The general idea here is that a transgression is not forgiven until the actor expresses a changed attitude, implying that the same kind of deviancy will not occur again. A simplified representation of such a system is

$$U_A \longrightarrow A \underset{c}{\overset{a}{\rightleftarrows}} B \longleftarrow U_B$$

where **a** represents the transformation of favorable attitudes into favorable behavior, **c** represents the transformation of deviancy into inverted attitude change, and U_A and U_B are unspecified sources of variation in attitudes and behaviors. The **a** should be positive in value; **c** should be negative to represent the reversal in transforming deviant acts to attitude change. Thus the system corresponds to the type analyzed in **4.21**. Consequently the correlation between attitudes and behaviors may take on nearly any value, and this correlation provides no basis for deciding whether attitudes do determine behavior.

SOURCES AND ADDITIONAL READINGS

Sewall Wright summarized his classic work on path analysis in "The Method of Path Coefficients," *Annals of Mathematical Statistics*, **5** (1934), 161–215. Key articles by Wright and others which expand the scope of path analysis are collected conveniently in Hubert M. Blalock, Jr., Ed. *Causal Models in the Social Sciences* (Chicago: Aldine-Atherton, 1971).

EXERCISES

1.* The amount of convict aggression in felon prisons depends on characteristics of the inmate population and on characteristics of the prison as an

---

* This exercise was developed from D. Ellis, H. Grasmick, and B. Gilman, "Violence in Prisons: A Sociological Analysis," *American Journal of Sociology*, **80**, No. 1 (July 1974).

institution. Some possible relationships are reflected in the following path diagram:

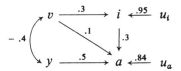

Variables are as follows:

  v: proportion of inmates sentenced for violent crimes;
  i: isolation—proportion of inmates without visitors for more than a year;
  y: inmate youthfulness—proportion younger than 21 years;
  a: rate of inmate aggressions that lead to official discipline.

(a) Compute the expected correlations among the variables.

(b) What proportion of the variance in a is explained by the other variables? Does this figure set a bound on the effectiveness of programs aimed at reducing a by changing i, v, or y?

(c) What is the expected effect on a if a prison's population is increased one standard unit in youthfulness, whereas the proportion of violent offenders is maintained without change? What is the expected result if the proportion of youths is increased without worrying about types of offense?

(d) Using the three independent variables here, define the kind of prison that would generate the most disciplinary problems. What is the profile for a prison with low inmate aggressiveness?

2.   Imagine a population in which there are variations in education, occupational prestige, and income but no relation among the variables; for example, suppose the variances on all variables are 1.0 and all three correlations are 0.0. Suppose now that social operators are created so that persons' occupations are dependent on their educations and incomes are dependent on occupations. In this system education is an input variable and the original variations in occupation and income constitute unexplained disturbances. For heuristic purposes assume that the structural coefficient for each of the new operators is 1.0.

(a) What are the variances and covariances of the variables after the new social system has been established? What are the correlations among the variables?

(b) What are the values of the system's (standardized) path coefficients in the final population? Do these path coefficients suggest anything different from the original structural coefficients? (Note that the superimposed operators change the character of the population by increasing variance in occupational prestige and income.)

(c) Social stratification exists in a population when status differences are ordered such that each individual person's (or family's) set of statuses is internally consistent. Judging from this exercise, what are some requisites for the development of stratification? Which statuses in a social system will have the most inequality?

3. Assume that the social system in exercise 2 includes an additional operator such that a given level of income generates mobility to an occupation of corresponding prestige (e.g., such a relation would exist if jobs could be bought). Assume that the structural coefficient for this operator is .5 (compared with the values of 1.0 for the other two operators). Again calculate the variances, covariances, and correlations of the status variables after the new system is imposed. What effect has the amplifying loop on the variances of variables in the loop? On the correlation of loop variables?

4. In the diagram that follows think of $\hat{x}$ as a set of standardized scores representing persons' true attitudes toward abortion and x_1 and x_2 as the standardized scores obtained from two questionnaire measures of this attitude. Arrows from true scores to the indicators mean that persons' true attitudes determine their responses on particular questionnaire measures. However, questionnaire responses depend on a variety of other factors— moods, interviewer effects, distractions, and misunderstandings. All such sources of measurement error are viewed together as disturbances d_1 and d_2. Variable $\hat{y}$ represents persons' true levels of knowledge about abortion. Again, the variable is standardized and is a source of two questionnaire measures of knowledge, y_1 and y_2. These indicators are presumed to be subject to measurement errors e_1 and e_2. Coefficients on the arrows indicate

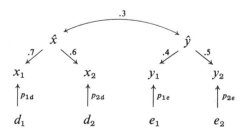

that somehow we know the correlation $\rho_{\hat{x}\hat{y}}$ between the true scores as well as the relations between the true scores and their indicators.

(a) What is the expected correlation between the two indicators of $\hat{x}$? Between the two indicators of $\hat{y}$? Why is the correlation between two measures of the same variable not 1.00?

(b) What are the correlations between indicators of $\hat{x}$ and indicators of $\hat{y}$? If you knew the values of these correlations but not the value of $\rho_{\hat{x}\hat{y}}$, what might you conclude about the relations between attitudes and information in this case?

(c) What proportion of the variance in each indicator is due to errors of measurement? If the errors are viewed as standardized, what are the values of the p coefficients on their arrows?

(d) The coefficients on the arrows from true scores to indicators can be called validity coefficients. Suppose you know only the correlation between two indicators $\rho_{x(1)y(1)}$ and the validity coefficients for x_1 and y_1. Use these figures to estimate the correlation between the true scores $\hat{x}$ and $\hat{y}$.

5. In exercise 4 it was assumed that the measurement errors for different indicators were uncorrelated. If, however, all four questions are presented during the same interview, that may not be the case. Continue with the model specified in exercise 4 but suppose that the errors in each indicator correlate .30 with the errors for each of the other indicators.

(a) Use the parameters from exercise 4 and these additional figures to reestimate the correlations among all indicators. What is the overall trend in results compared with those obtained in exercise 4? Would this be the usual effect of correlated errors?

(b) Again apply the procedure in exercise 4d to estimate the true correlation $\rho_{\hat{x}\hat{y}}$. Now use the validity coefficients for x_1 and y_1 and the "observed" correlation $\rho_{x(1)y(1)}$ obtained in part (a) of this exercise. Might this lead to erroneous conclusions?

(c) Suppose that x_1 represents scores on an opinion question in which intensity of disagreement or agreement is coded in just five levels—1.0 through 5.0. There is reason to suspect that the errors d_1 for this measure might be correlated negatively with the true attitudes $\hat{x}$. Explain why.

6. A system was presented in **4.20** in which talent is transformed into accomplishments (operator **a**) and accomplishments lead to status (operator **c**). It also was allowed that a control operator (**d**) may evolve such that more status produces fewer accomplishments. The statistical implications of these specifications were worked out when structural coefficients **a**, **c**, and **d** were assigned arbitrary values of 1.0, 1.0, and $-.25$, respectively. Now suppose that **a** and **d** remain the same but the system's reward mechanism **c** is doubled in strength so that the coefficient has a value of 2.0. What is the impact of the greater rewards on status variability in a system in which the control mechanism has not yet developed (i.e., when $d = 0$)? What is the impact on status variability in a system that includes the control mechanism ($d = -.25$)? From these results interpret the functions and dysfunctions of the control mechanism.

7.* A heritability coefficient indicates the proportion of variance on an observable trait that can be explained by variations in genetic constitution. Ordinarily, genetic variables cannot be measured directly; therefore a heritability coefficient must be estimated indirectly. The following diagram shows the basic logic in many heritability studies.

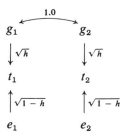

Variables subscripted with 1 refer to one member of a pair of identical twins. Variables subscripted with 2 apply to the other member. Thus the analysis treats a pair of identical twins as the basic unit of analysis. Variable g represents a person's value on the relevant genetic variable. (Actually almost any trait depends on numerous genetic variables and g is really an aggregate variable comparable to a disturbance term.) Variable t stands for a person's value on the trait of interest (e.g., height or intelligence). Variable e represents the nongenetic, or environmental, sources of variation in t. Note that g_1 and g_2 are shown as correlating 1.0. Analyses are limited purposely to identical twins so that this is known to be true. Identical twins have exactly the same genotypes. Also note that $\sqrt{h}$ is shown as the path coefficient from g to t. This must be the case if heritability is the proportion of trait variance genetically determined (see exercise 1b).

---

*This exercise has been drawn from materials reviewed in D. Heise, *Personality: Biosocial Bases* (Chicago: Rand McNally, 1973).

(a) Given the above model, what observable statistic provides a direct estimate of the heritability h of a trait?

(b) Why do heritability researchers prefer to study twins who have been raised apart?

(c) The heritability of intelligence sometimes is cited as about .80. Does this mean that for all practical purposes environments cannot be manipulated to increase intelligence?

(d) Suppose trait t is measured with error. What would the expected effect be on estimates of heritability?

(e) Suppose a sociocultural system is gradually becoming more heterogeneous in the sense that its environmental diversity is increasing. Will heritabilities of most traits increase, decrease, or stay the same?

8. Suppose that a researcher interested in aesthetic values obtains data from all students registered in the humanities in a large state university. He finds that a precise measure of aesthetic values correlates only negligibly in this population with parental statuses and numerous indicators of childhood cultural experiences. Can he conclude that parental statuses and childhood cultural experiences do not affect aesthetic values?

9. Suppose a valid test of musical interest has been included in a battery of tests widely administered to high school students for a number of years. A researcher makes up a study population of people who took the test years ago, half of whom are now professional musicians and half randomly selected. He finds a strong correlation between the test scores and a measure of present musical skills. He then replicates the study on a population made up only of laymen and finds a much lower correlation. What is a likely explanation for this pattern of findings?

5 IDENTIFICATION AND ESTIMATION

The full power of causal analysis for explanation, prediction, and interdiction cannot be attained until the structural parameters of a causal system are estimated numerically. Sometimes, in engineering, operators are designed to have specific quantitative effects, in which case numerical estimation of coefficients poses no distinct problem. But social systems are often evolved rather than designed, and the social laws and basic constants underlying system operations typically are unknown. So the parameters of a social system must be estimated from empirical observations on the system rather than deductively from available knowledge.

The principles of path analysis presented in Chapter 4 provide a lead into an important set of procedures for empirical estimation of system parameters. The basic logic of these *least-squares procedures* is elaborated here with reference to the simple system defined in **5.1**.

5.1 The theoretical system consists only of X and Y with X affecting Y via an operator whose linear effect is **a**. The covariance term indicates that X may be coordinated with other unspecified determinants of Y within the population of interest.

$$\sigma \dashrightarrow U_Y$$
$$X \xrightarrow{\ a\ } Y$$

First, the values of X and Y are measured for all cases that have been subjected to the system operation. From these measurements the following statistics are calculated: variance of $X(\sigma_X^2)$, variance of $Y(\sigma_Y^2)$, and the covariance of X and $Y(\sigma_{XY})$.

These calculations directly provide one parameter needed for analyzing the distributional outcomes of this simple system σ_X^2. If there were additional specified sources, their variances and covariances would also be known at this point.

Path analysis can be used to express the values of the remaining observed statistics in terms of basic system and population parameters.

$$\sigma_{XY} = a\sigma_X^2 + \sigma_{XU(Y)}$$
$$\sigma_Y^2 = a^2\sigma_X^2 + \sigma_{U(Y)}^2 + 2a\sigma_{XU(Y)}$$

The first equation can be solved for **a**, giving a formula that expresses the value of **a** in terms of population statistics:

$$a = \frac{\sigma_{XY} - \sigma_{XU(Y)}}{\sigma_X^2}$$

Two of the quantities on the right (σ_{XY} and σ_X^2) are known because their values have been calculated directly from data. The value of the third quantity $\sigma_{XU(Y)}$, however, is not directly measurable, and because this is an unknown the formula does not uniquely identify the value of **a**.

Similarly, the second equation, with the third, can be solved to provide an equation for the variance of the disturbance variable $\sigma_{U(Y)}^2$.

$$\sigma_{U(Y)}^2 = \sigma_Y^2 - \frac{\sigma_{XY}^2 \sigma_{XU(Y)}^2}{\sigma_X^2}$$

This equation also contains the unknown quantity $\sigma_{XU(Y)}$ and so does not uniquely identify $\sigma_{U(Y)}^2$.

Suppose a restrictive condition is stated. These formulas may be applied only when X is uncoordinated with any disturbance of Y. Then the unknown quantity in these formulas has a "known" value, $\sigma_{XU(Y)} = 0$, and the formulas simplify to the following:

$$\left.\begin{array}{c} a = \dfrac{\sigma_{XY}}{\sigma_X^2} \\[3em] \sigma_U^2 = \sigma_Y^2 - \dfrac{\sigma_{XY}^2}{\sigma_X^2} \end{array}\right\} \text{if } \sigma_{XU(Y)} = 0$$

Thus in restricted situations (i.e., when X and U_Y are uncoordinated) both coefficient **a** and the disturbance variance $\sigma_{U(Y)}^2$ are uniquely identified in terms of observable statistical quantities. Consequently the formulas might be used to estimate these parameters from empirical statistics.

This example spotlights a characteristic difficulty in least-squares estimations. The path analysis yields two equations that can be solved for unknown parameters, but these equations contain three unknowns. Thus a unique solution for any of the unknowns is not possible until the value of one unknown is determined on a nonempirical basis. The general predicament of no unique solution is known as the *identification problem*. Systems that yield fewer path analytic equations than there are unknowns are said to be *underidentified*.

REGRESSION ANALYSIS AND IDENTIFICATION

A second example illustrates other features of the least-squares logic. Though the system considered is only slightly more complex, the algebra complicates rapidly, and two simplifying assumptions are made beforehand. First, it is assumed that all variables are measured on scales with standardized units. This is not a restrictive assumption (essentially the same results could be obtained without it). However, it has the heuristic value of making all variances equal to 1.0 and the variances need not be represented explicitly in formulas. In addition, it is assumed that disturbances of a variable are uncorrelated with the variable's specified sources. This is a restrictive assumption in that the results apply only in situations in which the assumption is true. However, this particular restriction is exactly what is needed to develop the least-squares logic further.

The system to be considered is presented in **5.2**.

5.2   All variables are measured in standard units and the disturbances are uncorrelated with x or with one another.

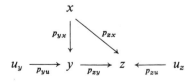

Again measurements are made on each variable over the cases of interest and the key statistics are calculated. Because variables are standardized, the variances of all variables are equal to 1.0 and the covariances are the same as the correlations. Path analysis specifies the correlations as

$$\rho_{xy} = \rho_{yx}$$
$$\rho_{yz} = \rho_{zy} + \rho_{yx}\rho_{zx}$$
$$\rho_{xz} = \rho_{zx} + \rho_{yx}\rho_{zy}$$

and solving for the unknown p's yields the following formulas:

$$p_{yx} = \rho_{xy}$$

$$p_{zy} = \frac{\rho_{yz} - \rho_{xy}\rho_{xz}}{1 - \rho_{xy}^2}$$

$$p_{zx} = \frac{\rho_{xz} - \rho_{xy}\rho_{yz}}{1 - \rho_{xy}^2}$$

These formulas, however, are exactly those that define standardized partial regression coefficients (see **3.32** and **3.33**). If we regress y on x and z on x and y together, the results of the regressions estimate the system operators:

$$p_{yx} = \beta_{yx}$$
$$p_{zy} = \beta_{zy \cdot x}$$
$$p_{zx} = \beta_{zx \cdot y}$$

Path analysis of variances can be conducted as usual if we remember that all variances have a value of 1.0.

$$\sigma_y^2 = 1 = p_{yu}^2 + p_{yx}^2 = p_{yu}^2 + \rho_{xy}^2$$
$$\sigma_z^2 = 1 = p_{zu}^2 + p_{zy}^2 + p_{zx}^2 + 2\rho_{xy}p_{zy}p_{zx}$$

By using a number of the preceding results in substitutions the following formulas can be derived:

$$p_{yu}^2 = 1 - (\beta_{yx}^2)$$
$$p_{zu}^2 = 1 - (\beta_{zy \cdot x}^2 + \beta_{zx \cdot y}^2 + 2\beta_{zy \cdot x}\beta_{zx \cdot y}\rho_{xy})$$

Here the quantities in parentheses are precisely the expressions for coefficients of determination (see **3.34**). Path coefficients from disturbances can also be obtained directly from the results of regression analyses:

$$p_{yu}^2 = 1 - R_{y \cdot x}^2$$
$$p_{zu}^2 = 1 - R_{z \cdot xy}^2$$

A general principle has been illustrated. *Under restricted conditions a system's parameters can be estimated by conducting a series of regression analyses.* This parallelism between system estimation and regression analysis holds *only* when source variables and disturbances are uncorrelated. Regression procedures are mathematically defined to eliminate correlation between predictor variables and the residuals from predictions. If source variables and disturbances actually are correlated, regression coefficients do not correspond to system parameters.

The Need for Theory

The examples given serve to emphasize that empirical observations can lead to inferences about the nature of a system only in the context of theoretical assumptions. A formula can be used to estimate a parameter if the formula uniquely identifies that parameter in terms of measurable statistics. In general this is true only if some quantities are eliminated from the formula on a theoretical basis; for example, it must be *known* that a source variable is not affected by the dependent variable before a causal interpretation is given to a regression of the one on the other. Further, it must be *known* that any spurious coordination between two variables is absent or controlled before a regression coefficient can be interpreted as a valid estimate of a causal effect. Various estimation methods mentioned later offer some variety in the choice of theoretical assumptions needed for system identification, but some kind of theoretical information is needed before data can be interpreted. Mere observations of a system are not enough to identify it, and the identification problem can never be solved merely by collecting observations on more cases. Underidentification is a theoretical rather than a statistical problem.

It is presumed throughout most of this chapter that variances and covariances are calculated on the basis of all cases in a population in order to bypass complications created by probabilistic inference from samples. In practice, parameter estimates can be calculated from observations on samples —and this economy is exploited routinely in social research. When working with samples, an increase in the sample size generally does improve the accuracy of estimations. (Problems of sampling and statistical inference are discussed briefly at the end of the chapter. These matters are covered at length in statistical and econometric textbooks.) Nevertheless, an estimation is not possible at all unless a formula exists that provides a unique mathematical identification of the desired parameter. Such formulas are obtained only by making assumptions of a theoretical nature.

RECURSIVE SYSTEMS

The following definition presents a concept that is convenient for a more detailed development of estimation methods by ordinary regression analyses.

V.1 *A relation between two variables is called recursive if it is linear, if the two variables are not in a loop, and if the source variable is uncoordinated with the disturbances of the dependent variable. If all the causal relations in a system are recursive, the entire system is said to be recursive.*

"Recursive" is simply a name for a kind of causal relation in which parameters are identified in terms of ordinary regression formulas. Because of the ease with which the parameters can be estimated, recursive relations do warrant some special attention.

The matter of linearity was discussed in Chapter 1 and is not considered further here. Ascertaining that two variables are not in a loop amounts to an inference that no causal effect exists from one variable to the other. The bases for such causal inferences were discussed in Chapter 1 and need not be repeated. Discussion here is focused only on the matter of coordination between sources and disturbances.

Viewed from a theoretic perspective, three conditions outlined in **5.3** can create correlations between a source variable and the disturbances of a dependent variable.

5.3 A linear relation from X to Y is nonrecursive if the disturbances of the dependent variable are coordinated with the specified source variable; that is,

$$
\begin{array}{ccc}
\sigma & \cdots\!\rightarrow & U_y \\
\vdots & & \downarrow \\
\downarrow & & \\
X & \xrightarrow{\ a\ } & Y
\end{array}
$$

This coordination can develop in three ways:

1. A mutual source of X and Y has not been considered explicitly: it exists implicitly in the U_Y aggregate. This relation can be made recursive

by elaborating the specification of the system to include the mutual source explicitly; for example,

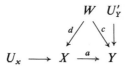

An implicit variable creates nonrecursiveness only if it determines both source and dependent variable. In particular, deleting an intervening variable in a recursive system does not create nonrecursiveness in the reduced system; for example, both of the following are recursive systems:

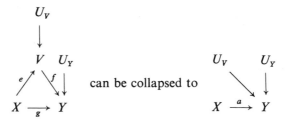

2. Some variable in the U_Y aggregate serves jointly with X in a gating mechanism, thereby creating artificial coordination between X and the other variable, say Z, in the population of interest. In this situation recursiveness could be established by removing Z from the disturbance aggregate and considering it explicitly because coordination among specified sources does not interfere with recursiveness.

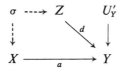

Gating directly on variable Y generates a negative correlation between X and U_Y', as pointed out in Chapter 4. This problem could be eliminated by examining the full population (both gated and ungated cases).

3. If X and Y are involved together in a loop in which Y is directly or indirectly a source for X as well as dependent on X, the disturbances of Y must be correlated with the values of X.

$$U_Y$$

$$\downarrow$$

$$X \overset{a}{\underset{d}{\rightleftharpoons}} Y$$

X and U_Y are coordinated by the path $(U_Y YX)$.
Here the coordination between X and U_Y is intrinsic and cannot be eliminated by further specification of the system.

Thus the relation between two variables can be treated as recursive only when (a) causality is unidirectional so that one variable is known not to affect the other and there is no ambiguity about which is the source and which is dependent; (b) any third variable that is a source for both is included explicitly in analyses; (c) the source variable (or one of its sources) is not involved in a gating mechanism along with any unspecified variable that affects the dependent variable and the population of interest has not been gated on the dependent variable.

Ordinary Least Squares (OLS)

The method of ordinary least squares, described in the next rule, gives unbiased parameter estimates only if the relations between a dependent variable and all its sources are recursive.

V.2 *If the relations between a system variable and its sources are all recursive, the structural coefficients for operators determining the variable may be estimated directly by regression analysis and the disturbance variance by the variance of the regression residuals. The appropriate regression is defined as follows:*

(a) *Write out the structural equation expressing the value of the dependent variable as a function of its immediate sources, the structural coefficients, and the disturbance term, for example $Z = aX + dY + U_Z$.*

(b) *This equation defines the multiple regression model—the dependent variable (Z) is regressed on all of its specified sources (X, Y).*

(c) *The resulting partial regression coefficients identify the structural coefficients; for example,*

$$a = b_{ZX \cdot Y} \qquad d = b_{ZY \cdot X}$$

and the residual variance, defined by the regression's multiple correlation coefficient, identifies the disturbance variance; for example,

$$\sigma^2_{U(Z)} = \sigma^2_{(Z-\hat{Z})} = (1 - R^2_{Z\cdot XY})\sigma^2_Z$$

The ideas involved in ordinary least squares are elaborated in **5.4**.

5.4 BASIC PARADIGM FOR ORDINARY LEAST SQUARES

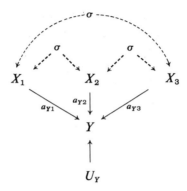

Restrictions: Y's relations with all of its sources are recursive. Theoretically, there is no restriction on the number of X variables or on their interrelations.

Procedure. Regress Y on X_1, X_2, and X_3. The partial regression coefficients identify the structural coefficients:

$$a_{Y1} = b_{Y1\cdot23}$$
$$a_{Y2} = b_{Y2\cdot13}$$
$$a_{Y3} = b_{Y3\cdot12}$$

The variance of the disturbance is identified by the multiple correlation coefficient and the variance of Y:

$$\sigma^2_{U(Y)} = (1 - R^2_{Y\cdot123})\sigma^2_Y$$

In a recursive system this paradigm may be applied repeatedly to identify and estimate all unknown parameters, as illustrated in **5.5**.

5.5 Here there are no loops and the U's are uncorrelated with V or W or among themselves. Hence ordinary least squares may be used to estimate parameters.

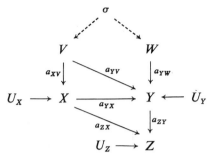

The procedure involves running the following separate regressions for each dependent variable:

$$V$$
$$a_{xv} \downarrow$$
$$U_X \longrightarrow X$$

defines the regression of X on V to identify $\mathbf{a}_{xv}$ and $\sigma^2_{U(X)}$.

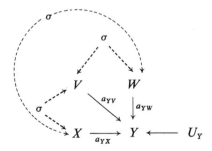

defines the regression of Y on V, W, and X to identify $\mathbf{a}_{yv}$, $\mathbf{a}_{yw}$, $\mathbf{a}_{yx}$, and $\sigma^2_{U(Y)}$. Note that the causal relationship between V and X is merely summarized by a covariance term (and implicitly by the variances of V and X), which indicate that the kind of relation existing between V and X is of no consequence in this step; that is, the regression procedure ignores the details of causal relationships among prior variables and takes into account the net effects of these processes reflected in the covariances and variances of the variables.

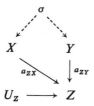

This diagram defines the regression of Z on X and Y to identify $\mathbf{a}_{ZX}$ $\mathbf{a}_{ZY}$, and $\sigma^2_{U(Z)}$. Again X and Y are treated as direct sources of Z. Their detailed causal relationships are ignored and treated in summary form by the observed covariance σ_{XY} and also, implicitly, by the observed variances σ^2_X and σ^2_Y.

Essentially the ordinary least squares method involves breaking a diagram down into a set of subdiagrams, each suitable for defining the variance of a single dependent variable in terms of the variances and covariances of its sources. Only the direct sources of the dependent variable are included in a subdiagram and relations among these sources are summarized by covariance terms.

Some illustrative situations in which ordinary least squares is *not applicable* are given in **5.6**.

5.6 Instances in which ordinary least squares *should not be used:*

$$\sigma \dashrightarrow U_Y$$

$$X \xrightarrow{a} Y$$

The disturbances of Y are coordinated with the specified source X. In this case the regression coefficient does not estimate $\mathbf{a}$. Rather

$$b_{YX} = a + \frac{\sigma_{XU(Y)}}{\sigma^2_X}$$

$$U_X \qquad U_Y$$

$$W \xrightarrow{a_{XW}} X \xrightarrow{a_{XY}} Y$$

Here the disturbances themselves are coordinated. Although $\mathbf{a}_{XW}$ can be estimated by ordinary least squares, $\mathbf{a}_{YX}$ is not uniquely identified. The appropriate subdiagram must reflect the correlation between X and U_y that exists via the disturbances of X:

$$\sigma \dashrightarrow U_Y$$
$$\downarrow \qquad \downarrow$$
$$X \xrightarrow{\ a_{YX}\ } Y$$

This, however, is the same diagram considered above.

$$U_X \qquad U_Y$$
$$\downarrow \qquad \downarrow$$
$$X \underset{a_{XY}}{\overset{a_{YX}}{\rightleftarrows}} Y$$

Both variables are involved in a loop and the regression of Y on X does not identify $\mathbf{a}_{YX}$. Rather the regression coefficient represents another quantity of no particular interest:

$$b_{YX} = \frac{a_{YX} + a_{XY}(\sigma_Y^2/\sigma_X^2)}{1 + a_{YX}a_{XY}}$$

Loop coefficients can never be estimated accurately by using ordinary least squares because loop parameters are not properly identified by simple regression statistics. It may be possible, however, to identify parts of a loop system by using OLS. In particular, the independent variables in a regression can be in loops without biasing results because a loop does not affect open paths leading away from the loop variables (see the "touching" rule—II.15).

5.7 $U_X \qquad U_Y$
$$\downarrow \qquad \downarrow$$
$$X \underset{a_{XY}}{\overset{a_{YX}}{\rightleftarrows}} Y$$
$$a_{ZX} \searrow \qquad \swarrow a_{ZY}$$
$$U_Z \longrightarrow Z$$

Ordinary least squares cannot be used to estimate $\mathbf{a}_{YX}$ or $\mathbf{a}_{XY}$ but it can be used to estimate the coefficients leading to Z because the subdiagram below accurately displays the information relevant to Z:

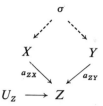

In other words, X and Y are recursive sources with respect to Z even though they are nonrecursive sources with respect to each other.

NONRECURSIVE SYSTEMS

Coefficients in nonrecursive relations can also be identified and estimated provided that the specification of the system includes some variables with certain restricted features. These "instrumental variables" (defined in the following rule) may be part of the original specification of the system or they may be added to the system specification merely as a matter of research design. Regardless of whether instrumental variables are considered practically relevant, their conceptualization at the time of theorizing is a matter of utmost importance. The structural coefficients in a nonrecursive system can be estimated from cross-sectional data *only* if adequate instruments are available.

Instrumental Variables

V.3   A. *A variable, X, is an instrument for Y in the nonrecursive relationship $Y \rightarrow Z$ if*

(a) *X has no direct effect on Z;*
(b) *X does affect Y, either directly or through an intervening variable that has no direct effect on Z;*
(c) *neither Y nor Z has a direct or indirect effect on X;*
(d) *no unspecified factor jointly affects X and Z and, in general, X is uncoordinated with the disturbances of Z.*

B. *A variable, X', that is merely correlated with Y also is an instrument for the Y → Z relation providing it fulfills conditions (a), (c), and (d) above.*

If X is an instrument for the relation $Y \to Z$, then the relation between X and Z is like a recursive relation in two ways; that is, Z has no effect on X and X has no coordination with the unspecified variables affecting Z (Z's disturbances). On the other hand, an instrumental source contrasts with an ordinary recursive source in that it definitely must not have a direct effect on Z—it must affect Z only through specified intervening variables and, in particular, through the variable Y.

An instrument, X, as defined by section A of the rule, must be a source for variable Y, but the X–Y relation need not be fully recursive because X may be correlated with the disturbances of Y. Section B extends the concept of instrument to include any variable that is merely correlated with Y, provided that the correlation is not due to a causal effect from Y and that the variable meets conditions (a), (c), and (d).

Examples of instrumental variables are presented in **5.8**.

5.8   EXAMPLES OF INSTRUMENTAL VARIABLES. In each case X is a valid instrument relative to the relation $Y \to Z$.

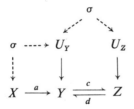

X may be correlated with U_Y but not U_Z. U_Y and U_Z may be correlated and Y and Z may be variables in a loop.

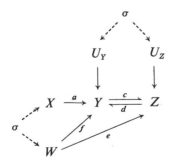

X may be correlated with other *specified* source variables affecting either Y or Z.

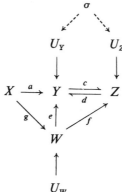

X may affect Z through intervening variables other than Y if they are included *explicitly* in the analyses.

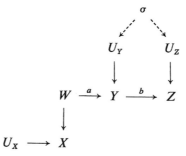

X is an instrument if its relations with Y and Z are mediated by the primary instrument W and if its disturbances are uncorrelated with Z.

Further understanding of instrumental variables can be obtained by examining some examples in which a variable fails to meet the defining conditions.

5.9   In the following examples X is *not* an instrument for the relation $Y \to Z$:

$$U_X \longrightarrow X \longleftarrow Y \longrightarrow Z \longleftarrow U_Z$$

$$U_Y$$

because Y affects X

$$U_X \longrightarrow X \xrightleftharpoons[d]{a} Y \xrightarrow{c} Z \longleftarrow U_Z$$

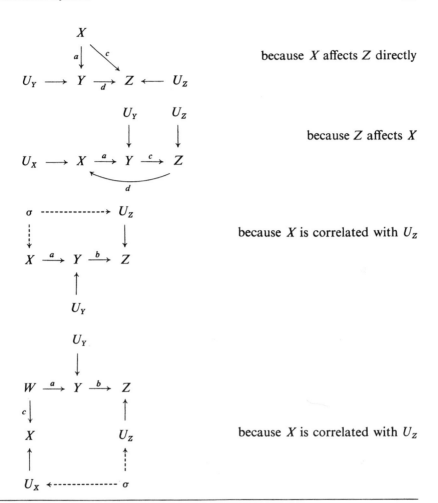

because X affects Z directly

because Z affects X

because X is correlated with U_Z

because X is correlated with U_Z

A variable may serve as an instrument for more than one relationship, as illustrated in the examples in **5.10**.

5.10   EXAMPLES OF MULTIPLE-PURPOSE INSTRUMENTS

X is an instrument for $V \rightarrow W$ and for $Y \rightarrow Z$.

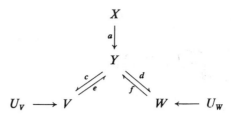

X is an instrument for $Y \to V$ and for $Y \to W$.

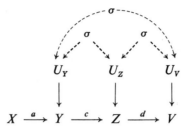

X is an instrument for $Y \to Z$; it is also an instrument for $Z \to V$.

$$
\begin{array}{ccccc}
U_V & & U_Y & & U_Z \\
\downarrow & & \downarrow & & \downarrow \\
X \xrightarrow{a} & V & \xrightarrow{c} & Y \underset{e}{\overset{d}{\rightrightarrows}} & Z
\end{array}
$$

X is an instrument for $Y \to Z$ and it would be an instrument for $V \to Y$ but no instrument is needed to deal with that recursive relationship.

$$
\begin{array}{ccccc}
U_Y & & U_Z & & U_V \\
\downarrow & & \downarrow & & \downarrow \\
X \xrightarrow{a} & Y \underset{c}{\overset{d}{\rightrightarrows}} & Z \underset{e}{\overset{f}{\rightrightarrows}} & V
\end{array}
$$

X is an instrument for $Y \to Z$; it is also an instrument for $Z \to V$.

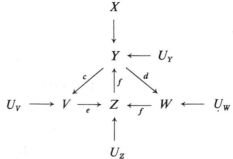

X is an instrument for $Y \to V$ and for $Y \to W$; also for $V \to Z$ and $W \to Z$.

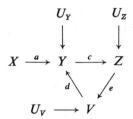

X is an instrument for $Y \rightarrow Z$; it is also an instrument for $Z \rightarrow V$.

X is an instrument for $Y \rightarrow Z$, for $Z \rightarrow V$, and for $V \rightarrow W$.

Instruments and Identification

Instrumental variables provide a net gain in the information for dealing with identification problems. An instrument brings some additional unknowns into an analysis. It also yields additional variances and covariances that can be path analyzed for supplementary identification equations.

5.11

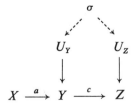

Without the instrument X there are just two path analysis equations available for identifying the unknowns of the system.

$$\sigma_{YZ} = c\sigma_Y^2 + \sigma_{U(Y)U(Z)} \tag{1}$$

$$\sigma_Z^2 = c^2\sigma_Y^2 + \sigma_{U(Z)}^2 + 2\sigma_{U(Y)U(Z)} \tag{2}$$

Because these two equations contain three unobservables, the system is underidentified. Adding the instrument adds one unknown quantity **a**, but it also adds three new observables and three new path analysis equations.

$$\sigma_{XY} = a\sigma_X^2 \tag{3}$$

$$\sigma_{XZ} = ac\sigma_X^2 \tag{4}$$

$$\sigma_Y^2 = a^2\sigma_X^2 + \sigma_{U(Y)}^2 \tag{5}$$

The following identification formulas can be obtained:

$$a = \frac{\sigma_{XY}}{\sigma_X^2} \qquad\qquad \text{[from (3)]} \quad (6)$$

$$c = \frac{\sigma_{XZ}}{\sigma_{XY}} \qquad\qquad \text{[from (4) and (6)]} \quad (7)$$

$$\sigma_{U(Y)U(Z)} = \sigma_{YZ} - \frac{\sigma_{XZ}\sigma_Y^2}{\sigma_{XY}} \qquad\qquad \text{[from (1) and (7)]} \quad (8)$$

$$\sigma_{U(Y)}^2 = \sigma_Y^2 - \frac{\sigma_{XY}^2}{\sigma_X^2} \qquad\qquad \text{[from (5) and (6)]} \quad (9)$$

$$\sigma_{U(Z)}^2 = \sigma_Z^2 - \frac{\sigma_{XZ}}{\sigma_{XY}}\left(\frac{\sigma_{XZ}}{\sigma_{XY}} - 2\sigma_Y^2\right) - 2\sigma_{YZ} \tag{10}$$

Thus the instrument adds enough equations to identify all unknowns. If the instrument X were correlated with U_Y, it would still provide enough information to identify key parameters in the original non-recursive relation, but the parameters relating the instrument to the other variables would not be identified uniquely; for example, adding a nonzero covariance between X and U_Y yields the following co-variance and variance equations:

$$\sigma_{XY} = a\sigma_X^2 + \sigma_{XU(Y)}$$
$$\sigma_{XZ} = ac\sigma_X^2 + c\sigma_{XU(Y)}$$
$$\sigma_Y^2 = a^2\sigma_X^2 + \sigma_{U(Y)}^2 + 2a\sigma_{XU(Y)}$$

These equations give rise to the same identification formulas for **c**, $\sigma_{U(Y)U(Z)}$, and $\sigma_{U(Z)}^2$. However, coefficient **a** and the statistical param-eters $\sigma_{U(Y)}^2$ and $\sigma_{XU(Y)}$ cannot be identified uniquely. Adding an instrument to an analysis can increase information enough to identify

important system parameters even when it is impossible to identify
the parameters relating the instrument to the system.

The last part of this example illustrates an important point. *The coefficient
linking a variable to its instrument cannot be identified accurately unless the
relation between the two is recursive;* that is, an instrument need not be
recursively related to its entry variable to be useful, but its effect on the entry
variable can be assessed correctly only if the relation between the two is
recursive.

A net gain in information also results when an instrument is available for
one of the relations in a loop.

5.12

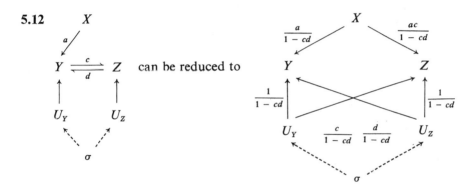

The following covariance formulas can then be obtained from the
reduced diagram:

$$\sigma_{XY} = \frac{a}{1 - cd}\sigma_X^2$$

$$\sigma_{XZ} = \frac{ac}{1 - cd}\sigma_X^2$$

Dividing the second by the first gives an identification formula for
coefficient **c**:

$$c = \frac{\sigma_{XZ}}{\sigma_{XY}}$$

It is interesting to note that the same result could be obtained by regressing Y on X, regressing Z on X, and then writing the final identification formula in terms of the regression coefficients that result:

$$c = \frac{\sigma_{XZ}}{\sigma_{XY}} = \frac{\sigma_{XZ}/\sigma_X^2}{\sigma_{XY}/\sigma_X^2} = \frac{b_{ZX}}{b_{YX}}$$

The generalized version of this technique is an estimation method called indirect least squares.

The last equation in **5.12** suggests that if loop variables are regressed on instrumental variables loop coefficients can be identified from the regression coefficients. This is the key idea in the method of indirect least squares. This estimation method, however, is not elaborated here because it has a basic practical weakness. If there is more than one instrument for a given relationship, several different estimates for a structural coefficient may be obtained with indirect least squares, but there is no set procedure that will combine them into a single best estimate.

Another manner of using instrumental variables leads to a general method of estimating unknowns in nonrecursive relations, even when a relationship is overidentified by more instruments than are needed for a single estimate of a particular coefficient.

Two-Stage Least Squares (2SLS)

A general method of estimating parameters in nonrecursive relations from cross-sectional data was developed in the 1950s by the econometrician Henry Theil. This method—two-stage least squares—is applicable when the disturbances of system variables are correlated, it is appropriate for estimating coefficients in loops, and it combines information from multiple instruments efficiently to obtain a single estimate of each structural coefficient.

In effect, the two-stage least squares method involves using instrumental variables in a first round of multiple regression analyses to define new system variables that are free of confounding effects from disturbances. These new variables are employed in a final round of regression analyses to estimate structural coefficients and the variances and covariances of disturbances. A graphical interpretation of two-stage least squares is provided later. First though, we shall consider the basic steps that can be followed to implement the procedure.

V.4 *Two-Stage Least Squares (2SLS) Estimation. If some of the relations between a system variable and its sources are nonrecursive but adequate instruments exist for them, the structural coefficients for operators determining the variable may be estimated:*

(a)   *Write out a structural equation that expresses the value of the dependent variable as a function of its immediate sources, the structural coefficients and the disturbance term.*

(b)   *Make up a list of predetermined variables consisting of all recursive sources in the equation and all instruments for the nonrecursive sources.*

(c)   *Regress each of the nonrecursive sources on all the predetermined variables to obtain a set of regression equations for "predicting" values on each nonrecursive source from values on the predetermined variables.*

(d)   *Return to the original set of observations and for each case calculate the predicted value for each nonrecursive source, using the formulas obtained in step (c). This procedure generates one new variable, called a "decontaminated source," for each of the original nonrecursive source variables.*

(e)   *Return to the equation defined in step (a) and estimate its coefficients by ordinary least squares, substituting the decontaminated source variables for the original nonrecursive sources.*

5.13   PROBLEM: Estimate **a**, **c**, and **d** from observations on T, V, W, X, Y, Z.

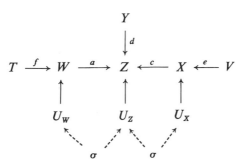

Ordinary least squares should not be used here because X and W are nonrecursive sources for Z: that is, they are coordinated with the disturbances in Z. Hence we turn to the 2SLS method.

STEP 1.   Write out the structural equation for Z.

$$Z = aW + cX + dY + U_Z$$

STEP 2.   Make up the list of predetermined variables relative to this equation. This list includes Y because Y is a recursive source for Z. It also includes T and V because they are instruments for the two nonrecursive sources of Z.

STEP 3.   Regress the nonrecursive sources on *all* the predetermined variables.

$$W = b_{WT \cdot VY}T + b_{WV \cdot TY}V + b_{WY \cdot TV}Y + e_W$$
$$X = b_{XT \cdot VY}T + b_{XV \cdot TY}V + b_{XY \cdot TV}Y + e_X$$

STEP 4.   Return to the original data and generate the decontaminated variables $\hat{W}$ and $\hat{X}$ by using the following formulas:

$$\hat{W} = b_{WT \cdot VY}T + b_{WV \cdot TY}V + b_{WY \cdot TV}Y$$
$$\hat{X} = b_{XT \cdot VY}T + b_{XV \cdot TY}V + b_{XY \cdot TV}Y$$

STEP 5.   Revise the equation in step 1 by substituting the decontaminated variables for the original sources

$$Z = a\hat{W} + c\hat{X} + dY + U_Z$$

and estimate the structural coefficients by using ordinary least squares.

The disturbance variance $\sigma^2_{U(Z)}$ is not estimated directly by the variance of residuals in the final regression but rather by a fairly complex transformation of the residual variance. The calculating formulas are not presented here.

5.14   2SLS ESTIMATION OF COEFFICIENTS IN A LOOP

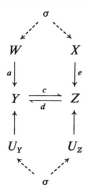

Relations $Y \rightarrow Z$ and $Z \rightarrow Y$ are nonrecursive; W and X, however, are instruments for these relations.

Step 1. The equations for Y and Z are

$$Y = aW + dZ + U_Y$$
$$Z = eX + cY + U_Z$$

STEP 2. W is a recursive source in the first equation and an instrument with respect to the second equation. Similarly, X is a recursive source in the second equation and an instrument for the first. Thus W and X constitute the set of predetermined variables for both equations.

STEP 3. Conduct the multiple regressions of Y on W and X and of Z on W and X to obtain the regression formulas

$$Y = b_{YW \cdot X}W + b_{YX \cdot W}X + e_Y$$
$$Z = b_{ZW \cdot X}W + b_{ZX \cdot W}X + e_Z$$

STEP 4. For each original observation calculate the predicted values of Y and Z, using the regression coefficients obtained in Step 2. This defines two new variables:

$$\hat{Y} = b_{YW \cdot X}W + b_{YX \cdot W}X$$
$$\hat{Z} = b_{ZW \cdot X}W + b_{ZX \cdot W}X$$

STEP 5. Use ordinary least squares to estimate the operators in each structural equation. Always regress onto $\hat{Y}$ or $\hat{Z}$ instead of Y or Z. Thus to estimate the coefficients in the structural equation

$$Y = aW + dZ + U_Y$$

conduct the following regression:

$$Y = b_{YW \cdot \hat{Z}}W + b_{Y\hat{Z} \cdot W}\hat{Z} + e_Y'$$

The resulting coefficients are unbiased estimates of the corresponding operator coefficients; that is,

a is estimated by $b_{YW \cdot \hat{Z}}$
d is estimated by $b_{Y\hat{Z} \cdot W}$

Similarly, to estimate the coefficients in

$$Z = eX + cY + U_Z$$

regress Z on X and $\hat{Y}$; then

e is estimated as $b_{ZX \cdot \hat{Y}}$
c is estimated as $b_{Z\hat{Y} \cdot X}$

Calculating Procedures

The procedure for 2SLS estimation defined by Rule V.4 requires two separate sets of regression analyses plus an intermediate step in which we return to the original data to create decontaminated variables. Actually the intermediate step can be accomplished without returning to the original observations by using procedures outlined in exercise 6 of this chapter.

Mathematical formulas that define 2SLS as a single-step analytic procedure are available. The matrix equations are much too complex to present here and too complex to be used for manual calculations. Many computer installations maintain a 2SLS program that incorporates the mathematical solution and can be called routinely to handle various problems, however.

The use of 2SLS computer programs is recommended in terms of economy and greater numerical accuracy. In addition, these programs ordinarily calculate statistics for testing the statistical significance of coefficient estimates when data consist of observations on a sample rather than of observations on a whole population. Moreover, computer programs make routine provision of 2SLS estimates of the variances and covariances of disturbances. Formulas for calculating these quantities have not been given here because of their complexity.

Graphical Interpretation of 2SLS

A system graph can be transformed to correspond to the procedures in a two-stage least squares analysis. Such graphical manipulations are helpful toward an understanding of the basic logic of this method.

5.15   PROBLEM: Obtain a single unbiased estimate of coefficient **c**, given the two instruments W and X.

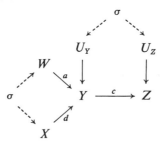

The values of Y that are predictable just from the instruments W and X could be used to define a composite instrumental variable $\hat{Y}$, and this variable can be entered explicitly on the diagram.

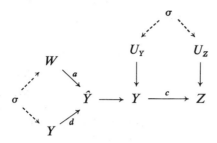

$\hat{Y}$ is defined by the multiple regression of Y on W and X, and values of $\hat{Y}$ for each observed case can be obtained by applying the regression formula to values of W and Y. Variables Y and Z in the above diagram can now be reduced onto $\hat{Y}$, U_Y and U_Z (see rule II.17).

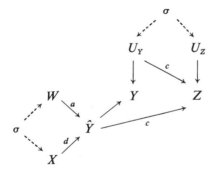

In this transformed diagram $\hat{Y}$ is revealed as a determinant of Z that is uncorrelated with any disturbance of Z. Hence ordinary least squares may be applied. Z is regressed on $\hat{Y}$ and $\mathbf{c}$ is estimated by the regression coefficient $b_{z\hat{y}}$.

The key idea clarified by the graphical approach is that the values of $\hat{Y}$ represent an extraction of real variations in Y that are in no way contaminated by, or correlated with, the disturbances of Z. Hence the relation between Z and this "purified" Y is recursive and coefficient $\mathbf{c}$ can be estimated by ordinary least squares.

This example with two instrumental variables for the relation $Y \rightarrow Z$

is of special interest because the $Y \to Z$ relation is *overidentified*. From the original graph seven equations can be written to express the values of observable covariances and variances in terms of the unknowns and the observable variances of W and X. There are only six unknowns, however—three structural coefficients and three disturbance parameters. If the seven equations were solved for the six unknowns, two different estimating formulas would be obtained for coefficient **c**. It is unlikely that these two formulas would always give exactly the same result if we were working with real data, and there would be the problem of merging the different estimates of **c** into a single best value. Two-stage least squares solves the overidentification problem by creating a single composite instrumental variable $\hat{Y}$ that optimally combines the variance extracted from Y using each instrument.

Two-stage least squares estimation of loop coefficients can also be represented graphically if the dependent variable of interest is extricated first (rule II.19).

5.16   PROBLEM. Obtain a single unbiased estimate of the loop coefficient **c**, given instruments W and X.

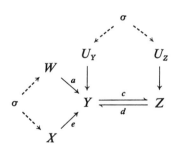

First the variable Z is extricated from the loop (by rule II.19).

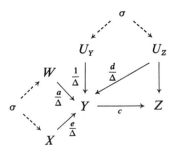

where $\Delta = 1 - cd$. This is then transformed, as in the preceding example, to give

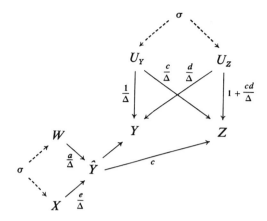

Again a regression of Y on W and X defines the variable $\hat{Y}$ and a regression of Z on $\hat{Y}$ estimates coefficient **c**.

As this example shows, extrication of variables in a system with loops converts the diagram to one without loops in which key relations still remain nonrecursive. Thus the problem of estimating a loop coefficient does not differ in nature from the problem of estimating the coefficient in other types of nonrecursive relations, though graphically it does involve the extra step of extrication.

Identification Problems

A loop does create additional difficulties by complicating the identification problem; for example, coefficient **c** in **5.16** was identified, given the instruments W and X. In fact, it was overidentified because there were two instruments for the one relation, $Y \to Z$. It remains impossible, however, to identify the operator **d** in the system defined in **5.16**. This can be seen by extricating Y instead of Z.

5.17 EXTRICATION OF Y FROM THE LOOP SYSTEM IN **5.16**

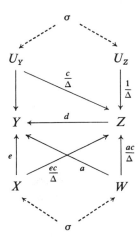

Now Z clearly is correlated with U_Y and **d** cannot be identified by ordinary least squares. Moreover, there is no instrument for the relation $Z \to Y$; therefore it is impossible to create a decontaminated variable $\hat{Z}$ that can be used to estimate **d** by a multiple regression of Y on $\hat{Z}$, X, and W. It is *not* possible to use X and W to create a useful $\hat{Z}$ because both variables have direct effects on Y. More specifically, coefficient $b_{Y\hat{Z} \cdot WX}$, which presumably would estimate **d** in a final ordinary least squares analysis, can be viewed as the coefficient obtained by regressing the residuals of Y (removing all predictions from X and W) on the residuals of $\hat{Z}$ (removing all predictions from X and W). However, because $\hat{Z}$ is created solely from X and W, these two variables predict it perfectly, and no residuals of $\hat{Z}$ exist after predicting it from W and X. Hence the coefficient $b_{Y\hat{Z} \cdot XW}$ is undefined and **d** is not identified.

At this point the simple idea of counting up equations and unknowns has broken down as a basis for deciding whether a system is identifiable. In the above example there are seven definable equations and a total of seven unknowns, but because there are two redundant instruments for the relation $Y \to Z$ and none for $Z \to Y$, only one of the loop operators can be identified. The system as a whole remains underidentified.

Moreover, it is clear now that *the two-stage least squares procedure may break down when no instrument is available for a nonrecursive relation.* The applicability of rule V.4 must necessarily be constrained by another rule that states under what conditions the coefficients in an equation may be identified.

Identifiability

V.5 *If a variable is in a loop and its disturbances are correlated with the values of its sources, then all the coefficients in its structural equation are identified only if conditions (a) and (b) hold:*

(a) *At least one instrument is available for every nonrecursive relation represented in the equation.*

(b) *If the equation involves several nonrecursive sources—say the number is M—there must be at least M different instruments for the relations between the dependent variable and its sources. (Each of the instrumental variables may serve as an instrument for more than one of the M relations.)*

If each nonrecursive source is associated with a variable that is an instrument for relations involving that source only, the structural coefficients are always theoretically identified.

Condition (a) states, in effect, that the coefficient in a particular nonrecursive causal relation is identified only if at least one instrument is available for that particular relation.

5.18

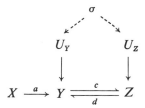

Coefficient **c** is identified because there is an instrument (X) that applies specifically to the $Y \rightarrow Z$ relation. Coefficient **d** is not identified because there is no instrument for the $Z \rightarrow Y$ relation.

Note that the same instrument may serve repeatedly in the analysis of different equations.

5.19

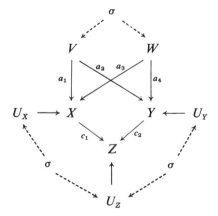

All coefficients are mathematically identified because the W–X relation is recursive and **a** is identified by an ordinary regression coefficient; W is an instrument for the $X \rightarrow Y$ relation and **c** is identified; W is also an instrument for $Y \rightarrow Z$ and **d** is identified.

In other words, it is not necessary to have a *separate* instrument for every nonrecursive relation in a system.

Condition (b) relaxes the requirements even more when a dependent variable is involved in several nonrecursive relations. There must be an instrument for every relation, but it is not required that each instrument apply to only one.

5.20

V is an instrument for both the $X \to Z$ and $Y \to Z$ relations. Similarly, W is an instrument for both nonrecursive relations. Nevertheless, condition (b) is fulfilled, and ordinarily it would be possible to estimate all the coefficients: the $\mathbf{a}$'s by ordinary least squares and the $\mathbf{c}$'s by 2SLS.

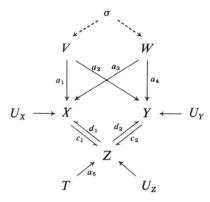

This is a variation of the above situation, and all coefficients ordinarily are identified. V and W are instruments that identify the $\mathbf{c}$'s and T is an instrument that identifies the $\mathbf{d}$'s. The $\mathbf{a}$'s are also identified in terms of statistics from 2SLS analyses.

Following are examples in which one of the necessary conditions for identifiability is fulfilled but not the other.

5.21

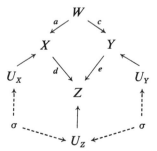

W serves as an instrument for both nonrecursive relations, $X \to Z$ and $Y \to Z$, and condition (a) is fulfilled, but because there is only one instrument for the two nonrecursive sources of Z condition (b) is not fulfilled.

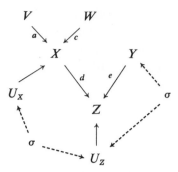

Z is involved in two nonrecursive relations and there are two instruments, V and W; hence condition (b) is fulfilled. No instrument is available, however, for the $Y \rightarrow Z$ relation and condition (a) is unfulfilled.

Conditions (a) and (b) in rule V.5 are necessary for identifiability. All coefficients in a nonrecursive system cannot be identified unless these conditions are fulfilled, but they are not sufficient conditions. Instances do occur in which conditions (a) and (b) are met and still some structural coefficients cannot be estimated at all or they are subject to such large errors that they are useless practically; for example, this would be true if by chance $\mathbf{a}_1 = \mathbf{a}_3$ and $\mathbf{a}_2 = \mathbf{a}_4$ in **5.20**.

The last part of the rule defines a sufficient condition for identifiability. If each nonrecursive source is the "entry point" for an instrument that has no other entry points, then all structural coefficients are identified mathematically.

5.22

$$X_1 \qquad\qquad X_2$$

$$U_1 \longrightarrow Y_1 \underset{c_2}{\overset{c_1}{\rightleftarrows}} Y_2 \longleftarrow U_2$$

$$Y_3 \longleftarrow U_3$$

$$X_3$$

All the coefficients are mathematically identified because a unique instrument is associated with each of the variables in the loop complex.

Indeed, this condition is *over*sufficient. If defines a useful goal in the theoretical specification of a system rather than a practical necessity because instances occur (in large systems especially) in which all coefficients in a block can be identified without fulfilling the condition. (A more preceise, just-sufficient condition for identifiability is presented routinely in econometrics textbooks, but its formulation requires familiarity with matrix algebra.)

Full-Information Methods

Ordinary least squares and two-stage least squares are "single-equation methods" of estimation, meaning that they involve the estimation of coefficients in just one structural equation at a time in contrast to full-information methods that estimate all coefficients in a system simultaneously. Whereas single-equation methods depend on retracing causal paths only one or two links from a dependent variable, full-information methods use information on extended causal chains. This yields one of the major advantages of full-information methods. They make more efficient use of valid theory, literally incorporating all such knowledge into the estimate of each system parameter so that the estimates are more precise. The major disadvantage of full-information methods is that they similarly incorporate any erroneous theory into calculations. If part of a system has been misspecified, all coefficient estimates may be affected rather than just a few, as in a single-equation method. Thus, in general, the full-information methods are most appropriately used in later stages of research when there is a high level of confidence in the theoretical specification of a system.

Full-information methods can also make use of *a priori* knowledge about disturbance covariances, which leads to extra power in identification. The following simple example illustrates the logic involved:

5.23 Both coefficients in a loop are identified with a single recursive instrument if the disturbances of the loop variables are known to have zero covariance.

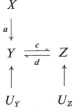

Using the instrument X, we identify coefficient **c** as indicated in **5.12**.

$$c = \frac{\sigma_{XZ}}{\sigma_{XY}}$$

Because X, U_Y, and U_Z are uncorrelated, the covariance σ_{YZ} can be defined purely in terms of the variances of Y and Z. The algebra to demonstrate this point is not given here, but the following expression is the result:

$$\sigma_{YZ} = \frac{c\sigma_Y^2 + d\sigma_Z^2}{1 + cd}$$

Substituting $(\sigma_{XZ}/\sigma_{XY})$ for **c** and solving for **d** gives

$$\sigma_{YZ} = \frac{(\sigma_{XZ}/\sigma_{XY})\sigma_Y^2 + d\sigma_Z^2}{1 + (\sigma_{XZ}/\sigma_{XY})d}$$

$$d = \frac{\sigma_Y^2\sigma_{XZ} - \sigma_{YZ}\sigma_{XY}}{\sigma_{YZ}\sigma_{XZ} - \sigma_Z^2\sigma_{XY}}$$

In many routine applications, however, full-information methods are applied only to improve estimation efficiency rather than to achieve extra identification power. Indeed, one of the procedures—three-stage least squares (3SLS)—incorporates a 2SLS analysis as a preliminary to its final analysis. Ordinarily it simply gives more efficient estimates of coefficients that have been estimated by the 2SLS method. The analytic procedures for full-information methods are complex and can be described succinctly only by using a higher level of mathematics than is available for this book. Econometric textbooks provide detailed discussions of these techniques.

Self-Loops

No procedure is available for identifying the coefficients for self-loops from cross-sectional data. Moreover, when self-loops are assumed to be absent when actually they are present, the identification of some other coefficients necessarily is affected, as indicated in **5.24**.

5.24   EFFECT OF A SELF-LOOP ON IDENTIFICATION

Assume for convenience that

$$\sigma_W^2 = \sigma_X^2 = 1.0 \qquad \sigma_{WX} = 0$$

In which case

$$\sigma_{WY} = .515 \qquad \sigma_{XY} = .059$$
$$\sigma_{WZ} = .145 \qquad \sigma_{XZ} = .588$$

Now suppose that the system is misspecified as

The two-stage least squares estimates of these coefficients would be

$$a_{ZY} = .281 \qquad a_{ZX} = .571$$
$$a_{YZ} = .100 \qquad a_{YW} = .501$$

The structural coefficients determining Y are estimated accurately (within rounding error) but those affecting Z are too large. In fact, $\mathbf{a}_{ZY}$ and $\mathbf{a}_{ZX}$ are systematically biased such that they must be multiplied by the return difference of the self-loop (i.e., $[1 - .3] = .7$) to obtain the correct values.

As the example suggests, the existence of an unspecified self-loop on a variable leads to biased estimates for coefficients in that variable's structural equation. The resulting errors are relatively benign, however, because the estimated coefficients are in the right proportions relative to one another and they do reproduce accurately all static relations in the system.

Lagged Variables as Instruments

Earlier measurements of a variable are sometimes included in a system specification as an aid to identification under the assumption that the variable measured earlier is an instrument for the same variable measured at a later time. This usage can lead to false inferences if stability in the key variable is maintained mainly by stability in other system variables, as shown in **5.25**.

5.25 $x_1 \xrightarrow{.5} y_1 \longleftarrow U_y$

$\quad\quad\quad \downarrow {\scriptstyle .8}$

$\quad\quad x_2 \xrightarrow{.5} y_2 \longleftarrow U_y$

$\quad\quad\quad \uparrow$

$\quad\quad U_{x(2)}$

Subscripts on x and y indicate the time of measurement. The .8 is the stability coefficient for the x variable over the time interval; the lack of a path from y_1 to y_2 indicates the lack of stability in y except via its dependence on x. Now suppose that the relation between x and y is unknown and y_1 is used as an instrument to identify c in the following diagram:

$$U_{x(2)} \quad\quad\quad y_1$$
$$\downarrow \quad\quad\quad\quad \downarrow$$
$$x_2 \underset{c}{\overset{a}{\rightleftarrows}} y_2 \longleftarrow U'_{y(2)}$$

$\rho_{y(1)y(2)} = .2$, $\rho_{y(1)x(2)} = .4$. The value of c would be estimated as $(.4/.2) = 2.0$, which is a grave error (the true value is zero). This error could have been avoided by including x_1 in the analysis, in which case y_1 would be revealed as an inadequate instrument for the $y_2 \rightarrow x_2$ relation because it has no correlation with y_2 when the value of x_1 is controlled.

The major lesson here is that lagged values of a variable cannot be used routinely to identify its relations with other variables. In particular, we must know beforehand that the focal variable is a source for the others or the lagged variable may not be a meaningful instrument. If such knowledge is lacking, overtime measurements must be made on *all* the variables to gain information about the system's structure from temporal coordination. Such a longitudinal design is a combination of the cross-sectional approach we have already discussed and time-series analysis, discussed in Chapter 6.

FACTORS AFFECTING ESTIMATES

Sampling Error

Many complications have been avoided by assuming that data are collected for every case in the population of interest. In practical problems, however, we typically examine a *sample* of cases from the population. Sample variances and covariances are likely to be somewhat different from the true values in the population because of idiosyncracies in the particular subset of cases under examination. Substitution of the erroneous variances and covariances into identification formulas naturally yields somewhat erroneous estimates of structural coefficients as well.

A sample of three cases has a high likelihood of being idiosyncratic and unrepresentative of a population. Just by chance, for example, all three cases may be above the population mean on one variable and below it on another. Samples of 10 cases have less chance of being idiosyncratic because it is less likely that so many cases will be in the same directions. As we move to samples of hundreds or thousands, the chances of idiosyncracy and nonrepresentativeness decrease even more (and this is true whether the population size is 10,000, a million, or a billion). Thus the larger the sample, the more likely it is that its statistical characteristics will match those of the population as a whole. Consequently the expected error of parameter estimates decreases regularly with increasing sample size. The minimal useful sample size depends on how much error in estimation we are willing to tolerate, on the number of variables, on the strength of relations in the system, on which estimation procedures are being used, and on a number of other factors considered below. A sample of 100 cases is usually necessary before estimations have much credibility when dealing with social systems; the number must be larger if the system is large, if measurements are poor and correlations are weak, and if estimation is by 2SLS rather than OLS. There are situations in which a sample smaller than 100 cases can yield interesting information, but ordinarily a larger—even a much larger—sample is needed to get results of value.

In addition to being large enough, a sample must be drawn without biases that could create nonrandom idiosyncracies. Appropriate sampling procedures and other methodological aspects of sampling are discussed in textbooks on the topic (see chapter references).

Strength of Relations

The structure of a system may make it difficult to estimate parameters accurately unless large samples are available; for example, the following simple system (shown with all variables standardized) presents problems in the accurate estimation of some of its coefficients from sample data.

5.26 $x \xrightarrow{\ .9\ } y \xleftarrow{\ .44\ } u_y$

$\quad\quad\ \ _{.5}\searrow\ \ \swarrow_{.2}$

$\quad\quad\quad z \xleftarrow{\ .73\ } u_z$

True correlations are

$$\rho_{xy} = .90 \qquad \rho_{xz} = .68 \qquad \rho_{yz} = .65$$

A set of hypothetical sample correlations might be

$$r_{xy} = .91 \qquad r_{xz} = .70 \qquad r_{yz} = .62$$

The identification formula for p_{zy} is

$$p_{zy} = \frac{\rho_{yz} - \rho_{xy}\rho_{xz}}{1 - \rho_{xy}^2}$$

Applied to the true correlations, this gives

$$\frac{.65 - (.90)(.68)}{1 - (.90)^2} = .2$$

Applied to the sample correlations, the formula gives

$$\frac{.62 - (.91)(.70)}{1 - (.91)^2} = -.1$$

Thus in this case the sample data provide an inaccurate estimate of the value of p_{zy} by indicating a negative relationship when the true relationship is positive.

The erroneous result in this example is largely due to the high degree of *collinearity* among the determinants of z (ρ_{xy} = .90). This exaggerates the impact of the errors in the sample correlations (which are not atypical of those obtained in even fairly large samples).

A collinearity problem exists when the correlations between two or more determinants of a dependent variable are much higher than the correlations between the dependent variable and the determinants. Accurate estimation of structural coefficients then requires that estimates of true correlations have little error which implies the need for extremely large samples.

The strength of relations also influences the accuracy of estimates based on instrumental variables, as shown in **5.27**.

5.27

$$U_y \qquad U_z$$

$$\downarrow \qquad \downarrow$$

$$x \xrightarrow{\;.05\;} y \underset{.20}{\overset{.30}{\rightleftarrows}} z$$

True correlations are

$$\rho_{xy} = .053 \qquad \rho_{xz} = .016 \qquad \rho_{yz} = .471$$

A set of "observed" correlations based on a hypothetical sample is

$$r_{xy} = .068 \qquad r_{xz} = .005 \qquad r_{yz} = .463$$

An identification formula for p_{zy}, using x as an instrument, is (from **5.11**)

$$p_{zy} = \frac{\rho_{xz}}{\rho_{xy}}$$

Applied to the true correlations, this gives .30 (within rounding error). Applied to the hypothetical sample correlations it gives

$$\frac{r_{xz}}{r_{xy}} = \frac{.005}{.068} = .074$$

Hence the weak instrument in conjunction with even relatively small sampling errors in the values of correlations can yield an inaccurate estimate of the structural coefficient.

A problem of weak instruments exists whenever an instrumental variable has a near-zero correlation with its dependent variable (in the above example this correlation is just .068); sampling errors in the observed correlations are magnified in the process of estimating parameters and the estimates are unreliable. If only one weak instrument is available in a problem, accurate parameter estimates can be obtained only by using a large number of cases so that sampling errors will be small.

If additional instruments are available for the same relation, they can be treated together as a set in the 2SLS procedure, and the measure of adequacy is the multiple correlation (R) between the instruments and the dependent variable. Sometimes it is possible to make R large enough by using a number of instruments that would be inadequate separately.

Measurement Imprecision

Even if a whole population is being examined, the true values of variances and covariances cannot be obtained if variables are measured imprecisely. Hence empirical estimates of system parameters can be accurate only if measurements are accurate.

Analyses of the measurement problem usually begin by assuming that measurement errors are unpredictable (random) disturbances in the observed values of a variable. This model translates readily into a path diagram.

5.28

$$X \to \tilde{X} \leftarrow \varepsilon$$

X represents true variations; $\tilde{X}$ represents the observed variations obtained on an operational scale; ε represents the aggregate of random measurement errors. Ordinarily it is assumed that X and ε are uncorrelated.

In standardized form

$$x \xrightarrow{\ v\ } \tilde{x} \xleftarrow{\ \sqrt{1 - v^2}\ } e$$

The validity coefficient **v** measures the correlation between the true scores and the observed scores.

The causal interpretation of the measurement problem can be integrated with the ordinary analysis of a system, as indicated in the simple example in **5.29**.

5.29

$$X \xrightarrow{a} Y \longleftarrow U_Y$$
$$\downarrow \qquad \downarrow$$
$$\tilde{X} \qquad \tilde{Y}$$
$$\uparrow \qquad \uparrow$$
$$\varepsilon_X \qquad \varepsilon_Y$$

Both variables are assumed to be measured with error and the errors are assumed to be uncorrelated.

Ordinarily to identify **a** we might use the formula in **5.1**:

$$a = \frac{\sigma_{XY}}{\sigma_X^2}$$

Path analysis shows that the observed covariance of $\tilde{X}$ and $\tilde{Y}$ is equal to the covariance of the true scores.

$$\sigma_{\tilde{X}\tilde{Y}} = \sigma_{XY} = a\sigma_X^2$$

However, the variance of X is not accurately estimated by the empirical measurements:

$$\sigma_{\tilde{X}}^2 = \sigma_X^2 + \sigma_\varepsilon^2$$

Hence, if we substituted the observed quantities based on fallible measurements into the identification formula, we would get

$$\frac{\sigma_{\tilde{X}\tilde{Y}}}{\sigma_{\tilde{X}}^2} = \frac{\sigma_{XY}}{\sigma_X^2 + \sigma_\varepsilon^2}$$

Here we would underestimate the magnitude of **a**, the more so as the errors in measuring X are greater. Note that errors in measuring the *dependent* variable do not affect the accuracy of estimating an unstandardized structural coefficient. Such errors, however, would bias the estimate of a path coefficient because it is standardized on the basis of both the independent and dependent variable.

Parameter estimates made from imprecise measurements generally are biased, a problem that can never be solved by just increasing sample size. In essence, measurement imprecision is an aspect of the identification problem. To get unbiased parameter estimates, we must estimate the variances of measurement errors in addition to all the other parameters in the system, and ordinarily not enough information is available. The solution to the measurement problem is to use instrumental variables or multiple indicators.

5.30 The example in **5.29** could be dealt with by adding an instrument—even one that itself is measured imprecisely.

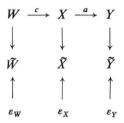

By applying the usual formula for estimation from an instrument **(5.12)**, we have

$$\frac{\sigma_{\tilde{Y}\tilde{W}}}{\sigma_{\tilde{X}\tilde{W}}} = \frac{ca\sigma_W^2}{c\sigma_W^2} = a$$

Thus the estimate of **a** using the instrument is unbiased.

Alternatively, the problem could be handled by obtaining additional indicators of X.

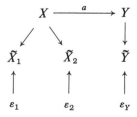

For convenience in the illustration it is assumed that the two indicators are equivalent in scale units so that both are related to X by a coefficient of 1.0. Now an unbiased estimate of the variance of X may be obtained from the path analysis formula for the covariance of the indicators.

$$\sigma_{12} = \sigma_X^2$$

This could be used to obtain two estimates of **a**:

$$\frac{\sigma_{1\hat{y}}}{\sigma_{12}} \quad \text{or} \quad \frac{\sigma_{2\hat{y}}}{\sigma_{12}}$$

Efficient procedures for combining such multiple estimates are given in more advanced references.

Theoretically only one variable (i.e., one instrument or one extra indicator) need be added to obtain unbiased parameter estimates in a situation like that above. Most practical problems, however, are confounded by sampling as well as measurement errors, and the use of a single weak instrument or just two weak indicators would have the effect of magnifying sampling errors in calculations, thus producing final estimates too erratic to be of value. Hence the measurement problem must be attacked by including multiple instruments or multiple indicators in research design. Analyses must be correspondingly complex to incorporate all the information; for example, the use of instruments leads directly to 2SLS analyses (or an equivalent procedure), and the use of multiple indicators calls for other multivariate procedures such as factor analysis or canonical analysis (see references).

As shown above, the measurement problem can sometimes be transcended by using instruments and 2SLS. Conversely, *coefficient estimates based on 2SLS analyses are routinely unbiased by measurement errors, provided that the errors of measurement are uncorrelated across variables.* Thus instrumental variables are powerful research tools that give unbiased coefficient estimates for intricate and imperfectly measured systems.

Specification Errors

Certain patterns of causal structuring are required for the valid application of the estimation methods discussed in preceding sections. Recursive relations are required for ordinary least squares; valid instrumental variables are needed for 2SLS. A specification error occurs if a particular pattern is assumed to exist when it does not. *Specification mistakes that falsely define causal priorities or falsely eliminate disturbance correlations may lead to serious distortions in coefficient estimations and to grave errors in the understanding of a system.*

5.31   Suppose that the true system is

$$x \xrightarrow{.8} y \longleftarrow U_y \quad \text{so} \quad p_{yx} = .8 \text{ and } p_{xy} = 0$$

If it is wrongly assumed that y is prior to x, then ordinary least squares would lead to the following results:

$$p_{yx} = 0 \quad \text{(by assumption)} \quad \text{and} \quad p_{xy} = .8$$

This pattern of results is in grave error because it implies a causal pattern just opposite to what exists.

Suppose that the true system is

$$
\begin{array}{cc}
U_y & U_z \\
\downarrow & \downarrow
\end{array}
$$

$$U_x \longrightarrow w \xleftarrow{.6} y \xleftarrow{.5} z \xleftarrow{.8} x \quad \text{so} \quad P_{zy} = 0 \quad \text{and} \quad p_{yz} = .5$$

If it is wrongly assumed that w is an instrument for $y \to z$, then 2SLS would lead to the following results:

$$p_{zy} = .21 \quad \text{and} \quad p_{yz} = .35$$

These results are in grave error because a loop is implied when none exists.

Suppose that the true system is

$$-.4 \dashrightarrow U_z \qquad p_{yx} = .6 \quad \text{and} \quad p_{zy} = .3$$

$$x \xrightarrow{.6} y \xrightarrow{.3} z$$

$$\uparrow$$

$$U_y$$

If it is assumed that $\sigma_{xU(z)} = 0$ instead of $-.4$, then applying ordinary least squares gives the following estimates for the structural coefficients:

$$P_{yx} = .6 \quad \text{and} \quad P_{zy} = .06$$

If x were used as an instrument in 2SLS to allow for a possible correlation between U_y and U_z (the assumption being that $\sigma_{xU(z)}$ is zero), the estimates would be

$$p_{yx} = .6 \quad \text{and} \quad p_{zy} = -.37$$

The OLS results are seriously in error. The 2SLS results are gravely misleading.

Ordinary least squares does not give sensible results unless variables are entered in analysis according to their true causal priorities. Results from two-stage least squares analyses are inaccurate if the variables used as instruments do not, in fact, fulfill the requirements for instrumental variables.

ELABORATION IN SOCIAL RESEARCH

Research interest frequently centers on a core system of greatest theoretical or practical relevance. Initially it may seem a straightforward matter to obtain some empirical data and estimate the desired system parameters. In fact, matters are usually not so simple. The problems of identifying a system snowball, leading from one to another, so that an elaborate research scaffold may have to be constructed before modest ends can be achieved.

Leaving key variables out of the system specification creates correlated disturbances which eliminate system recursiveness and perhaps undermine the validity of instruments. To avoid the biased estimations that can develop from correlated disturbances either the key variables must be brought into the analysis or other variables must be entered that can serve as instruments for the contaminated relationships. Either way, more variables may have to be analyzed than originally were considered relevant. Similarly, the coefficients in loops can be identified only if enough adequate instruments are available. This may require expanding the system to include variables of little theoretical or practical interest, including them simply because they fit research needs.

Because social variables are rarely measured precisely by any single index, a measurement problem routinely exists in social research. This, perhaps more than any other factor, calls for manifold expansion of the number of variables that have to be considered. If measurements are imprecise but still of fairly high reliability, then at least two measurements are needed for every source variable in the system before there is any hope of obtaining unbiased estimations of system parameters (that is, each variable must be associated with two indicators or with one indicator and one instrument). In the more likely situation of moderate and low reliability measures, numerous indicators or instruments may be required for each source variable to estimate system parameters reliably.

Thus quantitative studies of even fairly simple social systems tend to expand into intricate research projects that require detailed planning, the collection of large quantities of data, and the use of sophisticated statistical techniques to extract the results.

ZERO COEFFICIENTS

An analysis may reveal that some of the coefficients in a structural equation are zero, which suggests that some of the conceivable causal relationships in the system actually did not occur in the population that was examined. Such causal inference operationalizes rule I.5, which stated that one event does not cause another if occurrences of the first do not imply occurrences of the second. A zero coefficient means that variations in a given source do not imply variations in a particular outcome. Consequently it is concluded that the first variable is not a direct cause of the second.

Whether the true value of a coefficient is zero actually may be somewhat ambiguous, given the results from an empirical study. Coefficient estimates are themselves subject to error (as discussed above) and a null effect from one variable to another may turn out to be associated with a coefficient estimate that is only near zero in value rather than exactly zero. This means that "small" coefficients, as well as zero values, must be regarded as indicating no effect. Yet the existence of errors in estimates also opens the possibility that an estimated coefficient is only accidentally small, the true value being substantially different from zero. If we were to treat all near-zero coefficients as zero, we might eliminate some relationships that actually are operative.

Statistical tests can be applied to assess the probability that an estimated coefficient corresponds to a true value of zero (see chapter references) and such tests should be used routinely to gain information for deciding whether an effect exists. Such tests, however, are only an aid to decisions, not a mechanical routine for decision making. If we are dealing with a small sample (or any other situation that tends to inflate the errors in coefficient estimates), a statistical test may be too insensitive for our purposes and will lead us to reject causal effects that actually exist. If we are working with a large sample, a statistical test may be so sensitive that it will lead us to retain minute coefficients that might be nonzero only because of minor biases in estimates (developing, for example, from unresolved measurement problems or from a sample containing a few cases in which operators failed to act). Thus, in addition to statistical information, a pragmatic element has to enter such decisions. A relationship should not be eliminated from a model if the coefficient indicates that the magnitude of the effect is comparable to other effects being considered, even if a statistical test suggests that the coefficient is not "significantly" different from zero. On the other hand, even if the coefficient is statistically significant, a relationship may be eliminated from a model if the magnitude of the effect is so small in relation to other effects that it has no practical or theoretical interest.

Eliminating relationships on the basis of near-zero coefficients permits the simplification of the system formulation. Arrows can be removed from the flowgraph and terms dropped from structural equations. The remaining coefficients in the simplified system should be reestimated to improve their precision; that is, the data should be reanalyzed by employing the new constraints to obtain improved estimates of the remaining system parameters.

SOURCES AND ADDITIONAL READINGS

Several articles that introduce least squares estimation techniques are reprinted conveniently in Hubert M. Blalock, Jr., Ed. *Causal Models in the Social Sciences* (Chicago: Aldine-Atherton, 1971). Kenneth C. Land, "Formal Theory," Chapter 7 in Herbert L. Costner, Ed., *Sociological Methodology: 1971* (San Francisco: Jossey-Bass, 1971), further elucidates the relations between theories, models, and data.

The various estimation techniques were developed mainly by econometricians, and econometrics textbooks provide the most comprehensive discussions of the procedures. An elementary treatment (though still employing matrix algebra—see Chapter 3 readings) is provided by Ronald J. Wonnacott and Thomas H. Wonnacott, *Econometrics* (New York: Wiley, 1970). The presentations of Arthur S. Goldberger, *Econometric Theory* (New York: Wiley, 1964), and Henry Theil, *Principles of Econometrics* (New York: Wiley, 1971), are mathematical but notable for their detail and authoritativeness.

The Goldberger and Theil texts pay considerable attention to sampling errors in estimation (as well as to other sources of error). Additional discussion of sampling problems from an operational perspective is available in Leslie Kish, *Survey Sampling* (New York: Wiley, 1965).

Sociologists have focused particularly on how the impact of measurement errors can be controlled when estimates of structural parameters are being obtained. A number of key articles are included in the Blalock reader cited above. Additional works are D. R. Heise and George W. Bohrnstedt, "Validity, Invalidity, and Reliability" Chapter 6 in Edgar F. Borgatta and G. W. Bohrnstedt, Eds., *Sociological Methodology: 1970* (San Francisco: Jossey-Bass, 1970), Robert M. Hauser and Arthur S. Goldberger, "The Treatment of Unobservable Variables in Path Analysis," Chapter 4 in Herbert L. Costner, Ed., *Sociological Methodology: 1971* (San Francisco: Jossey-Bass, 1971), and R. M. Hauser, "Disaggregating a Social-Psychological Model of Educational Attainment," *Social Science Research*, 1 (1972), 159–188; all depend on matrix aglebra in derivations. The classical psychometric approach to measurement is introduced lucidly by Jum C. Nunnally, *Psychometric Theory* (New York: McGraw-Hill, 1967). A detailed, authoritative reference on the psychometric tradition is provided by Frederic M. Lord and Melvin R. Novick, *Statistical Theories of Mental Test Scores* (Reading, Mass.: Addison-Wesley, 1968).

Making sense of a multitude of variables is a classical problem in social science research. Morris Rosenberg, *The Logic of Survey Analysis* (New York: Basic Books, 1968), provides an introduction to the problems with numerous illustrations. Mathematically derived approaches are presented in the papers by Hauser and Goldberger and by Hauser cited above. K. G. Jöreskog, "A General Method for Estimating a Linear Structural Equation System," Chapter 5 in A. S. Goldberger and O. D. Duncan, Eds., *Structural Equation Models in the Social Sciences* (New York: Seminar Press, 1973), introduces a model applicable to a great variety of problems involving multiple indicators and complex causal relations among abstract variables. (The Goldberger-Duncan book also contains exemplary empirical work on estimation of linear causal models.)

Multivariate analyses of a sample of cases observed at several times present a plethora of problems, some of which are considered in D. R. Heise, "Causal Inference from Panel Data," Chapter 1 in E. F. Borgatta and G. W. Bohrnstedt, Eds., *Sociological Methodology: 1970* (San Francisco: Jossey-Bass, 1970), Otis Dudley Duncan, "Unmeasured Variables in Linear Models for Panel Analysis," Chapter 2 in H. L. Costner, Ed., *Sociological Methodology: 1972* (San Francisco, Jossey-Bass, 1972), and K. G. Jöreskog, "Factoring The Multitest-Multioccasion Correlation Matrix," RB-69-62 (Princeton, N.J.: Educational Testing Service, 1969). Some models for pooling overtime data are presented mathematically in Jan Kmenta, *Elements of Econometrics* (New York: Macmillan, 1971), pp. 508–517.

EXERCISES

1. Can the following variables be organized into a recursive model: father's education, father's occupational standing, son's education, son's occupational standing? Discuss the various considerations.

2. The observed correlations among father and son status variables were as follows in one study (P. Blau and O. D. Duncan, *The American Occupational Structure*, New York: Wiley, 1967, p. 169).

	FaEd	FaOcc	SoEd	SoOcc
FaEd	1.000	.516	.453	.322
FaOcc		1.000	.438	.405
SoEd			1.000	.596
SoOcc				1.000

Suppose that a strict recursive model applies in the population being studied. Estimate all the relevant standardized parameters of the model. Use the specifications from exercise 5, Chapter 1. (A calculator is needed for this and some subsequent problems.)

3. Suppose a number of persons are brought to a task in which they can exchange deference and domination acts. Dyads are formed experimentally by pairing persons whose outside occupations are associated with various levels of social power. Ratings of the powerfulness of these occupations are obtained from participants before beginning the task. After extended interaction, the task is terminated, and a second set of ratings is obtained by asking each person to rate himself and his partner on the same powerfulness scale. The model on page 198 might be used to interpret the experimental results.

O_1 and O_2, power ratings for the occupations of persons 1 and 2, respectively, translate to initial estimates of interpersonal power (I_1 and I_2) by the multiplier ll with possibilities of judgmental disturbances U_1 and U_2. D is the perceived discrepancy between the power of self and other adjusted by one's personal tendency to see the self as stronger or weaker than others (P). Deferring or dominating acts are represented by **a**; for example, if a person

$$P_1$$

$$O_1 \qquad \downarrow {+1} \qquad O_2$$

$$D_1$$

$$k \downarrow \quad {+1} \nearrow \qquad \searrow {-a} \quad \downarrow k$$

$$U_1 \longrightarrow I_1 \quad {+a} \qquad {-1} \quad I_2 \longleftarrow U_2$$

$${-1} \searrow \qquad \nearrow {+a}$$

$${-a} \qquad \qquad {+1}$$

$$D_2$$

$$\uparrow {+1}$$

$$P_2$$

perceives an adjusted discrepancy of $+1.0$ (self more powerful than other), a dominant act is emitted, thus adding **a** units to self-power and subtracting **a** units from other's power. If a -1.0 discrepancy is perceived, a deferring act subtracts **a** units from self-power and adds the same amount to the other's power.

(a) Suppose the researcher regresses the terminal values of I_1 on O_1 and O_2 in the manner of ordinary least squares. What systemic parameters are estimated by the regression coefficients? Could an estimate of **a** be derived in this way?

(b) Suppose the O and I variables were assessed in terms of likeability or goodness instead of power. Then **a** might change sign, standing for acts of altruism and exploitation rather than dominance and deference; that is, perceiving a positive discrepancy in goodness leads to an act that transfers some of one's own worth to the other; perceiving a negative discrepancy leads to exploiting the other's goodness to improve one's own standing. With this change what would the expected effect be on the regression coefficients when I_1 is regressed on O_1 and O_2? Are problems of identification different in the new system?

4. Sociologists debate whether social structure is determined materialistically or by the force of ideologies. Suppose we decide to examine the issue empirically in the population of small societies that have been described by ethnographers. (Systematic data on more than 1000 cultures have been published in the journal *Ethnography*.) For heuristic purposes let us suppose that the relevant variables can be represented as follows.

S: the level of elaboration of a hierarchical social structure as reflected in the occurrence of classes, castes, and high political offices.

M: the society's materialistic advantages in the subsistence realm indexed by a scale of subsistence technology ranging from hunting and gathering to advanced agricultural techniques such as cereal agriculture with irrigation.

I: the development of an authoritative moral ideology for ordering social relations reflected in beliefs about the power of supernatural agents to sanction human behavior.

The task is to estimate structural coefficients $\mathbf{a}_{SM}$ and $\mathbf{a}_{SI}$ and, in particular, to determine whether one or the other of these coefficients is negligible in magnitude. The relationships may not be recursive, however. The elaboration of social structure conceivably could have a return effect on subsistence technology or moral ideology. Moreover, advances in all three areas might be achieved by way of cultural diffusion from other societies so that disturbances of the variables might be correlated. Accordingly, we must attempt to specify instruments that would allow us to identify the structural coefficients.

(a) Evaluate each of the following variables that characterize a society's locale as a possible instrument for identifying the structural coefficients $\mathbf{a}_{SM}$ and $\mathbf{a}_{SI}$.

- Average length of growing season
- Soil fertility
- Severity of everyday habitat (i.e., the extent of conditions threatening death by thirst, starvation, predators, drowning, and falling).
- Accessibility of metal ore deposits.

(b) Suppose that we find that the growing-season variable has a correlation of zero with the social structure variable S and also with the ideology variable I. Does this information help in deciding whether it is an adequate instrument for the relation $M \rightarrow S$?

5. At the end of Chapter 4 it was suggested that attitudes and behaviors might be related in a control loop. Thus identifying the effect of one on the other from survey data would require the use of instruments. Suppose that questions are designed that adequately measure a person's attitude toward alcoholic beverages and rate of alcohol use. The items are included in a survey of students at a large state university in a region in which the legal drinking age is 21 for hard liquor, 18 for beer. Other items determine whether the student was raised in a family with fundamentalist religious identification, the amount of weekly spending money the student has for entertainments, and the student's age. Evaluate the last three items as instruments for identifying the coefficients in the attitude-behavior loop for alcohol.

6. Statistics characterizing a weighted composite score can be calculated from the variances and covariances of its component variables; for example, suppose that we want to generate a new variable, $\hat{V}$, by adding together variables X and Y weighted by $\mathbf{w_1}$ and $\mathbf{w_2}$. If we know σ_X^2, σ_Y^2, and σ_{XY}, it is easy to define $\sigma_{\hat{V}}^2$, $\sigma_{X\hat{V}}$, and $\sigma_{Y\hat{V}}$. Moreover, suppose that originally we had another variable, Z, and we know σ_{XZ} and σ_{YZ}. Then it also is easy to define $\sigma_{\hat{V}Z}$. The logic can be seen by applying path analysis to the following diagram:

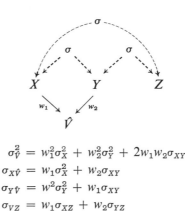

$$\sigma_{\hat{V}}^2 = w_1^2\sigma_X^2 + w_2^2\sigma_Y^2 + 2w_1w_2\sigma_{XY}$$
$$\sigma_{X\hat{V}} = w_1\sigma_X^2 + w_2\sigma_{XY}$$
$$\sigma_{Y\hat{V}} = w^2\sigma_Y^2 + w_1\sigma_{XY}$$
$$\sigma_{VZ} = w_1\sigma_{XZ} + w_2\sigma_{YZ}$$

This means that a two-stage least squares analysis can be conducted without actually going back to individual observations after the first round of regression analyses; for example, suppose that we have the following problem:

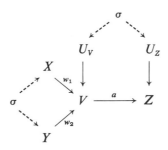

The values of $\mathbf{w_1}$ and $\mathbf{w_2}$ are estimated by regressing V on X and Y (or by the use of the regression coefficient formulas given in Chapter 3). Then, using the above procedures, we can estimate the variance of the predicted score $\hat{V}$ and its covariance with Z. These figures are sufficient to compute a second-stage regression estimating $\mathbf{a}$ (again referring to formulas in Chapter 3). Use these procedures to do a 2SLS estimation of the structural coefficients in the following model:

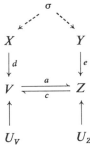

The variances and covariances of the variables are as follows:

	X	Y	V	Z
X	1.000	.300	.283	.235
Y	.300	1.000	−.113	.466
V	.283	−.113	1.068	−.164
Z	.235	.466	−.164	1.051

7. Minority racial groups in America might improve their socioeconomic position by working toward a higher average level of education, whereupon a higher average income would follow. It could also be argued that minority groups should demand better jobs and wages so that education and other forms of status can be bought. These arguments imply that theoretically we cannot eliminate a loop between average education and average income in a minority population. If, however, we could define suitable instruments, the issue could be examined empirically. We could estimate the coefficient from education to income and from income to education to assess which of the effects have operational support in American society. Data from a study of 63 standard metropolitan statistical areas (SMSAs) can be used to illustrate the kinds of results that might be obtained [Richard Child Hill, "Unionization and Racial Income Inequality in the Metropolis," *American Sociological Review*, **39** (1974) 507–22]. The variables listed were included in the study.

S: Presence of the SMSA in the South.
U: Extent of unionization within the SMSA.
P: Percent of the SMSAs population that is nonwhite.
M: Percent of the SMSAs labor force that is in manufacturing industries.
E: Median education among nonwhites in the SMSA.
I: Median family income among nonwhites in the SMSA.

The correlations among these variables in 1960 were reported as follows:

	S	U	P	M	E	I
S	1.000					
U	−.556	1.000				
P	.591	−.258	1.000			
M	−.253	.510	−.233	1.000		
E	−.574	.226	−.684	−.134	1.000	
I	−.749	.569	−.527	.185	.709	1.000

The author of the article did not focus on the issues raised here, but the following model might be proposed as a basis for analyzing the data. (The V's represent disturbances.)

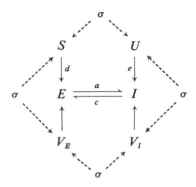

(a) Use the reported correlations and the diagram to estimate **a** and **c**. Use the procedures presented in exercise 6 to implement the 2SLS approach.

(b) Estimate **a** and **c** again, using the following model.

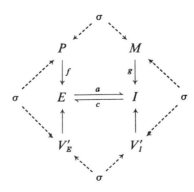

(c) Compare the results from (a) and (b). In particular, discuss the adequacy of the instruments and biases they might have produced. (Remember the sample size in your discussion.)

8. We continue with the variables and data given in exercise 7. Suppose now that we are willing to accept the following specification:

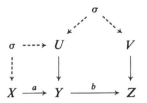

Use this model to reestimate coefficient **a** and **c**. Use the results from this analysis with the results from exercise 7 to formulate a strategy for improving the socioeconomic position of urban nonwhites.

9. Covariances among disturbances can be estimated fairly easily from observed variances and covariances if the system does not contain loops and if instruments are available; for example, suppose that we have the following simple system:

$$\sigma \dashrightarrow U \qquad V$$
$$X \xrightarrow{a} Y \xrightarrow{b} Z$$

An estimate of **b** is provided by $(\sigma_{XZ}/\sigma_{XY})$. The covariance of disturbances U and V is identified as

$$\sigma_{YZ} = b\sigma_Y^2 + \sigma_{UV}$$

or

$$\sigma_{UV} = \sigma_{YZ} - \frac{\sigma_{XZ}\sigma_Y^2}{\sigma_{XY}}$$

Typically we are dealing with variables that are measured imprecisely.

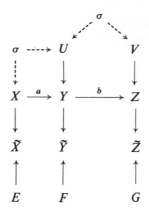

in which case key covariances and variances of the observed variables will have the following relations to the covariances and variances of the true variables:

$$\sigma_{\tilde{X}\tilde{Y}} = \sigma_{XY}$$
$$\sigma_{\tilde{X}\tilde{Z}} = \sigma_{XZ}$$
$$\sigma_{\tilde{Y}\tilde{Z}} = \sigma_{YZ}$$
$$\sigma_{\tilde{Y}}^2 = \sigma_{Y}^2 + \sigma_{F}^2$$

The empirically observed statistics are used to estimate system parameters. Hence in practice the estimate of the disturbance covariance would be

$$\tilde{\sigma}_{UV} = \sigma_{\tilde{Y}\tilde{Z}} - \frac{\sigma_{\tilde{X}\tilde{Z}}\sigma_{\tilde{Y}}^2}{\sigma_{\tilde{X}\tilde{Y}}}$$

Use the formulas given to define how imprecise measures affect estimates of disturbance covariances. Are we justified in trying to give theoretical interpretations to estimated disturbance covariances when variables have been measured with error?

6 DYNAMIC CONSIDERATIONS

A static analysis requires that the present values of a system's inputs have been maintained at the same levels for a period long enough to have their full causal repercussions felt throughout the system. Thus the observed outcomes reflect ultimate consequences of the inputs. However, social analysts may be interested not only in ultimate outcomes but also in the processes leading to these outcomes. The trends and wiggles of social system variables constitute history itself and are of immense personal significance to humans. Moreover, it may be necessary to consider a system's dynamics to identify undesirable processes that intervene between inputs and outputs or processes so extreme that they destroy the system before a static state can be achieved. Some consideration of system dynamics is needed also just to gain a better understanding of static analyses. The requirements that inputs are held constant and outcomes fully realized are not always present in reality: inputs may have values that vary over time or a system with stable inputs may not yet have generated the full consequences of these inputs. In either of these circumstances the usual statistical estimates of the system's parameters will be biased and we need to turn to dynamic analyses to comprehend the problem.

The study of system dynamics focuses on the period ignored in static analyses between the initiation of a new input and the final system outcomes. As in statics, there are both deductive and inductive matters for attention. At the deductive level dynamic analyses provide information about a system's adjustment phenomena. The results may be of particular interest because changes in the values of variables in a linear system are often complicated nonlinear functions of time. Also, the study of dynamics opens up a new topic—the processing of information in the form of time-varying input "signals" in order to determine how a system responds to temporal patterning of inputs and how it generates new configurations of its own. On the inductive or inferential side the study of system dynamics leads to additional procedures for identifying the structure of a system by using time-series data.

Although the topic of system dynamics is clearly important to social scientists, it cannot be treated systematically here. Even an elementary introduction would require more pages and more mathematics than we have already presented in this book. (Research on system dynamics literally involves a whole new dimension—time—which requires longitudinal elaboration of data-gathering procedures and which complicates analyses by drawing in the mathematics of complex variables.) This chapter has the modest aim of trying to deepen the understanding of static models by a brief consideration of a few selected issues in system dynamics. First, the dynamic characteristics of some simple linear systems are considered to gain an appreciation of their complexity. We then consider some ways that estimates of static-model parameters may be confounded by collecting data from systems that are dynamic rather than in a static state.

SIMPLE SYSTEM DYNAMICS

Causal Lags

There is usually at least a brief lag while operators construct effects from causes. Accordingly, causally related events are most often separated by some lag period, and systems typically respond to an input with some dynamic process, however simple or brief; for example, beginning with the instant a car's gas pedal changes position there is a small but definite period in which there is absolutely no change in the torque delivered to the wheels because the chain of effects has not yet reached that stage; or, following passage of a piece of legislation, there is a period of no effect for the general citizenry while administrators gear up to implement the policy. As an analytic convenience it is useful to assume that a causal lag always exists while allowing that in some instances the lag time may approach zero for all practical purposes.

Lag periods vary considerably according to the kind of system that is being considered. Psychological latencies usually can be measured adequately in hundredths-of-a-second, interpersonal latencies in terms of seconds or minutes, formal organization latencies in terms of hours or days, and community or societal latencies in terms of months or years. Thus we generally cannot expect to study the dynamics of different levels of organization within the same time framework. Processes that might interest a psychologist occur on a time scale that is useless to a sociologist and vice versa. Yet, with an adjustment for the different time scales that are appropriate for different phenomena, the formal characteristics of change may be quite similar, regardless of the level of analysis. Indeed, this is one of the basic findings of general systems theory.

A diagramming device is available to represent causal lags on flowgraphs and to show that lag periods vary for different operations. Following conventions that have developed in the system dynamics literature, a time delay is symbolized by the letter z and its relative magnitude is indicated by an exponent with a minus sign. To represent a causal lag period in a diagram we simply "attach" an appropriate time symbol to the symbol representing the causal operator, as illustrated in **6.1**.

6.1 $X \xrightarrow{az^{-2}} Y$

Operator **a** requires two units of time to transform a change in X into a change in Y.

The actual time scale is determined by the problem being considered; for example, the two units of time indicated in **6.1** may refer to two nanoseconds for an electrical engineer or to two years for a political scientist.

This representation of time lags is especially attractive when dealing with linear systems because all the usual rules of flowgraph analysis can be applied in a meaningful way. The time symbol is treated as if it represented a distinct linear operator with an unknown value that is subject to the usual multiplication and addition rules. The kinds of flowgraph interpretation displayed in **6.2** follow directly (remembering the special algebraic rule for multiplying exponentials; i.e., $z^m \cdot z^n = (z^{m+n})$.

6.2 $W \xrightarrow{z^{-1}} X \xrightarrow{z^{-3}} Y$ reduces to $W \xrightarrow{z^{-4}} Y$

A change in W causes a change in X one period later and a change in X causes a change in Y three periods later. Thus a change in W implies a change in Y four periods later.

$$W$$

$$X \xrightarrow{z^{-3}} Y \quad \text{reduces to} \quad W \xrightarrow{z^{-2}+z^{-4}} Y$$

A change in W causes a change in Y two periods later and generates an additional change in Y four periods later.

The graph reductions in **6.2** define the *transfer functions* for the simple systems illustrated. In a similar way the full battery of graph reduction rules can be applied to define the transfer functions for more complicated systems with loops. Making an interesting application of these results requires recognition of the symbol z as a complex number and carrying on with full-scale dynamic analysis. For present purposes it is enough that we have conventions for the graphic representation of the relations among system variables and the time element involved in system operations.

Elementary Dynamic Patterns

The trends and wiggles that become evident when the values of a system variable are plotted over time are referred to commonly as a *signal*. It is the configuration of values that consitutes the signal. One common problem in dynamic analysis is to describe a complicated signal by a relatively simple mathematical expression. A second is to find a relatively simple mathematical expression (the transfer function) that can be adapted to describing how a particular system transforms an input signal into an output signal with a different configuration. In this way we deal with the response of a given system to different inputs or with the treatment of a given input signal by different systems.

Because our concern here is still with systems that can be characterized as being typically in a static state, we can sidestep most of the analytic problems created by complex input signals. The usual presumption in working with static models is that inputs have been changed all at once at some earlier time and then held constant until the system operators have worked out all the outcomes. Thus the input signals of primary interest are the simple step functions illustrated in **6.3**

6.3   A STEP FUNCTION

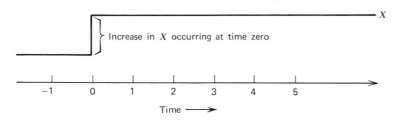

Increase in X occurring at time zero

The goal, then, is to develop some rough notions about how various kinds of system transform step changes in inputs into a variety of output signals during the transitional period before a static state is reached.

The simplest system consists of a *single operator* that generates a response all at once some time after the input signal has changed value. If a step function is provided as the input signal, a lagged step function is obtained as output, as shown in **6.4**.

6.4   The basic system is

$$X \xrightarrow{\frac{1}{2}z^{-2}} Y$$

Suppose the value of X is increased one unit at a point in time arbitrarily labeled zero. The system's input and output signals will have the following forms:

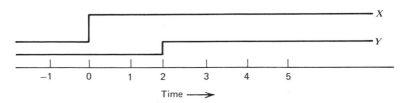

If the structural coefficient has a negative value, the output signal changes in the opposite direction from the input signal; that is, if a step function is applied to the following system

$$X \xrightarrow{-\frac{1}{2}z^{-2}} Y$$

we would get the following configuration:

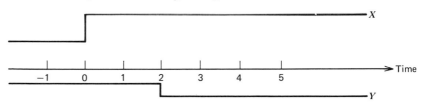

The only interesting feature in the dynamics of such a simple system is the waiting period between input and output changes.

A *recursive* array of operators can generate a more complex output signal because the effects generated along different paths will usually arrive at the output variable at different times. If all the operators in the system have positive effects, the final values of the output variable will tend to cumulate monotonically over time. If some negative paths exist between the input and output, the value of the output may move both up and down before it reaches its static state. Both points are illustrated in **6.5**

6.5   The system

$$X$$

$$\frac{z^{-1}}{2} \Bigg\downarrow \quad \searrow^{\frac{z^{-1}}{2}} \qquad \text{reduces to} \quad X \xrightarrow{\frac{1}{2}(z^{-1}) + \frac{1}{2}(z^{-2})} Y$$

$$W \xrightarrow[\frac{z^{-1}}{2}]{} Y$$

A step change in the input would produce the following signals.

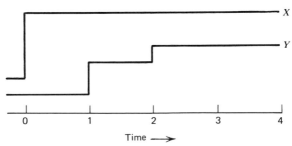

If the operator between X and Y had a negative effect, the reduced system would be

$$X \xrightarrow{\quad -\frac{1}{4}(z^{-1}) + \frac{1}{4}(z^{-2}) \quad} Y$$

and the input-output signals would have the following configuration:

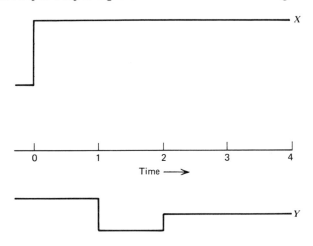

Some social processes can be described in terms of recursive diffusion through a social network (e.g., adoption of a technological innovation), in which case any outcome that is dependent on these changes (e.g., productivity) will tend to change incrementally following a step increase in the input. A simple illustration is given in **6.6**

6.6 This flowgraph might represent a hierarchical influence network in a small group of farmers:

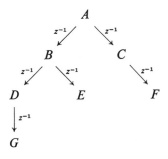

Variables A through G could be interpreted as a measure of the agricultural technology of each farmer, and all of them might be related additively to a community variable such as agricultural surpluses (S); besides the above arrows, we have the following:

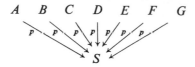

where **p** indicates the quantitative relation between a farmer's technology in a given year and community surpluses in the same year. When the two diagrams are combined and reduced, we get the following relation between A and S:

$$A \xrightarrow{\; p(1 + 2z^{-1} + 3z^{-2} + z^{-3}) \;} S$$

A step increase in the level of A's technology at time zero would produce the following pattern of change in community surpluses:

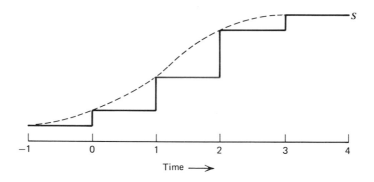

The output pattern of change can be roughly represented by the continuous "sigmoid" curve shown as a dotted line. The continuous-curve approximation is not precise in such a small community, but the appearance of fit would be better if surpluses were constituted by small contributions from hundreds of farmers.

The example in **6.6** illustrates that even those systems lacking feedback can produce relatively complex transformations of input signals. Even more intricate output signals than those shown could be obtained by including negative relations in the system considered in **6.6**—negative relations might represent competitive, exploitive, or deceptive relations among farmers. With such negative operators, structures could be defined in which A's increase in technology leads to fluctuation or even a net reduction in community surpluses over time.

Feedback Effects

Systems with feedback always generate relatively complicated output signals from step changes in inputs. Indeed, feedback systems can be designed to transform a step input into an output signal of nearly any desired degree of complexity and matching nearly any desired pattern. Here we focus on only a few basic types of pattern that are produced by relatively simple feedback structures.

Amplification—the simplest type of feedback phenomenon—is produced by a loop with positive return effect. In Chapter 2 the net effect or final outcome from such a loop was examined. Now interest focuses on the series of changes that culminates in the final outcome. In general, these changes occur in the cumulative monotonic pattern illustrated in **6.7**

6.7 Suppose we have a system in which a change in W causes a change in X three periods later, any change in X causes a change in Y two periods later, and any change in Y causes a change in X one period later. Assume further that all structural coefficients are positive, in which case the loop has a positive return effect, and it is an amplifier. Assignment of some arbitrary values to the coefficients produces the following system:

$$W \xrightarrow{\ z^{-3}\ } X \underset{.6z^{-1}}{\overset{.5z^{-2}}{\rightleftarrows}} Y$$

Mason's theorem (rule II.16) could be applied as usual to reduce X and Y on to W, but then to employ the results in graphing output signals we would have to recognize z as a complex number and carry out some advanced mathematical analyses. Instead, we simply follow the system's operations through the first few periods after a change in W in order to characterize its dynamics. Suppose that before the change in W all three variables have a value of zero. At time zero W increases in value to 1.0; X and Y still would remain unchanged because of the three-period lag between changes in W and X. From then on values of X and Y will change as shown in the following table. (Read Δ as "the change in"; a subscript i is read "at time i.")

Time	Value of X	Value of Y
1	0	0
2	0	0
3	$0 + 1(\Delta W_0) = 1$	0
4	1	0
5	1	$0 + .5(\Delta X_3) = .5$
6	$1 + .6(\Delta Y_5) = 1.3$	.5
7	1.3	.5
8	1.3	$.5 + .5(\Delta X_6) = .65$
9	$1.3 + .6(\Delta Y_8) = 1.39$	.65
10	1.39	.65
$\vdots$		
∞	1.43	.71

The values for ∞ are obtained by applying rule II.16 to the static system (in which case the z's are ignored). Graphing the system variables over time gives the following:

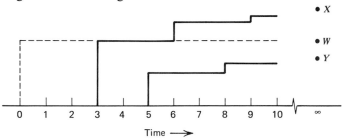

The loop in **6.7** is an amplifier because it takes the initial change in X (or Y) and works it up into a larger final change. The growth process does not occur all at once but in steps. As changes circulate around the loop again and again, they increment the values of the variables a bit more on each cycle. In the example *most* of the growth occurs during the first few cycles. The size of the increments is less and less as time goes on until at some point they can be ignored and for all practical purposes the variables have attained their final values. This is generally true of stable amplifying loops (unstable loops are considered later). Change occurs in conformity with an "exponential curve" that levels off toward some constant value.

6.8 Stable amplifying loops produce continually decreasing growth as a response to an initiating change. The developmental period can be characterized approximately by a smooth exponential curve, as shown by the dotted line.

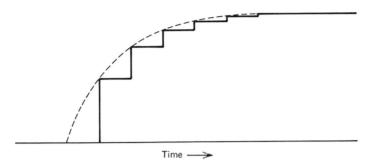

Time ⟶

An amplifying loop responds to a decrement in an input value (rather than an increment) with the same kind of process, except that the exponential curve is "upside down" and the value of the loop variable declines in a stepwise pattern.

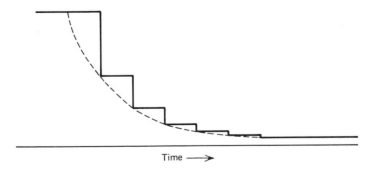

Time ⟶

A stable loop with a negative return effect is a *control structure* because it tends to counteract change and eventually system outcomes are less affected by changes in system inputs than they were at the beginning. Dynamic processes are especially significant in control loops because recovery is not a smooth monotonic process. Controlled system variables recover from disturbances by a process of oscillation, as indicated in **6.9**.

6.9 The following system tends to counteract effects of changes in W. The controlling nature of the system is reflected in the negative return effect for the loop—$(.9)(-.8) = (-.72)$.

$$W \xrightarrow{z^{-1}} X \xrightarrow[-.8z^{-2}]{.9z^{-1}} Y$$

Assume that all variables have values of zero before W is changed one unit at time zero. Then values of X and Y at later times are as follows:

Time	Value of X	Value of Y
1	$0 + 1(\Delta W_0) = 1$	0
2	1	$0 + .9(\Delta X_1) = .9$
3	1	$.9$
4	$1 + (-.8)(\Delta Y_2) = .28$	$.9$
5	$.28$	$.9 + .9(\Delta X_4) = .25$
6	$.28$	$.25$
7	$.28 + (-.8)(\Delta Y_5) = .80$	$.25$
8	$.80$	$.25 + .9(\Delta X_7) = .72$
⋮		
∞	$.58$	$.52$

Thus the values of the output variables have the following patterns over time:

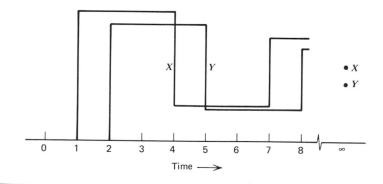

When the value of a variable in a stable control system is changed, a sequence of adaptations in that variable is triggered which culminates in a final change that is less extreme than the beginning change. But in the process of getting to the final state the value of the variable swings too far one way, then too far the other way, only gradually homing in on the ultimate resting point. As with amplifying loops, a stable control loop generates the biggest shifts at the beginning of the process. After some point in time the oscillations are small enough to ignore, and for all practical purposes the value of the variable has attained its final state.

As indicated in **6.10** the oscillations in a controlled variable conform to a sinusoidal curve that is damped with time. This fact is used extensively in mathematical analysis of dynamic control systems.

6.10 The sinusoidal curve underlying changes in a control loop.

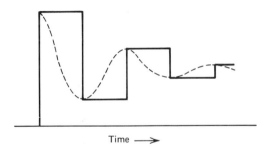

Time ——→

A loop that is isolated from other loops is *unstable* if its return effect is greater than or equal to 1.0 (in amplifiers) or less than or equal to −1.0 (in control loops). Unstable loops show the same general patterns in their output signals as stable loops, *except* that the changes generated become larger with time rather than smaller. (Changes continue at the same level if the return effect happens to be exactly 1.0 or −1.0.)

6.11 Possible output from the unstable amplifying loop:

$$X \underset{-1.2z^{-1}}{\overset{-1.4z^{-1}}{\rightleftarrows}} Y$$

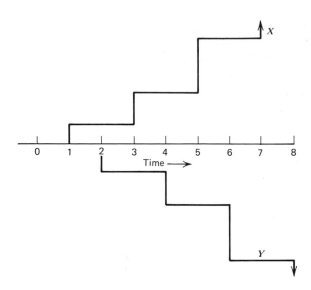

Graph of a possible output signal at X from the unstable "control" loop:

$$X \underset{1.2z^{-1}}{\overset{-1.4z^{-1}}{\rightleftharpoons}} Y$$

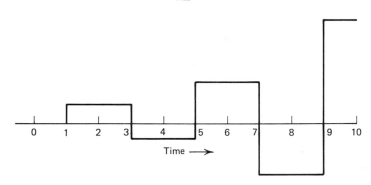

The growth produced by unstable amplification is still exponential but now explosively so. Similarly, the changes produced by an unstable loop with a negative return effect still conform to an underlying sinusoidal curve but now the swings become wilder with time.

The stability characteristics of a system with multiple loops cannot be discerned by examining the stability of each loop in isolation, as illustrated by an example to follow. The stability question can be answered if all the system's structural and time parameters are known. However, the required analyses involve advanced mathematical treatment of the system's transfer function.

Unstable processes never last long (though the meaning of "long" depends on the time scale of the system being examined—seconds for electronic equipment, centuries, perhaps, for societies). This is a matter of material necessity, as can be seen by viewing the value of a variable as the rate of certain events occurring on a lower level—a perspective introduced in Chapter 1. When a variable takes on an extreme value, the lower level operators are being worked near their limitations. Thereafter no further increases in rates of lower level events are possible because the lower level operators can do no more. At this point there are two possibilities. Relations among system variables may become nonlinear—a change in one variable no longer has the usual effects on other variables—which in effect stops the explosive process. Alternatively, the lower level operators may begin failing, in which case all processing falters and the system collapses.

Instability is almost always considered a serious problem and something to be avoided. A system grinding on at the limits of its capacity is no longer adaptive; variations in input signals can no longer be responded to differentially. Such a system amounts to an insensitive and useless devourer of energy. The inconveniences of the alternative possibility of collapse are obvious, especially if one's own social-ecological system is being considered. Thus, if a system is unstable, it is useless or doomed until and unless the instability is eliminated. One way of solving the problem is to reorganize the system to eliminate the unstable loop or loops. The second fundamental method is to add higher order control loops that counteract the instability produced by lower order loops.

Higher Order Feedback

A nest of loops creates *higher order feedback* when the return times for the various loops in the nest are different (a "return time" is the time required to complete one cycle). Higher order feedback produces additional complications in output signals. All the possibilities cannot be discussed here, but it is useful to consider a few examples to appreciate the diversity in output signals that may be obtained merely by adding a second-order loop. The simple second-order system shown in **6.12** is used to generate illustrative materials by applying a step function input at W and examining the output signal at Y.

6.12   The following is a simple system with second-order feedback (the vertical arrows might represent communication operations):

$$R \xleftarrow{bz^{-1}} S$$

$$z^{-2}\downarrow \qquad \uparrow z^{-2}$$

$$T \xleftarrow{az^{-1}} U$$

$$z^{-1}\downarrow \qquad \uparrow z^{-1}$$

$$W \xrightarrow{z^{-3}} X \xrightarrow[z^{-1}]{} Y$$

All coefficients except **a** and **b** have been set at 1.0 for heuristic purposes. The signs of **a** and **b** can be made either $+$ or $-$ to create different types of systems. The above can be reduced to

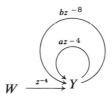

which corresponds to the "difference equation"

$$Y_k = a Y_{k-4} + b Y_{k-8} + W_{k-4}$$

in which subscripts indicate the time at which a variable is observed; for example, the value of Y at time eight equals **a** times Y at time four, plus **b** times Y at time zero, plus the value of W at time four.

To generate example output signals from this second-order system the absolute value of **a** was set at $\frac{1}{2}$ and of **b** at $\frac{3}{4}$. The values of all variables were presumed to be zero before time zero, when W was increased one unit and held there. The signs of **a** and **b** were varied to create the following kinds of system: **a** positive and **b** positive—first and second-order amplification; **a** positive and **b** negative—first-order amplification with second-order control; **a** negative and **b** positive—first-order control and second-order amplification; both **a** and **b** negative—first- and second-order control. Output signals were obtained by substituting each set of **a** and **b** values into the difference equation in **6.12** and then applying the formula repeatedly to generate sequential values of Y. The calculating details are tedious and only the graphed results are given in **6.13**.

6.13 EXAMPLE OUTPUT SIGNALS FROM SECOND-ORDER SYSTEMS

First- and second-order amplification:

$$Y_k = \tfrac{1}{2}Y_{k-4} + \tfrac{3}{4}Y_{k-8} + W_{k-4}$$

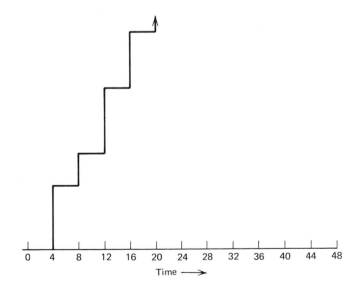

First-order control, second-order amplification:

$$Y_k = -\tfrac{1}{2} Y_{k-4} + \tfrac{3}{4} Y_{k-8} + W_{k-4}$$

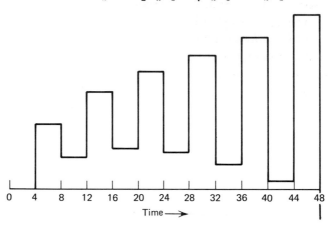

First-order amplification, second-order control:

$$Y_k = \tfrac{1}{2} Y_{k-4} - \tfrac{3}{4} Y_{k-8} + W_{k-4}$$

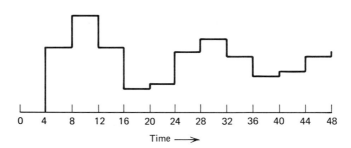

First- and second-order control:

$$Y_k = -\tfrac{1}{2} Y_{k-4} - \tfrac{3}{4} Y_{k-8} + W_{k-4}$$

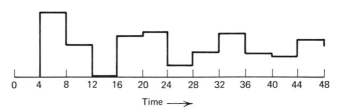

The first two graphs in **6.13** illustrate the important point that second-order amplification may create unexpected instabilities. The last two graphs display the complicated output signals that are often produced by the presence of higher order control.

The second graph deserves particular attention because it illustrates how system dynamics may be nonintuitive. The system consists of a first-order control loop and a second-order amplifying loop, the combination of which produces unstable oscillation. This result might be considered surprising for three reasons. First, either of the two loops would be completely stable in isolation. The instability occurs only when they are connected hierarchically, with the amplifier at the second level. Second, the creation of such a system might seem completely rational in everyday life; for example, work-group norms may be holding productivity within a restricted range (the first-order control loop), so management superimposes its own incentive program (the second-order amplifier); but if the management reaction to productivity is only half as fast as the work-group response the results could be far different than desired, as the graph shows. Third, a static formulation of the system would give no hint of its dynamic instability. Indeed, in the static formulation of the system (which can be obtained by removing all the z's from the diagram in **6.12**), it would appear that the two loops largely cancel one another, with the amplifier dominating somewhat. The instability can be predicted only when we have information on time lags and know, in particular, that the amplification operation takes twice as long as the control operation.

Complex Inputs

In the preceding examples the characteristics of system output signals were examined when a simple step change in value was applied at a single input variable. The results showed a variety of output signals whose complexity depended on the system being considered. Now it is time to acknowledge that changes in inputs do not always conform to simple step functions. Indeed, in many social systems such input variation may be the exception rather than the normal case. Moreover, most interesting systems have multiple source variables rather than just a single input.

Even the simplest system can produce a complicated output signal if it is operating on a complicated input signal. This is illustrated by assigning an intricate input signal to the single-operator system defined in **6.4**. The result is an equally intricate output signal that shows the same pattern of changes as the input, though delayed to later points in time and somewhat attenuated by the system operation.

6.14   Possible input and output for the system in **6.4**.

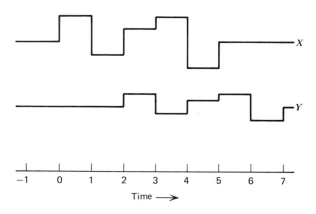

If a simple system sums the values of two input variables to produce its outcome, the output signal typically will not correspond to either input signal but to a weighted average of both. Although we ordinarily expect such an output to be more complicated than either of the inputs, it is also possible for the output signal to have a simpler pattern of variations if the two inputs tend to cancel each other. (This is the basic idea employed by engineers in designing signal "filters"—to get rid of any unwanted signal pattern generate a complementary pattern and add.)

A feedback system operates on a complex input signal in a convoluted way to produce an output signal that may have little obvious similarity to either the input signal or to the system's step-function response. This is because the system responds to every change in the input signal with a whole sequence of adjustments. Therefore the output at any instant is not a singular outcome but instead represents the cumulation of system responses to all of the preceding changes in input (the more recent responses being weighted more in a stable system). Obviously, if a feedback system has multiple inputs, the output signals would be even more complex functions of the inputs and the system's characteristics.

Despite these complications, linear systems of any degree of intricacy retain a provocative feature. If we have a full description of the input signals and a full description of the system, it *is* possible to derive a full description of the output signal. Thus dynamic system analysis remains a determinate discipline. Perhaps it is even more significant that any two of the three descriptions (i.e., of input signals, of output signals, or of the system's response characteristics) can be used to derive the third. This principle provides a foundation for methods of system identification using over-time data, and such techniques supplement the static methods discussed in Chapter 5. The same principle allows characterization of past input signals from knowledge of a system and its outputs, a fact that is fundamental in communications (allowing us to reconstruct the thoughts of others from what we see or hear) and might permit social analysts to do historical reconstructions of some variables by using their knowledge of a given social system and its outcome events. (It must be noted, however, that valuable descriptions of signals and systems usually are mathematical expressions and that rather complicated mathematical procedures are routinely involved in such derivations.)

System identification from over-time data is too complex a topic to broach here (see chapter references) but one general point deserves attention. Such identification is possible only when there is knowledge of *both* the input and the output signals. When dealing with personality or social systems, laymen and scholars alike are sometimes guilty of diagnosing system ills only in terms of outcomes that have been produced. Similarly, it is frequently presumed that studying only a system's products—its behavioral career or its historical record—permits discerning its structure, the "implied" personality or the "necessary" social organization. When such analyses are reported, assumptions about environmental inputs have been made implicitly or the conclusions are untrustworthy. Historical study of a system's outputs permits inferences concerning the system's structure only when the record of inputs is considered simultaneously, and then somewhat complex analyses may be required to disentangle the data.

DYNAMIC CONFOUNDING IN STATIC ANALYSES

Having considered a few elementary features of system dynamics, we can now turn to a related issue of practical significance for contemporary social science. In what ways is cross-sectional research on static models confounded by systems in a transition phase rather than in steady state at the time of observation? It is convenient to divide the problem into two aspects. First, we consider systems that have not yet completed their response to a set of inputs which is being maintained at constant levels. Second, we consider systems that are continuously dynamic because some of their inputs vary over time.

Equilibration

In cross-sectional research data are collected on multiple instances of the same system by measuring values of system variables for each case at a particular time. Inputs presumably have been set at different levels for different cases, and outcome variables will also display variations across cases. Consequently the patterns of variations over variables and across cases should reveal the workings of the system. There is a waiting period, however, after system inputs have been set before related consequences can be observed. If observations are made too soon, the outcome variables may show little or no relation to values of the inputs because system operators have not yet had a chance to complete their work.

The problem can be seen in simple form by reconsidering the system in **6.4** in which there are two variables X and Y and an operator that produces its effect after a lag of two time periods. Suppose that input X is set at a new value for all cases at time zero. Clearly, there is no sense in observing the values of the two system variables at time one because at that point X has its new values, whereas Y still has its old values (which are responses to the preceding values of X). Only by waiting at least until time two, when the dynamics are over and the cases are "equilibrated," it it possible to observe values of X and values of Y that are meaningfully related by the causal operation. Thus *all observed cases must be equilibrated if cross-sectional analyses are to be meaningful.*

An individual case is ready for observation when it has completed all responses to the given inputs and thereby reached a state of equilibrium. Although there is always a period after inputs have been set during which a case is *not* ready for static analysis, once a case has equilibrated it remains in equilibrium until its inputs are reset. Consequently *all equilibrated cases may be considered together in the same analysis; they do not need to have had their inputs set at exactly the same time.*

Equilibration Time

The length of time required for equilibration depends on the lag periods of individual operators in the system. Equilibration time, however, may be considerably more than the lag periods for separate operators in systems with chains of effects or feedback loops.

Cross-sectional observations of recursive systems have to be delayed until the repercussions of the given outputs have had a chance to cascade over the longest path in the system. "Middle" variables in a system cannot be treated simply as inputs for following variables, ignoring dynamic processes in prior variables. Unless the system as a whole has equilibrated, the settings of the "middle" variables may change before their causal effects are observed.

This can be illustrated by a simple chain system: $W \to X \to Y$, where each causal link is associated with a lag of one time period. Suppose W is reset in a sample of cases at time zero and held constant thereafter. Observations made at time one are adequate for estimating the effect from W to X because the values of W have been maintained through time one and the values of X are the effects produced by these same values of W at time zero. The observations at time one are not adequate for studying the $X \to Y$ relation. The observed values of Y are responses to the values of X at time zero but those values of X have not been maintained through time one. Indeed, the observed values of X at time one have no logical relation to the time-one values of Y. On the other hand, if observations are delayed until time two, both relations in the system can be studied. The values of W and X continue the same as they were at time one and the $W \to X$ effect can be estimated as before; and the Y values are responses to X values at time one, which have been maintained through time two, so the $X \to Y$ effect can also be estimated.

The matter of equilibration time is complicated when a system contains feedbacks because theoretically loops keep adjusting indefinitely. This might suggest that such cases never equilibrate because they never finish developing the consequences of a given input. It was pointed out earlier, however, that the adjustments produced by a stable loop are completed for all practical purposes in a relatively short time. Thus a period generally can be defined after which a stable feedback system is essentially static in the sense that observations made after that period give parameter estimates containing errors less than some tolerable amount. The tolerable amount of error would be an arbitrary quantity that might vary for different purposes, but theoretically it can be set as small as desired. It is in this practical sense that static analyses of feedback systems are feasible.

Analyses of a feedback system to illustrate how cross-sectional studies after a change in inputs lead to errors in parameter estimates are presented in **6.15**. The system in **6.15** is simple and the results complicated, but even so it permits some insight into the main features of equilibration when dealing with feedback systems.

6.15 Suppose we want to estimate parameters in the following system:

$$X \xrightarrow{az^{-1}} Y \overset{bz^{-1}}{\underset{cz^{-1}}{\rightleftarrows}} Z$$

This specification yields the following difference equations (assuming heuristically that Y and Z have no disturbances):

$$Y_t = aX_{t-1} + bcY_{t-2}$$
$$Z_t = abX_{t-2} + bcZ_{t-2}$$

We assume that the system is in a static state before time one and in particular that $X_i = X_0$ for $i < 0$.

Then at time one X is changed to a new value which is maintained thereafter so that $X_i = X_1$ for $i > 1$. Because of the causal lags, the value of Y will not be affected by the change in X until time two and the value of Z will not be affected until time three. Therefore before these times Y and Z will be dependent solely on X_0:

$$Y_i = \frac{aX_0}{1 - bc} \quad \text{for} \quad i < 2$$

$$Z_i = \frac{abX_0}{1 - bc} \quad \text{for} \quad i < 3$$

These specifications allow us to write the following formulas to express the value of the outcome variables at various times:

Time	Y	Z
1	$\dfrac{aX_0}{1 - bc}$	$\dfrac{abX_0}{1 - bc}$
2	$a(X_1 - X_0) + \dfrac{aX_0}{1 - bc} =$ $\dfrac{a}{1 - bc}[X_1(1 - bc) + bcX_0]$	$\dfrac{abX_0}{1 - bc}$

3    $\dfrac{a}{1-bc}[X_1(1-bc)+bcX_0]$ $\dfrac{ab}{1-bc}[X_1(1-bc)+bcX_0]$

4    $\dfrac{a}{1-bc}[X_1(1-b^2c^2)+b^2c^2X_0]$ $\dfrac{ab}{1-bc}[X_1(1-bc)+bcX_0]$

5    $\dfrac{a}{1-bc}[X_1(1-b^2c^2)+b^2c^2X_0]$ $\dfrac{ab}{1-bc}[X_1(1-b^2c^2)+b^2c^2X_0]$

6    $\dfrac{a}{1-bc}[X_1(1-b^3c^3)+b^3c^3X_0]$ $\dfrac{ab}{1-bc}[X_1(1-b^2c^2)+b^2c^2X_0]$

Given data on a cohort of cases, we might estimate the value of parameter **b** by using the formula in **5.12**:

$$b = \frac{\sigma_{ZX}}{\sigma_{YX}}$$

To apply this formula at different times after the change in X we must obtain the expressions for the covariances at times two, three, four, etc. (using procedures like those outlined in **4.17**). The results are as follows:

Time	σ_{YX}	σ_{ZX}
2	$\dfrac{a}{1-bc}[\sigma^2_{X(1)}(1-bc)$ $+bc\sigma_{X(0)X(1)}]$	$\dfrac{ab}{1-bc}\sigma_{X(0)X(1)}$
3	$\dfrac{a}{1-bc}[\sigma^2_{X(1)}(1-bc)$ $+bc\sigma_{X(0)X(1)}]$	$\dfrac{ab}{1-bc}[\sigma^2_{X(1)}(1-bc)$ $+bc\sigma_{X(0)X(1)}]$
4	$\dfrac{a}{1-bc}[\sigma^2_{X(1)}(1-b^2c^2)$ $+b^2c^2\sigma_{X(0)X(1)}]$	$\dfrac{ab}{1-bc}[\sigma^2_{X(1)}(1-bc)$ $+bc\sigma_{X(0)X(1)}]$
5	$\dfrac{a}{1-bc}[\sigma_{X(1)}(1-b^2c^2)$ $+b^2c^2\sigma_{X(0)X(1)}]$	$\dfrac{ab}{1-bc}[\sigma^2_{X(1)}(1-b^2c^2)$ $+b^2c^2\sigma_{X(0)X(1)}]$
6	$\dfrac{a}{1-bc}[\sigma^2_{X(1)}(1-b^3c^3)$ $+b^3c^3\sigma_{X(0)X(1)}]$	$\dfrac{ab}{1-bc}[\sigma^2_{X(1)}(1-b^2c^2)$ $+b^2c^2\sigma_{X(0)X(1)}]$

Thus the estimates of **b** from data collected at these times (after simplifying) would be

Time	Estimate of b
2	$b \left[\dfrac{\sigma_{X(0)X(1)}}{(1 - bc)\sigma^2_{X(1)} + bc\sigma_{X(0)X(1)}} \right]$
3	b
4	$b \left\{ \dfrac{(1 - bc)\sigma^2_{X(1)} + bc\sigma_{X(0)X(1)}}{[1 - (bc)^2]\sigma^2_{X(1)} + (bc)^2\sigma_{X(0)X(1)}} \right\}$
5	b
6	$b \left\{ \dfrac{[1 - (bc)^2]\sigma^2_{X(1)} + (bc)^2\sigma_{X(0)X(1)}}{[1 - (bc)^3]\sigma^2_{X(1)} + (bc)^3\sigma_{X(0)X(1)}} \right\}$

What seems to be a serendipitous result needs to be examined first. It would appear that if we choose our timing right we could obtain unbiased estimates of loop parameters even while the system was quite unequilibrated. In **6.15** the estimate of **b** is exactly right at times three and five. The trouble is that we typically would not know if our observations were being made at the "right" time because the necessary information about causal lags in the system was unavailable. Thus estimates derived from such unequilibrated cases might be biased or unbiased, but we would not know which. Moreover, in a more complicated system with multiple inputs and multiple loops such opportune times for making observations frequently would not even exist.

The fact that the unbiased estimate appears at intermittent times is significant. It reveals that observations of unequilibrated cases can yield parameter estimates that are extremely erratic. Repeated examination of the same cohort of cases during its early period of development might suggest that the system itself is nonstationary, its parameters in a state of flux or oscillation. This nonstationarity is not real but is caused by errors in estimation, and we want to eliminate unequilibrated cases from analyses to avoid precisely such problems. Moreover, the same fact suggests that conservatism is warranted in deciding whether a system has become nonstationary. When sequential cross-sectional analyses of a system suggest that a system has become time varying, it is possible that the system remains stationary but inputs have shifted so that cases are unequilibrated.

Errors in estimating the parameters of a stable feedback system from cross-sectional data are reduced by waiting until the system has gone through a larger number of cycles of adjustment following a step change in inputs. The results in **6.15** clearly indicate that improvement is not necessarily monotonic (because in that example, **b** could be estimated without error at times three and five). On the other hand, the worst possible error does decrease with time. This can be seen for the system in **6.15** by assigning convenient values to the key unknowns and then examining the value of the estimate at different times; for example, if $(b \cdot c) = .5$, $\sigma_{X(0)X(1)} = .0$, $\sigma^2_{X(1)} = 1.0$; the bracketed quantity then equals .0 at time two, .67 at time three, and .86 at time five. The decreasing difference between these numbers and 1.0 indicates that the maximum error in estimating **b** is smaller at later times.

The number of cycles required for equilibration varies somewhat across systems and in different circumstances. The closer loop return effects are to zero, the faster the estimation errors decline, and systems with powerful feedback have longer equilibration times. Also, the results in **6.15** show that biases in the estimate depend on the statistical quantities $\sigma^2_{X(1)}$ and $\sigma_{X(0)X(1)}$. Although detailed interpretations of these effects are involved, one important result can be stated simply. The greater the changes that have been made in inputs, the longer it takes for cases to equilibrate again.

Time-Varying Inputs

The logic of estimating structural coefficients from cross-sectional data requires that the values of inputs be maintained at constant levels. In natural situations, however, the values of inputs often do not remain perfectly stable over time. The values of an effect, Y, corresponding to values of a cause, X, may be observed at a given time, but the relevant values of X occurred in the past and may no longer be observable when their Y effects appear. Consequently the cross-sectional data do not contain the necessary information for a static analysis. They do not reveal accurately how present values of Y relate to values of X.

If the values of inputs are totally unpredictable from one instant to another, there is no possibility of meaningful parameter estimation from cross-sectional data, but in many actual situations matters are not so bleak. For example, the graph of the time-varying input X in **6.14** shows that although **X** does move about it still tends to stay within a limited range. It maintains an "essentially constant" average value over time. In fact, the same is true of the outcome Y. It also maintains an essentially constant average value over time. Moreover, it appears that the Y average is related to the X average by the structural coefficient for the causal relationship (.5 in this example).

Let us say that X in **6.14** is an essentially constant signal with a time-varying signal superimposed. Thus an observation of X at any instant usually does not measure the average value of X directly but with some amount of error. Of course, X's superimposed noise signal is not error in the usual sense—it does produce variations in Y. But the time-varying component does not affect Y until after we have completed an observation, so for practical purposes the temporal variation in X might be treated as if it were just "measurement error." By taking this perspective we confront a more familiar problem: estimating system parameters when variables are measured imprecisely.

Two basic suppositions here are that the X signal can be partitioned into two components—one constant and one time-varying—and that they can be analyzed independently to reveal the structure of the system. In fact, it can be demonstrated mathematically that any signal may be partitioned into a summation of component signals, including, particularly, a constant component. It can also be shown that an output signal produced by a linear system operating on a composite input signal equals the sum of output signals from identical systems operating on the components of that composite input signal. Proofs of both principles are provided in texts on system dynamics (see chapter references). Thus there is justification for attempting to identify a system's structure by analyzing the constant component of the input signal. The same structure is identified by analyzing this constant component as would be identified were we to deal with the full input signal in all its complexity.

By this reasoning the problem of time-varying input signals can be translated to a problem of predetermined variables measured with error, assuming the constant components of signals vary across cases. Then the problem of time-varying inputs can be attacked in several ways. First, because the constant components of signals amount to averages over time, we could actually extend the research design to include repeated observations of the inputs, which then could be averaged. Of course, such a design is not really "cross-sectional," and a considerable number of longitudinal observations on the inputs are required to obtain precise measures of the temporal mean. Note, however, that it is not necessary to obtain repeated observations on the outcome variables. Their temporal fluctuations merely constitute "disturbances" that do not bias parameter estimates. Moreover, repeated observations of the inputs could be made after the outcomes have been measured, as long as it can be presumed that the average values of the inputs remain unchanged.

Sometimes environments can be manipulated to set the constant component of a variable at a particular level for all members of a population exposed to that environment. In such a case the value of the constant component might be estimated from the mean of a cross section of observations; for example, an attitude stimulus might be presented to the members of a homogeneous group during interviews and a measure made of their attitudinal responses. The constant component of the attitude toward the stimulus characterizing any member of the group could then be estimated from the mean of the measurements over all group members, thus allowing individuals' transients to cancel one another. The requirements for employing this tactic are a standard generating element in the environment (e.g., the attitudinal stimulus), assurance that all observed units are effectively exposed to the generator (e.g., by presenting it explicitly during an interview), assurance that all units are equivalent in response (e.g., by studying only members of a homogeneous group), and lack of synchronization in transients (which might be handled in an attitudinal survey by varying the times, circumstances, and demand characteristics of interviews).

Somewhat similar procedures are the basis of "ecological correlation" in which geographic populations are used to obtain a set of mean values on each of several variables so that the relations of the variables can be analyzed. The problems with the geographical approach to aggregation are that the population in a region may not be homogeneous, all members may not be exposed uniformly to standard generating elements, and members may be synchronized in transients at a particular time. In addition, because a generating factor is implicitly assumed but often completely unspecified, there can be little confidence that a given factor sets the values of just one of the variables being studied. If the same generator is a factor in several variables, the observed correlations between the variables would be spurious to some degree. Detailed discussions of aggregation and ecological correlation are cited in the chapter references.

A third approach is the familiar strategy of using instrumental variables when confronted with an imperfectly measured source variable; that is, for each of the fluctuating inputs we find another variable that is a predictor of its average value over time (and is causally unrelated to system outcomes except through that input). Thus by moving the set of input variables back one step it is possible to obtain unbiased estimates of all the structural coefficients of interest despite the time-varying inputs. The selection of instruments was discussed at length in Chapter 5, and the same principles apply here, with the understanding that values of an instrument should correlate with the constant component of an input signal but not with the time-varying component.

Dynamics of Lagged Variables

Sometimes it is possible to construct an instrument from lagged observations on the input variable itself. Although this tactic is a common one, its applicability is restricted to special circumstances, as illustrated in **6.16** (and by the discussion of lagged variables as instruments in Chapter 5).

6.16   Given the following simple static model

$$X \xrightarrow{a} Y \longleftarrow U$$

the variable Y can be expressed as a function of a time series of X values:

$$Y_t = \left(\sum_{i=0}^{-\infty} a_i X_{t-i} \right) + U$$

where $\sum_{i=0}^{-\infty} a_i = a$, it being assumed heuristically that the disturbances for Y are constant over time. The assumption that the X series has an "essentially constant" component means that the value of X at any time k can be expressed as follows:

$$X_k = \bar{X} + x_k$$

where $\mathscr{E}(x) = 0$. With this definition Y_t becomes

$$Y_t = \left(\sum_{i=0}^{-\infty} a_i(\bar{X} + x_{t-i}) \right) + U$$

$$= a\bar{X} + \left(\sum_{i=0}^{-\infty} a_i x_{t-i} \right) + U$$

Suppose we observe values of X at some earlier time $(t - k)$. Assume also that variations in the constant component of X are uncorrelated with the time-varying variations in X and that the disturbances of Y are uncorrelated with X. Then

$$\sigma_{X(t)X(t-k)} = \sigma_X^2 + \sigma_{x(t)x(t-k)}$$

$$\sigma_{Y(t)X(t-k)} = a\sigma_X^2 + \sum_{i=0}^{-\infty} a_i\sigma_{x(t-i)x(t-k)}$$

If X_{t-k} were used as an instrument, an estimate of coefficient **a** would be

$$\frac{\sigma_{Y(t)X(t-k)}}{\sigma_{X(t)X(t-k)}} = \frac{a\sigma_X^2 + \sum\limits_{i=0}^{-\infty} a_i\sigma_{x(t-i)x(t-k)}}{\sigma_X^2 + \sigma_{x(t)x(t-k)}}$$

This would provide an unbiased estimate of the structural parameter if the effect from X to Y occurred all at once so that $a_i = 0$ for all but one value of i. However, the estimate would be biased in the more general case in which the effects of X on Y are distributed over time, unless the time-varying component of X has zero autocorrelation and the timing of the lagged observation is chosen such that $a_k = 0$.

Thus observations on an input variable at a different time should not be employed as an instrument unless (a) causal effects occur all at once or, if causal effects are distributed over time, (b) the time-varying component of the input signal is completely unpredictable from one time to another. If the latter case held, we would still have to be sure that the period between measurement of the dependent variable and the instrumental variable did not correspond to any causal lag period between the source and outcome.

Static and Dynamic Variance

Structural coefficients for a system that is essentially static, in the sense that its variables are maintained at constant average values over time, can be estimated from cross-sectional data by using the techniques noted above. However, an accurate assessment of disturbances in the dependent variables is not obtained ordinarily when inputs have time-varying components because unexplained variance in a dependent variable represents not only the effects of unspecified variables (i.e., the usual disturbances) but also lagged effects from the time-varying components of the specified inputs. Theoretically, the latter *would* be explained by the model if it were applied dynamically.

Suppose, for example, that engaging in creative work causes a person to become more liberal (as proposed in the sociological literature). Because of differing occupations, individuals vary in the average amount of creative work they do, and because of this essentially constant component in the source variable there is variance among persons. This perhaps could be used to estimate the structural coefficient relating creative work to liberalism. On the other hand, the amount of creative work done by an individual may vary considerably on a week-to-week or month-to-month basis because of shifting job demands, demands of personal life, or changes in mood. These fluctuations should also affect liberalism. Indeed, the net effect of such temporal variation in level of creative work is defined by the same structural coefficient that can be estimated from the constant component in the data. Nevertheless, if the effect occurs only after a lag, the time-varying component of liberalism will appear to be unexplained in a cross-sectional study. By the time liberalism has adapted to a level of creative work the level of creative work may have shifted to another level, so an individual's liberalism might be out of line with the source variable because it reflects the effect of a past level of creative work. Given just the observation at that single time we cannot distinguish this accountable deviation from a disturbance caused by completely extraneous and unspecified sources. Thus the variation in the dependent variable that is due to past fluctuations in the source variable is grouped with the variation due to unspecified disturbances, and the specified causal relation seems to explain less of the variation in the dependent variable than it really does.

This problem is severer in simpler systems. If we have a single causal relation with lag, the time-varying component of the input signal will be transmitted with considerable fidelity to the outcome variable. A more elaborate recursive system in which outputs are a response to input signals at several points in time generates overtime averages of the input signals, thereby beginning to eliminate their fluctuations. Consequently the outcomes contain less variance due to input fluctuations. The output from a feedback loop at any given time is always a weighted average of the past values of inputs. Therefore the effects from the time-varying components of the inputs tend to be averaged out, and the outcome variance is only moderately affected by fluctuations in input signals. Even with stable feedback systems, however, there will generally be some dynamic variance in outcomes associated with the most recent fluctuations in inputs.

By the same reasoning a system that accounts for most of the variations in its outcome variables under static conditions may seem to provide a less adequate model if inputs go into flux. Indeed, if the transient variation in inputs becomes considerably larger than the constant variation across cases, the system formulation may seem to lose nearly all its explanatory power. Yet it is conceivable, and even probable in such circumstances, that the system continues to determine most of the variation in outcomes. Using cross-sectional data alone, the problem is that we cannot distinguish the transient variation in outcomes from the unaccountable disturbances.

The inputs to many social systems probably have some time-varying components. Consequently theoretical models—especially simpler models—may be undervalued because of their poor performance in explaining variance in cross-sectional data. Thus, even though structural coefficients can be estimated from cross-sectional studies, we may eventually have to turn to experimental, longitudinal, and simulation studies in which explicit consideration is given to time in order to identify dynamic aspects of system structure and to evaluate theories with confidence.

SOURCES AND ADDITIONAL READINGS

An elementary treatment of systems dynamics is provided by Alpha C. Chiang, *Fundamental Methods of Mathematical Economics* (New York: McGraw-Hill, 1967), especially parts 3 and 5. James A. Cadzow, *Discrete-Time Systems: An Introduction With Interdisciplinary Applications* (Englewood Cliffs, N.J.: Prentice-Hall, 1973) is a rewarding text that deals with more advanced topics; like all texts on systems dynamics, it involves mathematics, but Cadzow depends on elementary algebra and makes a conscientious effort to address beginning students. Methods of extending flowgraph analysis into the dynamic realm are presented (along with examples) by W. H. Huggins and Doris R. Entwisle, *Introductory Systems and Design* (Waltham, Mass.: Blaisdell, 1968).

The statistical analysis of time series, for the sake of projections and system identification, is examined in Gwilym M. Jenkins and Donald G. Watts, *Spectral Analysis and Its Applications* (San Francisco; Holden-Day, 1968), and George E. P. Box and G. M. Jenkins, *Time Series Analysis: Forecasting and Control* (San Francisco: Holden-Day, 1970). Brief introductions to the same topics are available in Douglas A. Hibbs, Jr., "Problems of Statistical Estimation and Causal Inference in Time-Series Regression Models," and

Thomas F. Mayer and William Ray Arney, "Spectral Analysis and the Study
of Social Change," Chapters 10 and 11, respectively, in Herbert L. Costner,
Ed., *Sociological Methodology: 1973–1974* (San Francisco: Jossey-Bass,
1974). Daniel Graupe, *Identification of Systems* (New York: Van Nostrand
Reinhold, 1972) provides an advanced treatment of methods used in
engineering.

Recently psychologists have been developing models to describe growth
curves from data on cohorts. Some major issues in this area are surveyed in
John R. Nesselroade and Hayne W. Reese, Eds., *Life-Span Developmental
Psychology: Methodological Issues* (New York: Academic, 1973). A variety
of sociological time series are described and analyzed in Robert L. Hamblin,
R. Brooke Jacobsen, and Jerry L. L. Miller, *A Mathematical Theory of
Social Change* (New York: Wiley, 1973).

Aggregation procedures are discussed in Mattei Dogan and Stein Rokkan
Eds., *Quantitative Ecological Analysis in the Social Sciences* (Cambridge,
Mass., MIT Press, 1969), and Michael T. Hannan, *Aggregation and Disaggre-
gation in Sociology* (Lexington, Mass.: Heath, 1971).

EXERCISES

1.   Consider a specific sociological topic such as attitude-balance theory,
sociometric analysis, or modernization. The amount of research (R) on the
topic in a given year might be measured as the total number of researchers
who have devoted some minimal amount of time to the topic. The total
number of publications (P) in a year is roughly proportional to the amount
of research on the topic about three years before (allowing time for manuscript preparation and publication lag). Publications tend to generate more
research, at least after about two years (allowing time for readers to discover
the articles and set up projects of their own). Meanwhile, federal policy
directing funds (F) to the topic increases research, allowing about two years
to broadcast the policy and for preparation and processing of proposals.
Availability of federal funds may be influenced by an assessment of whether
grants will be identified with future publications. Assuming this to be true,
federal funding might be proportional to the rate of growth (G) of literature
on the topic—measured, say, as the difference between the number of publications last year and the number five years ago. Finally it might be supposed
that a major source of new research on a topic is the innovation (I) of a new

idea, technique, or perspective from a largely unrelated area of study. The input itself is probably best viewed as a relatively short-lived impulse which has to be sustained by activity within the new field of application. More important innovations (having larger values of I) would be those generating a larger amount of research a year or so after introduction.

(a) Make up the flowgraph for this system. (The *change score G* can be represented on the linear graph.) Represent each structural coefficient as a subscripted **a**, give its sign in parentheses, and follow with the delay operator properly superscripted; for example, the label for one arrow would be $\mathbf{a}_{RI}(+)$ z^{-1}. Ignore disturbances.

(b) From an examination of the diagram describe manifest and latent functions of federal funding agencies for the development of scientific literature on a topic.

(c) What is the shortest period that must pass before research being done now will stimulate new research?

2. For heuristic purposes let the absolute value of each coefficient in the system in exercise 1 equal 1.0.

(a) Redraw a reduced flowgraph in which variable G is eliminated.

(b) Write out the difference equations that define the dynamic system; for example:

$$R_t = I_{t-1} + P_{t-2} + F_{t-2}$$

(c) Use the difference equations to trace the 20-year impact of a unit impulse in I at time zero (that is, I has a value of 1.0 at t_0 and a value of zero thereafter). Assume that R, P, and F are measured as deviation scores and that the topic has had "average" attention, publications, and funding in the last few years, reflected by assigning values of zero to all variables (except I) at t_0 and relevant years before. The values of the variables at t_0 and one year after are shown below for guidance.

Time	I	R	P	F
0	1	0	0	0
1	0	1	0	0

3. Suppose that the following dynamic model represents the over-time relations of a person's education (E), occupational level (Q), yearly income (I), and savings (S), with disturbances ignored.

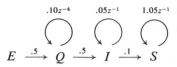

that is, education determines occupational level, which has a direct effect on income, and yearly income creates small increases in savings. The loop on Q suggests that about every four years promotions increase occupational level. The loop on I indicates that a person receives a base rate of pay corresponding to occupational level plus a percentage of last year's income. The loop on S indicates that savings and real property are maintained and incremented by interest, dividends, or appreciation. Assume that $t = 0$ is the year in which formal education and training are completed and that the variables have the following values at that time:

E_0: to be specified.
Q_0: dependent on E_0; zero before $t = 0$.
I_0: dependent on Q_0; zero before $t = 0$.
S_0: dependent on I_0; to represent educational and home-establishment debts we also make it dependent on E_0:

$$S_0 = .10 I_0 - .25 E_0$$

(a) Write the difference equations that express the value of each variable in terms of present and past values of variables in the system.

(b) Following is the equation for Q at (t_{-4}):

$$Q_{t-4} = .50 E_{t-4} + .10 Q_{t-8}$$

Substitute this equation into the equation for Q_t to get another expression for the value of Q at time t. How far could such substitutions be carried? Does this provide another way of representing the loop on Q?

(c) Assume that education is set at 10.0 at time zero and remains the same thereafter. Use the three difference equations to trace the growth of Q, I, and S over 15 years. (Remember the debts.) A desk calculator will be helpful here. Now assume that education is set at 1.0 at time zero and remains the same thereafter. Calculate the values of the variables over 25 years. This is tedious, but the results are instructive and are used below. (Answers are not provided for this second analysis.)

(d) Suppose that a level 10 education is a Ph.D. and that this is ordinarily acquired at age 26. Suppose a level 1 education represents the two years of high school attained at age 16. At what age does a doctor catch up in savings with a high school dropout, given the above system? Does a doctor ever acquire significantly greater savings than a high school dropout?

4. We continue with the system defined in exercise 3. Now suppose that more education leads to dissatisfaction with the establishment, whereas more occupational status, more income, and more savings all lead to pro-establishment attitudes. In particular, suppose for heuristic purposes that attitude toward the establishment is determined as follows:

$$A = -.2E + .2Q + .2I + .4S$$

(It is assumed that these effects on attitude are almost instantaneous.)

(a) Graph the establishment attitudes from age 26 to age 40 of a Ph.D. and of a high school dropout (use results from exercise 3).

(b) Suggest the kind of population (defined in terms of age, education, occupational level, etc.) in which one is most likely to find an anarchist, a "progressive" or liberal, and a conservative. Are lower class persons likely to be radical (right or left) in their youth? In their old age?

5. Consider the following simplified "class-conflict" system in which coefficients have been assigned arbitrary values and disturbances ignored:

$$P \xrightarrow{.5} I \underset{.4z^{-1}}{\overset{.4z^{-1}}{\rightleftarrows}} L \underset{-.8}{\overset{.4z^{-1}}{\rightleftarrows}} D$$

By this specification production surpluses (P) increase social inequality (I). The effect is almost instantaneous, compared with the time scale of other operations in the system (this is a heuristic simplification). An increase in social inequality generates legislation favoring the privileged (L), allowing a time lag for the privileged class to manipulate the composition and opinions of those in power roles. Such legislation also increases social inequality, again allowing time for socially exploitative projects to be planned and implemented. On the other hand, a large increase in discriminatory laws increases civil disturbance (D), once comprehension of the laws diffuses to the masses. Those in positions of power are quick to respond to such threats to social order by moderating the form or administration of the laws to make them less inflammatory.

Flowgraph analysis can be used to find the transfer function from P to each of the system variables; for example, in the case of I we would get the first expression below, which can be manipulated algebraically as shown.

$$T_{IP} = \frac{.5(1 + .32z^{-1})}{1 + .32z^{-1} - .16z^{-2}} = \frac{.50z^2 + .16z}{z^2 + .32z - .16}$$

$$= \frac{.50z^2 + .16z}{(z - .271)(z + .591)} = \frac{.343z}{(z - .271)} + \frac{.157z}{(z + .591)}$$

The last expression is a "partial-fraction expansion" of the transfer function (see chapter references for the method involved). It indicates that as far as I is concerned the original system could be replaced with the sum of two simpler systems and the results would be exactly the same. Moreover, we can immediately see that both simpler systems are stable—the return effects of the single loop in each is between -1.0 and $+1.0$. Thus we now know that the original system is stable. The last expression allows us to employ the notion of a "z transform" from advanced systems theory (again see references). Application of the z transform gives us an expression for the value of I in terms of present and past values of P:

$$I_t = \sum_{i=0}^{-\infty} [.343(.271)^i + .147(-.591)^i]P_{t-i}$$

$$= .50P_t + .00P_{t-1} + .08P_{t-2} - .03P_{t-3} + .02P_{t-4} - .01P_{t-5}\cdots$$

By the same procedures

$$L_t = \sum_{i=0}^{-\infty} [.232(.271)^i - .232(-.591)^i]P_{t-i}$$

$$= .00P_t + .20P_{t-1} - .06P_{t-2} + .05P_{t-3} - .03P_{t-4} + .02P_{t-5}\cdots$$

$$D_t = \sum_{i=0}^{-\infty} [-.499\delta + .342(.271)^i + .157(-.591)^i]P_{t-i}$$

(where $\delta = 1$ when $i = 0$ and is zero otherwise)

$$= .00P_t + .00P_{t-1} + .08P_{t-2} - .03P_{t-3} + .02P_{t-4} - .01P_{t-5}\cdots$$

In all these summations the coefficients for terms beyond P_{t-5} are zero when rounded to two places.

(a) Use the summation formulas above to estimate the values of I, L, and D at time zero if P has had a value of 1.0 from time $(t - 5)$ up to and including time t.

(b) Compare the results obtained in (a) with results you obtain from a static analysis of the same system, again assuming that P has a constant value of 1.0. What can you conclude about the equilibration time for this system?

6. Over-time configurations of change in a single variable are of fundamental interest in the study of physical systems; for example, mechanical vibrations with a particular configuration over time generate a characteristic sound, a fact that is of basic importance in engineering. In the social sciences significance is more likely to be attached to a multivariate configuration of states at a single time or over a brief period; for example, it is largely by considering a cross section of a society's events that we decide whether it is industrialized, at war, democratic, and so on. Theoretically, however, a multivariate profile of outcomes can always be redefined in terms of strictly historical configurations in the system's inputs. Suppose that we define a populist reformation, or revolution, as a period of intense civil disturbance, followed soon after by a collapse in social inequality. Given the single-input system specified in exercise 5, it is possible to get such a reformation only if production surpluses have had a particular historical configuration.

(a) Use the summation formulas in exercise 5 to define what the features of this historical configuration must be. (Assume that the definition above requires a large value of D_{-1} and a small value for I_0).

(b) As it turns out, reformation, as defined above, is largely an epiphenomenon in this system. The collapse of inequality is due more to economic circumstances than to preceding civil disturbances. Suppose, instead, that we defined reformation as a period of civil disturbance followed by at least two periods during which laws favoring the privileged were reduced (D_{-1} large, L_0 and L_1 small). What is the required historical configuration of surpluses now?

7. Attitudes can be viewed as having a relatively stable component, based on accumulated socialization, and also a transient component that varies with recent experiences. Thus at a particular moment we might represent a person's net attitude toward an object as a summation of the stable and transient components:

$$A_S \rightarrow A_N \leftarrow A_T$$

If we were to examine the same person a short time later, we would expect the stable component to be almost the same. The transient component, however, might have changed and thus the net attitude might also be different.

(a) Write the expression for the variance of A_N in a cross-sectional study of a population. Give a verbal interpretation to the components of variance and indicate some social conditions in which one component might be larger than the other.

(b) Modify the above diagram to allow for selective exposure—people exposing themselves to events that confirm their predispositions. How would this phenomenon affect the observed variance in the cross-sectional study?

(c) Give a formula for the correlation between attitude measurements made at two times with a short interval between. (Ignore the possibility of selective exposure in your derivation.) What social conditions would produce a relatively large value for the correlation? Assume that attitudes at the moment determine behavior toward the attitude object at that time. What social conditions would enhance the accuracy of predictions from attitudes measured at one time to behaviors observed later?

8. At the end of Chapter 4 it was suggested that attitudes and behaviors might be related in a control loop. Attitudes determine behaviors but behaviors deviating from norms invoke social control mechanisms that change attitudes. By disregarding the directionality of behavior deviation we can reconceptualize this system in terms of deviations and social punishments:

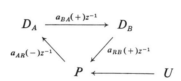

that is, deviation from an attitudinal norm produces behavioral deviation, which, in turn, produces punishment, but we allow that punishments are not regularly related to deviations by entering the disturbance U. Finally, punishment reduces attitudinal deviations. (Arbitrary delays have been assigned for heuristic purposes.) Ignoring attitudes, we could reduce this system to one involving only behavior deviations and social punishments:

$$U_P \longrightarrow P \xrightarrow[a_{RB}(+)z^{-1}]{c(-)z^{-2}} D_B$$

Reduce the system still further to one involving just behavioral deviations and disturbances in punishments. Express behavioral deviancy at time t as a function of irregularities in punishments at earlier times. What theoretical perspective is suggested by the result?

ANSWERS
TO EXERCISES

CHAPTER 1

1. The use of heroin—the later condition—implies the use of marihuana—the earlier condition. This statement suggests a developmental process rather than causation. A causal relationship could be inferred only if almost all marihuana users went on to heroin, and we would still have to specify an operator to account for the relationship.

2. If the privileged acts of a person constitute status, that person is the relevant operator. His status might be changed by increasing the material and social resources for privileged acts which amounts to a change in inputs, or his disposition to construct privileged acts from available resources could be increased. This motivational adjustment makes the person a stronger operator for converting resources into status. If status is constituted from acts of deference, then interaction partners are the operators producing one's own status. Perhaps others defer because they have learned that doing so gains rewards or prevents punishments. So we might increase A's status by taking away the material basis of B's satisfactions, making B more anxious to please A. Alternatively, we might teach B to deliver more deference for a given level of need, thus making B a more powerful operator for generating status.

3. Later events cannot cause earlier events (rule I.4). Thus the education and occupational statuses of sons do not affect the father variables. If we are willing to assume that formal education is almost always completed before a career is begun, the same rule would eliminate a causal relation from occupational status to education for both fathers and sons. We cannot eliminate the possibility of a relation from education to occupational status (for fathers or sons). The timing is appropriate and we can think of an explanation for such a link, which suggests that operators actually may be available.

We are left with relations from the father variables to the son variables, all of which pass the time-ordering test. It is conceivable that fathers with higher occupational statuses have contacts that directly help their sons to achieve higher levels of occupation. Thus, in general, we cannot eliminate the possibility of a causal relation. (Note, though, that we might be able to invoke rule I.3 if we were studying sons who had migrated beyond their fathers' fields of influence.) Similarly, it is plausible that fathers with higher status occupations have the money and influence to ensure better educations for their sons, a link that cannot be eliminated. Better educated fathers might give their sons an educational advantage in an enriched home environment. Also they might provide better guidance in coping with educational institutions. The possibility that father's education directly influences son's education cannot be disregarded. It is more difficult to imagine how a father's education can directly affect his son's occupational status. Most of the plausible explanations for such a link (e.g., father's contacts) seem actually to be indirect effects that pass through father's occupational status or through son's education. We might be willing to invoke rule I.2 to dismiss the possibility of a direct link here.

4. On the basis of this extra information, we might invoke rule I.5 to conclude that in modern America a father's occupational status has no direct causal effect on his son's occupational status.

5. A set of machines is a flow in the sense that each machine has a specific life span, and a constant aggregate size can be maintained only if there is replenishment. (Of course, the flow must be measured in years rather than minutes.) If we assess an air force in terms of number of planes, the force is linearly related to its sources—50 planes from the United States and 20 planes from Sweden constitutes a force of 70. Even if we used a more sophisticated basis of assessment, such as firepower, we would probably still have a linear dependence but might have to recognize that gains in firepower are proportionately different for planes from different sources. For purposes of propaganda, routine surveillance, and combat against an unsophisticated enemy, the planes could be treated as a homogeneous aggregate, regardless of their source. Logistically, and in battle with a technologically advanced enemy, the Swedish and American planes might have to be treated as separate forces.

6. The normative level of a variable frequently serves as the practical zero point in social systems. When phenomena occur in accordance with norms, people typically react as if nothing were happening at all. The normative zero is not a true zero in the sense of indicating an absence of flow. Nevertheless it does lead to lack of response in *subsequent* operators. Similarly, the "negative" values below the normative zero do not imply inhibition of positive flow on the original variable, but their occurrence may cause some *subsequent* flows to be inhibited.

7. In the first case advanced education yields antiestablishment attitudes and no inhibitory responses are generated by the possession of wealth; presumably such a person is radically antiestablishment. In the second case no education effect inhibits satisfaction with the establishment produced by money; hence this combination should yield a person who is radically proestablishment. In the status-consistent person the positive effect of money and the negative effect of education tend to cancel, yielding a more or less neutral attitude. Neutrality, however, is psychologically different for the poor illiterate person compared with someone who is educated and materially comfortable. Presumably the poor illiterate person has almost no attitude at all because the states generating attitudes toward the establishment are nearly absent. The wealthy educated person, however, is neutral because mutually inhibiting feelings are in conflict.

8a. For convenience let us suppose that each of the city's M families has been assigned an index number, $i = 1, 2, 3, \ldots, M$, and that variables are abbreviated as follows:

C: City's level of commerce in year 1.
S_i: Family i's surpluses in year 2.
B_i: The number of babies born in family i in year 3.
K: Size of the city's five-year-old cohort in year 8.
T: The number of grade school teachers in the city in year 9.

Assuming a large number of families, it is not practical to draw all the relevant chains of arrows. The essentials of the system could be represented as follows.

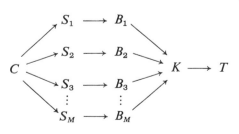

Of course, the diagram represents only selected processes. Family surpluses have more sources than the local economic situation; noneconomic factors also affect reproduction; the size of K depends on infant mortality and migrations as well as on local births five years earlier; the number of grade school teachers is determined by the size of all school age cohorts, among other things. Later such "disturbances" in causal formulations are considered more explicitly.

8b. Using the causal approximation, we can define two new variables.

L: The standard of living in the city in year 2. Essentially, this is the average level of surplus for all families in the city.

N: The total number of newborns in the city in year 3. This birth index is simply the sum of the births in all the city's families that year.

With these two new variables and by employing the notion of a causal approximation the system might be represented as follows:

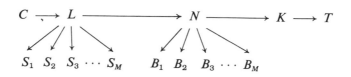

This simplification may be an adequate representation for many policy purposes. It might also be a preferred representation for analyses if measures of L and N are routinely available. On the other hand, the simplified system yields new explanations for events in individual familes; for example, why did the Smiths enjoy unusual surpluses in year 2? Because the standard of living was particularly high that year (i.e., the explanation is not directly in terms of the city's recent commercial boom). Why did the Smiths have two births in year 3? Answer: the birth rate was high that year (rather than because the Smiths had enjoyed unprecedented surpluses the year before and decided to accelerate their family growth). Such explanations may be adequate for some purposes, though they tend to conceal the actual operators in the system.

9. We might represent the relations between different living standards and different reproduction rates as follows:

Standard of Living	Activities Related to Reproduction	Reproduction Rate
Very high	→ Seek physician's help to enhance fertility	→ Very high
High	→ Increased intercourse for reproductive purposes	→ High
As expected	→ Normal sexual activity	→ Average
Low	→ Reduced sexual activity	→ Low
Very low	→ Use of contraceptives	→ Very low

At the extremes the relationship between living standard and reproduction rate is maintained by invoking new programs of medical or pharmaceutical intervention. Such qualitative shifts in operator activity are not found in most common machines, in which increased input simply leads to increased operator activity, which in turn yields an increase in the output. (According to the diagram, sexual behavior does function this way in the middle range.)

   Despite the qualitative shifts in functioning, we could speak of a single reproduction operator that presumably maintains a monotonic relationship between living standards and birth rates. This functional continuity is the important sense in which it can be treated like other operators subject to systems analysis.

10a.   The described relations create a loop between P and R.

$$P \underset{d}{\overset{c}{\rightleftharpoons}} R$$

10b.   Since an increase in P causes reduction in R, the sign of **c** must be negative (i.e., $c < 0$). Similarly, because an increase in R causes a decrease in P, the sign of **d** also must be negative. Because both coefficients are negative, their product is positive and the loop is an amplifier rather than a controller; that is, any shift in population composition will be accentuated rather than attenuated over time by the action of the loop.

10c.   If the absolute values of both coefficients are greater than 1.0 and we already know their signs are both negative, the product of **c** and **d** must be greater than 1.0. Thus the initial increase in R will be amplified over and over until the size of R is very large. That is not all, however. This is a "double negative" amplifier, and the increases in R will be accompanied by ever-growing decreases in P. (Trace the causes and effects around the loop for a few cycles to see how this happens.) Ultimately P will go to zero and the population will consist entirely of R's. At that point the loop self-destructs in the sense that one of its variables becomes nonexistent.

CHAPTER 2

1. The comparison between man A and man B suggests that sons get three schoolyears of education per 20 NORCS of father's occupation. The structural coefficient can be defined as

$$\frac{3 \text{ son school years}}{20 \text{ father NORCS}} = \left[.15 \frac{\text{son school year}}{\text{father NORC}} \right]$$

Note that "son" and "father" are included as part of the units of measurement to make clear what variables are being measured.

2. If F is father's status, E is son's education, and **a** is the structural coefficient relating them, the expected son's education is **a** times F, or

$$\left(.15 \frac{\text{son school year}}{\text{father NORC}} \right) \times 60 \text{ father NORCS} = 9 \text{ son school years}$$

Thus the man's son can be expected to achieve about a ninth-grade education.

3. As noted in Chapter 1 (I.6), a linear structural equation, with its constants deleted, can be applied to a change of input as well as to the absolute level of input. The structural equation in this case is

$$E = \left(.15 \frac{\text{son school year}}{\text{father NORC}} \right) F$$

and so the change equation is

$$\Delta E = \left(.15 \frac{\text{son school year}}{\text{father NORC}} \right) \Delta F$$

Applying this to the particular problem, we have

$$\Delta E = \left(.15 \frac{\text{son school year}}{\text{father NORC}} \right) (- 10 \text{ father NORCS})$$
$$= -1.5 \text{ son school year}$$

Thus the father's misfortune leads to an expected loss of 1.5 school years in son's education.

4. By the chain rule (II.8), a son's occupational level should be

$$S = \left(.15 \ \frac{\text{son } \cancel{\text{school year}}}{\cancel{\text{father NORC}}}\right)\left(5.0 \ \frac{\text{son NORCS}}{\cancel{\text{son school year}}}\right)(80 \ \cancel{\text{father NORCS}})$$

$$= 60 \text{ son NORCS}$$

5a.

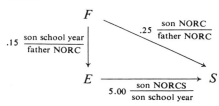

5b. The above reduces to

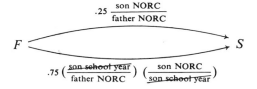

$$F \ \xrightarrow{\quad .25 \ \frac{\text{son NORC}}{\text{father NORC}} \ + \ .75 \ \frac{\text{son NORC}}{\text{father NORC}} \quad} \ S$$

or

$$F \ \xrightarrow{\quad 1.0 \ \frac{\text{son NORC}}{\text{father NORC}} \quad} \ S$$

from which we get the equation

$$S = \left(1.0 \ \frac{\text{son NORC}}{\text{father NORC}}\right) F$$

5c. $\quad S = \left(1.0 \ \dfrac{\text{son NORC}}{\cancel{\text{father NORC}}}\right)(80 \ \cancel{\text{father NORCS}}) = 80 \text{ son NORCS}$

6. According to the propositions

$$\mathbf{d} > 0 \ (\text{i.e., it is positive})$$
$$\mathbf{e} > 0 \ (\text{positive})$$
$$\mathbf{f} < 0 \ (\text{negative})$$

The units attached to each coefficient would be as follows (deleting the phrases "number of" and "in city" because they always occur).

Units for **d** are units of C per unit of I or

$$\frac{\text{crimes}/\text{dweller}}{\text{impoverished}/\text{dweller}} = \frac{\text{crimes}}{\text{impoverished}}$$

For **e** we have units of P per unit of C or

$$\frac{\text{police}/\text{dweller}}{\text{crimes}/\text{dweller}} = \frac{\text{police}}{\text{crime}}$$

For **f** it is units of C per unit of P or

$$\frac{\text{crimes}/\text{dweller}}{\text{police}/\text{dweller}} = \frac{\text{crimes}}{\text{police}}$$

The flowgraph is as follows:

7. The return effect of the loop in problem 6 is

$$L_{CP} = \left(e\,\frac{\text{police}}{\text{crime}} \right) \times \left(f\,\frac{\text{crime}}{\text{police}} \right) = ef$$

Therefore the return effect has no units at all. Since the return effect is unit free, it is unaffected by any linear transformation of the measurement scales for variables in the loop (such as adding or subtracting a constant or multiplying or dividing by a constant). In particular, the procedures used in problem 6 can be used to show that if the crime rate is measured as crimes per 1000 dwellers the three coefficients can be expressed as follows:

$$.001\left(d\,\frac{\text{crime}}{\text{impoverished}} \right)$$

$$1000\left(e\,\frac{\text{police}}{\text{crime}} \right)$$

$$.001\left(f\,\frac{\text{crime}}{\text{police}} \right)$$

and the return effect of the loop is exactly the same. Thus the return effect is a constant way of characterizing the nature of a loop regardless of the units used in measuring variables.

8a. The minimum income program constitutes an effort to reduce the *I* (impoverished) variable to zero. If the system is correctly specified, this would drive the crime rate down (though probably not to zero because undoubtedly there are other sources of crime besides the one specified here). By using flowgraph analysis it can be shown that this approach to crime reduction leads to a reduction in the police ratio as well.

8b. We might suppose that making the lives of the impoverished more comfortable would weaken the causal mechanisms between poverty and crime. If so, this program would reduce the size of the **d** coefficient. By reducing the dependency of crime on poverty it would tend to have the same effects discussed in answer 8a.

8c. Increasing the efficiency and salience of the police presumably enhances their deterrent function, thereby magnifying the negative value of coefficient **f**. In effect, this diminishes the relation between crime and poverty as shown in the reduced form equation

$$C = \frac{d}{1 - ef} I$$

Thus the crime rate will be lower for a given level of poverty. Similarly, the change ultimately leads to a lower police ratio for a given level of poverty.

8d. On a flowgraph we would have to represent the new program by adding a variable—federal support of police—and an arrow from this variable to the police ratio.

$$I \xrightarrow{d} C \underset{f}{\overset{e}{\rightleftarrows}} P \xleftarrow{g} F$$

(Coefficient **g** has a positive sign.) While the program is being instituted, the federal-support variable goes from zero to some positive value, which leads in turn to an increase in the police ratio and a reduction in the crime rate. These effects would be especially noticeable at first. Later, as the system regained equilibrium, the crime rate and the police ratio would move back somewhat toward their original positions.

9. Without politicalization the law enforcement system might be represented as follows (continuing the assumptions from exercise 6):

$$I \xrightarrow{d} C \xleftarrow{f} P \xleftarrow{h} S$$

Here *S* stands for public support at the local level and **h** is a positive coefficient that represents the transformation of public support for law enforcement into a standing police force. Theoretically, crime might be eradicated in this system if public support for the police were at a level high enough to balance the pressures for crime among the impoverished; that is, if

$$S = \frac{d}{fh} I$$

The problem with the above system is that it is not responsive to major increases in crime. The police, with their constant level of support, cannot mobilize to meet new demands. Politicalization solves this problem. Strangely, however, the creation of a "control" loop between crime and police by politicalization guarantees a continuing crime problem—at a low chronic level if the system remains stable and linear or in the form of intermittent spurts if on occasion the police are able to eliminate crime entirely. This is because politicalization as a causal operator also leads to *de*mobilization when the crime rate declines.

10. Using flowgraph analysis, we see that the relations between crime and its major source in the first plan would be

$$C_1 = \frac{d(1 - L)}{1 - ef - L} I$$

With the second plan the relations would be

$$C_2 = \frac{d}{1 - ef - L} I$$

Thus we can see that

$$C_1 = C_2(1 - L)$$

Because L is a negative number (it is the return effect for a control loop), the quantity in parentheses has a value greater than one. Thus the first plan will end up with a higher crime rate than the second plan even though the control loops are of equal strength. In the language of flowgraphs this result occurs because the control loop in plan one does not touch the open path from poverty to crime. Consequently it does not have full impact on that relationship. In ordinary language, plan one leads to the following process: whenever an increase in crime causes the local community to mobilize more police, some of the federal support is removed, thereby undercutting the local mobilization. Consequently the reaction to a crime wave is always muted. (On the other hand, locally inspired decreases in police are somewhat counteracted by more federal support. Therefore the loop does exert some control over crime by adding police when local support is too low.) On the other hand, federal intervention in plan two directly controls crime rather than the strength of local police forces. Its impact on crime is greater.

11a.

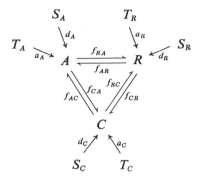

The structural equations are

$$A = a_A T_A + d_A S_A + f_{AR}R + f_{AC}C$$
$$C = a_C T_C + d_C S_C + f_{CR}R + f_{CA}A$$
$$R = a_R T_R + d_R S_R + f_{RA}A + f_{RC}C$$

11b. There are five distinct loops: (AR), (RC), (AC), (ARC), and (ACR). Note that each loop touches all the others. In specifying the system, it was assumed that every operator transforms an increase in one variable into an increase in another variable. Consequently all the structural coefficients must have positive signs. Because there are no negative coefficients, there can be no control loops and all the loops are amplifiers.

11c. $$T_{AS(A)} = \frac{d_A(1 - f_{RC}f_{CR})}{1 - f_{RA}f_{AR} - f_{RC}f_{CR} - f_{AC}f_{CA} - f_{RA}f_{CR}f_{AC} - f_{CA}f_{RC}f_{AR}}$$

Because each of the positive return effects is subtracted in the denominator, each reduces the size of the denominator and thereby increases the magnitude of $T_{AS(A)}$. Taking each loop separately, we see that this happens as follows: a scientific advance in America leads to an initial increment in America's military strength by way of military-industrial development ($\mathbf{d}_A$). This initial increment ultimately is magnified because it sets off a chain of response in the other two superpowers. Seeing America's increased military power, Russia has to increase hers, which in turn is viewed by Americans as a threat; America must therefore beef up its own forces another increment (loop AR). Moreover, Russia's military expansion is disturbing to the Chinese who feel obliged to increase their own military power. This obvious threat to

American security demands further expansion of the American military force (loop ARC). On the other side, we have similar processes. America's initial increment worries the Chinese into increasing their own forces, a move that demands a response by America (loop AC). Moreover, this same Chinese buildup forces the Russians to increase their strength again, which is seen as still another provocation that demands a strong American response (loop ACR). Of course, each of these increments spins further around the system to produce still more increments. The final effects are represented in the equation above. Loop (RC) is a special case. The initial increment by the Russians causes a Chinese increment, which not only disturbs the Americans, it further disturbs the Russians (who after all were only responding to an American threat). Thus they must increment their power to respond to the Chinese, thereby completing a cycle of loop (RC). (Similarly this loop transforms the initial Chinese increment into a Russian escalation which must be met by the Chinese.) This dyadic escalation between Russia and China has some effects on America because it increases the level of provocation from both Russia and China. Thus the return effect of loop (RC) is in the denominator of the above equation. On the other hand, the dyadic competition between those countries is once removed from America and the loop has less impact than if America were involved directly. This is represented by the subtraction of the (RC) return effect in the numerator; that is, an adjustment is made in the numerator to reflect the fact that the (RC) loop does not operate with its full force on America's military power.

12. An **f** coefficient of no more than .5 implies that when one nation increases its military power by a certain amount another nation's initial reaction is to increase its strength by no more than half that amount. A sophisticated scale for measuring military power would have to take into account the capacity and efficiency of delivery systems besides firepower, but an impression of the implication here can be gained from an example that involves a simpler scale: if Russia adds 100 tanks to her arsenal, the United States and China in their responses must not add more than 50 tanks to their arsenals. This system will produce an uncontrolled arms race if nations respond to one another's moves more vigorously. Certainly instability is likely if each nation attempts to match or exceed another's gain. On the other hand, a number of factors could lead to attenuated responses that would encourage stability; for example, poor intelligence services leading to underestimates of the gains of others, or alliances by which two countries share their response to the third.

These and other considerations might enter into an overall judgment of the system's stability.

13a.

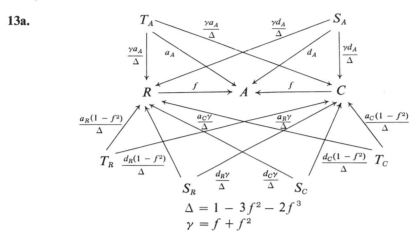

$$\Delta = 1 - 3f^2 - 2f^3$$
$$\gamma = f + f^2$$

13b. Arrows $(S_A R)$ and $(S_A C)$ imply that advances in American science lead directly to more military power for the Russians and Chinese. Perhaps the person supposes that espionage is the means by which this happens. Arrows $(S_R C)$ and $(S_C R)$ might be explained similarly or in terms of the alliance and cooperation between two communist nations. Note that there are no arrows $(S_R A)$ or $(S_C A)$: America does not spy on or benefit from science in other nations. Arrows $(T_A R)$ and $(T_A C)$ indicate that America's territory is directly responsible for the maintenance of Russian and Chinese arms. Perhaps this would be explained in terms of the greed and envy of others and their wish to occupy our land. The same kind of acquisitiveness accounts for arrows $(T_R C)$ and $(T_C R)$. Note that America does not prepare to occupy any other nation—there are no arrows $(T_R A)$ or $(T_C A)$.

Therefore, an American scientific advance naturally would lead directly to a stronger American military. However, this in no way is a cause for any Russian or Chinese response. What happens is that the Russians and Chinese steal our scientific secrets and use them to build their own might. When this happens, America of course meets the challenge by incrementing her strength still more. A Russian scientific advance would lead to a more powerful Russian military and also to a more powerful Chinese military (whether by sharing or spying). America would not steal Russian secrets, but she would have to respond directly to the Russian and Chinese military escalations.

The extricated model does make accurate predictions of what happens in the long run. This is its single strength when applied to the international situation. On the other hand, it might mislead someone into expecting a simple pattern in international dynamics. Also it would be highly misleading in suggesting that counterespionage efforts could have a major effect on the character of the system.

CHAPTER 3

1. Because there is only one president at a time, it is not possible to do the usual kind of cross-sectional study in which we examine repeated examples of the same operator type. For some purposes it might be satisfactory to assume that a president is a constant operator throughout his presidency and each of his completed episodes of a given type can be examined as a static configuration characterizing that president. The set of all such episodes could be examined statistically. This form of analysis has been called "comparative statics."

2a.

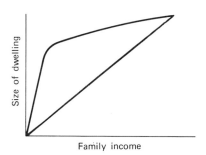

Family income

2b. A strictly linear system could not produce such a joint distribution. The disturbances in dwelling size are much greater for low-income families than for high-income families and there is no way to achieve this effect with strictly linear equations. Such a phenomenon might occur in a causal system if another variable—say, size of family—interacted with income to determine dwelling size, as suggested in the following equation:

$$\text{dwelling size} = a \cdot (\text{family income}) \cdot (\text{family size})$$

According to this formulation, some low-income families are forced to get large dwellings because their numbers are so large. The distribution can be viewed as evidence that "high income implies a large dwelling." To interpret this developmentally, however, we would have to suppose that occupying a large dwelling is a necessary antecedent for acquiring wealth and that is a dubious postulate in most contemporary societies.

2c. A linear relation is possible if the distributions of both variables are skewed, as suggested by the following graph:

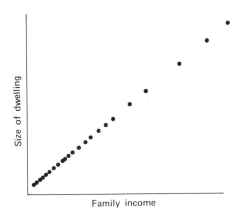

3. One way to interpret this problem is to imagine a fleet of buses, each moving ideally at a given instant exactly at the safest speed and in the safest direction. The drivers, being human, add some perturbations or disturbances to the actual speeds and directions, removing each bus more or less from the ideal. A second driver would add additional perturbations. Thus, assuming that the actions of the drivers are in no way coordinated, disturbance variances due to two drivers would create a larger variance than either driver would produce alone. Consequently two-driver buses would deviate more from the ideal and would be more dangerous.

4a. Without hesitation, the researcher should carry out the calculations again. The product-moment correlation cannot have a value less than -1.0 or greater than $+1.0$.

4b. Assuming that the calculations are correct, this regression coefficient suggests that I.Q. can be estimated to some degree if we know the student's GPA (because the coefficient is different from zero), and in particular higher GPAs are associated with higher I.Q.'s (because the coefficient is positive). The fact that the coefficient is greater than 1.0 is not informative in this case because the value of an unstandardized regression coefficient depends on the units used to measure the variables. There are no mathematical bounds at all on an unstandardized coefficient. Note that the regression coefficient here might be useful for transforming one kind of information into another, yet does not directly represent the effect of a causal operator; that is we do not suppose that an operator exists for transforming GPAs into levels of I.Q.

5.

$$\mathscr{E}[(X - \bar{X})^2] = \mathscr{E}(X^2 - 2X\bar{X} + \bar{X}^2)$$
$$= \mathscr{E}(X^2) - \mathscr{E}(2X\bar{X}) + E(\bar{X}^2)$$
$$= \mathscr{E}(X^2) - 2\bar{X}\mathscr{E}(X) + \bar{X}^2$$

The last step is possible because the mean is a constant:

$$= \mathscr{E}(X^2) - 2\bar{X}^2 + \bar{X}^2$$
$$= \mathscr{E}(X^2) - \bar{X}^2$$

or, alternatively:

$$= \mathscr{E}(X^2) - [\mathscr{E}(X)]^2$$

Because the original expression defines the variance of X, the final expression also defines the variance, and we see that a variance may be calculated directly from original measurements without first converting to deviation scores.

6.

$$\mathscr{E}[(X - \bar{X})(Y - \bar{Y})] = \mathscr{E}(XY - Y\bar{X} - X\bar{Y} + \bar{X}\bar{Y})$$
$$= \mathscr{E}(XY) - \mathscr{E}(Y\bar{X}) - \mathscr{E}(X\bar{Y}) + \mathscr{E}(\bar{X}\bar{Y})$$
$$= \mathscr{E}(XY) - \bar{X}\mathscr{E}(Y) - \bar{Y}\mathscr{E}(X) + \bar{X}\bar{Y}$$
$$= \mathscr{E}(XY) - \bar{X}\bar{Y} - \bar{Y}\bar{X} + \bar{X}\bar{Y}$$
$$= \mathscr{E}(XY) - \bar{X}\bar{Y}$$

or alternatively

$$= \mathscr{E}(XY) - [\mathscr{E}(X)][\mathscr{E}(Y)]$$

Thus a covariance can also be obtained from original measurements without first converting to deviation scores.

7. First note that $\hat{X}$, the predicted value of a variable, is not generally a constant; its value varies from case to case.

$$\mathscr{E}[(\hat{X} + e)^2] = \mathscr{E}(\hat{X}^2 + 2\hat{X}e + e^2)$$
$$= \mathscr{E}(\hat{X}^2) + \mathscr{E}(2\hat{X}e) + \mathscr{E}(e^2)$$
$$= \mathscr{E}(\hat{X}^2) + 2\mathscr{E}(\hat{X}e) + \mathscr{E}(e^2)$$

Because both $\hat{X}$ and e are presumed to represent deviation scores, the above can be converted to

$$= \sigma_{\hat{X}}^2 + 2\sigma_{\hat{X}e} + \sigma_e^2$$

This expression defines the variance of a variable $X = \hat{X} + e$. Obviously the variance of X is equal to the variance of $\hat{X}$ plus the variance of e only if the middle term has a value of zero. This is true only if the covariance of $\hat{X}$ and e is zero; in other words, only if predicted values are uncorrelated with the errors in predictions.

8. Since β is a standardized coefficient, we can suppose that all variables have been standardized before beginning analyses. Thereupon, the partial regression coefficient can be interpreted as the result of three separate regression analyses. First, we regress father's occupational status on son's education in order to define a set of residual variations in father's status that cannot be "postdicted" from son's education. Second, we regress son's occupational status on son's education to define a set of residual variations in son's status that cannot be predicted from son's education. Third, we regress the residuals in son's status on the residuals in father's status. The regression coefficient from this third analysis is the same thing as $\beta_{SF\cdot E}$. In this way we see that $\beta_{SF\cdot E}$ measures the predictability of variations in son's status that cannot be explained by son's education, where the predictor variable consists of variations in father's status that are unrelated to son's education. Because we began by equalizing the scales of all variables by standardization and the reported value of $\beta_{SF\cdot E}$ is so small, we can conclude here that there is relatively little covariance between father and son statuses that is not interpretable by the level of son's education.

9. Given these correlations, the standardized partial regression coefficient from father's status to son's status is

$$\beta_{SF\cdot E} = +1.06$$

There is no mathematical condition restricting the values of standardized partial regression coefficients to the range of the correlation coefficient. On the other hand, beta values outside the minus one to plus one range are fairly unusual, and in fact they can occur only when some of the correlations among variables are negative. The above beta indicates that variations in father's status are associated with even larger variations in son's status when son's education is controlled. In this peculiar community the higher status fathers have sons with lower than average education (as revealed by the negative value of ρ_{FE}), and poor educations of these sons in turn are associated with lower than expected occupational statuses (as revealed by the positive value of ρ_{ES}). Thus the relationship through son's education tends to counter-act the direct relationship from father status to son status and the overrall correlation is merely moderate. A variable like son's education in this example is often called a "suppressor variable."

CHAPTER 4

1a. Expected correlations among the variables can be obtained by path analysis.

	v	i	y	a
v	1.00	.30	−.40	−.01
i	.30	1.00	−.12	.27
y	−.40	−.12	1.00	.42
a	−.01	.27	.42	1.00

Diagonal entries in a correlation matrix are always 1.00 because they repre-sent the correlation of a variable with itself or, alternatively, the variance of a standardized variable. Note also that correlations below the diagonal are simply a repetition of correlations above the diagonal. Because this is the case, a correlation matrix is frequently presented merely in terms of its upper or lower triangle of entries.

1b. Because disturbances of a are shown as uncorrelated with anything else, the variance of a can be expressed as follows.

$$\sigma_a^2 = (.84)^2 \sigma_{u(a)}^2 + S$$

where S represents the variance accumulated from all the specified sources. If you work out the full expression for the variance of a, you will see how S is composed and also prove that the equation is true. Because the disturbance variation is standardized, the equation can be rewritten

$$\sigma_a^2 = .71 + S \quad \text{or} \quad S = \sigma_a^2 - .71$$

Thus the absolute amount of explained variation is defined. To convert this to a proportion we divide the explained variance in a by the total variance in a.

$$\frac{S}{\sigma_a^2} = \frac{\sigma_a^2 - .71}{\sigma_a^2}$$

Of course, a is standardized with variance 1.00 and the above reduces to $(1 - .71) = .29$. (In general, when all variables and disturbances are being treated in standardized form and a disturbance is uncorrelated with anything else, the proportion of explained variance can be read almost directly off the diagram. It is 1.00 minus the squared coefficient on the path from the disturbance term to the variable of interest.) The proportion of explained variance simply indicates the extent to which existing differences on a variable are due to existing differences in specified causes. The figure does not necessarily set any bounds on how much a variable can be changed; for example, suppose that all prisons have relatively high rates of inmate aggression. Variations in prisoner isolation, type of conviction, and age are known to account for only a portion of the variations around the overall average. Nevertheless it is still theoretically possible to change, say, visitation policies in any prison so drastically that its aggression rate might be cut by half, a third, or more. (Alternatively, it should be possible to increase i, v, or y so that aggression rates double, triple, quadruple, or whatever.) The finding that i, v, and y explain just 29 percent of the variance in a *does* mean that we cannot eliminate aggression differences between prisons just by eliminating prison differences in inmate isolation, type of conviction, and age. Nevertheless, these variables could be used to eliminate the a variance by designing variations in i, v, or y so that their effects would cancel effects from unspecified sources of variation in a. This amounts to building in a negative correlation between u_a and i, v, or y. In practical terms it would involve, say, transferring young prisoners from high aggression to low aggression prisons.

1c. If a prison's age structure is changed and the composition of its offenders is held constant, the impact on aggression must be solely via path $(y \rightarrow a)$. A one-unit increase in y would lead to an expected 0.5 increase in inmate aggression. If the change in age structure is accomplished without regard to offender type, then we would expect the usual $-.40$ correlation between y and v to be maintained. A one-unit change in y probably would be associated with a $-.40$ decrease in v. The net impact on a of both changes would be

$$.5 + (-.4)[.1 + (.3)(.3)] = .42$$

Thus some of the expected increase in aggression due to more youthfulness is counteracted by the fact that now the prison contains less violent offenders.

1d. A warden's nightmare would be a remote prison (far from inmate visitors) devoted specially to young violent offenders. A pleasant relief for a warden would be a prison that had a hospital-like visitation policy and that was dedicated to middle-aged nonviolent local offenders.

2a. The system with its newly created operators can be represented as follows (E is education, P is occupational prestige, I is income):

$$U_P \qquad\qquad U_I$$
$$\downarrow \qquad\qquad \downarrow$$
$$E \xrightarrow{\;1.0\;} P \xrightarrow{\;1.0\;} I$$

where

$$\sigma_E^2 = 1.0, \quad \sigma_{U(P)}^2 = 1.0, \quad \sigma_{U(I)}^2 = 1.0$$

Using path analysis, we find

$$\sigma_P^2 = (1.0)^2\sigma_E^2 + (1.0)^2\sigma_{U(P)}^2 + 2(1.0)(1.0)(0.0) = 2.0$$
$$\sigma_I^2 = 2.0 + 1.0 = 3.0$$
$$\sigma_{EP} = (1.0)\sigma_E^2 = 1.0$$
$$\sigma_{EI} = (1.0)(1.0)\sigma_E^2 = 1.0$$
$$\sigma_{PI} = (1.0)\sigma_P^2 = 2.0$$

Using the formula for the correlation coefficient in **3.17**, we obtain

$$\rho_{EP} = \frac{\sigma_{EP}}{\sigma_E\sigma_P} = \frac{1.0}{\sqrt{1.0}\sqrt{2.0}} = .707$$

$$\rho_{EI} = \frac{1.0}{\sqrt{1.0}\sqrt{3.0}} = .577$$

$$\sigma_{PI} = \frac{2.0}{\sqrt{2.0}\sqrt{3.0}} = .816$$

2b. The path coefficients are the structural coefficients that account for the correlations among variables. The values of the correlations were calculated above. Thus it must be true that the path coefficients (represented here by **q**) satisfy the following equations:

$$\rho_{EP} = q_{pe}$$
$$\rho_{PI} = q_{ip}$$

Thus the path coefficients can be estimated directly from the correlations:

$$q_{pe} = \rho_{EP} = .707$$
$$q_{ip} = \rho_{PI} = .816$$

[Notice that in fact $(q_{pe}) \cdot (q_{ip}) = \rho_{EI}$.] Using the original metrics, we suppose that both new operators are of equal importance because their structural coefficients have a value of 1.0. On the other hand, with the variables standardized in terms of the final distributions, it might seem that the second operator is stronger than the first. Of course, the same operators are involved in both cases, which illustrates that it is not really sensible to compare coefficients that are based on different metrics.

2c. This example suggests that correlations among statuses develop from social mechanisms for transforming one kind of status to another, provided that there are some preexisting variations on the source statuses. Adding such mechanisms to a community leaves diversity in the source statuses unchanged but increases the diversity in outcome statuses. Therefore we might say that the greatest inequalities occur on the least central statuses.

3. The system now is

$$
\begin{array}{ccc}
U_P & & U_I \\
\downarrow & & \downarrow \\
E \xrightarrow{\ 1.0\ } P & \overset{1.0}{\underset{.5}{\rightleftarrows}} & I
\end{array}
$$

The loop's return effect is $L = .5$ and its "return difference" is $(1 - L) = .5$. Thus the semireduced system has the following form:

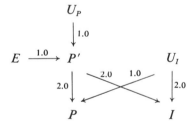

Path analysis gives the following results (recalling that $\sigma_E^2 = \sigma_{U(P)}^2 = \sigma_{U(I)}^2 = 1.0$).

$$
\sigma_P^2 = (2.0)^2 \sigma_{P'} + (1.0)^2 \sigma_{U(I)}^2 = (2.0)^2(2.0) + (1.0)^2(1.0)
$$
$$
= 8.0 + 1.0 = 9.0
$$

$$
\sigma_I^2 = (2.0)^2 \sigma_{P'}^2 + (2.0)^2 \sigma_{U(I)}^2 = (2.0)^3 + (2.0)^2 = 12.0
$$
$$
\sigma_{EP} = (1.0)(2.0)\sigma_E^2 = 2.0
$$
$$
\sigma_{EI} = (1.0)(2.0)\sigma_E^2 = 2.0
$$
$$
\sigma_{PI} = (2.0)\sigma_{P'}^2(2.0) + (1.0)\sigma_{U(I)}^2(2.0)
$$
$$
= (2.0)^3 + 2.0 = 10.0
$$

Note that the loop greatly increases the inequalities in occupations and incomes.

The correlations are calculated from the above:

$$\rho_{EP} = \frac{2.0}{\sqrt{1.0}\sqrt{9.0}} = .667$$

$$\sigma_{EI} = \frac{2.0}{\sqrt{1.0}\sqrt{12.0}} = .577$$

$$\sigma_{PI} = \frac{10.0}{\sqrt{9.0}\sqrt{12.0}} = .962$$

(Compare these values with the correlations obtained with the system in exercise 2.) The correlation between E and P is less here because P now has an additional source of variance—U_I. On the other hand, the presence of the amplifying loop increases the correlation of the two variables within the loop.

4a. Path analysis defines the correlations among the indicators:

$$\rho_{x(1)x(2)} = p_{x(1)\hat{x}}\sigma_{\hat{x}}^2 p_{x(2)\hat{x}} = .7(1.0).6 = .42$$
$$\rho_{y(1)y(2)} = .20$$

The two indicators of a variable (either $\hat{x}$ or $\hat{y}$) would correlate perfectly if both were determined by that variable alone. However, measurements on each indicator are also affected by measurement errors. The diagram indicates errors in one indicator are independent of errors in all other indicators. Thus the errors add to the variance of each indicator but contribute nothing to their covariances, thereby reducing their correlations.

4b. Path analysis defines the following correlations.

	y_1	y_2
x_1	.084	.105
x_2	.072	.090

Obviously the correlations between indicators of $\hat{x}$ and $\hat{y}$ are much smaller than the correlation between the true scores. Ordinarily, we calculate such correlations from a sample of cases, and there is some suspicion that their values would shift a bit if another sample were used. Thus we might be inclined to view the above correlations as negligibly different from zero, concluding that there is no attitude-information relation.

4c. Path analysis can be used to define the variance of each indicator; for example;

$$\sigma_{x(1)}^2 = (.7)^2\sigma_{\hat{x}}^2 + (p_{1d})^2\sigma_{d(1)}^2$$

Because all variables (including disturbances) are presumed to be standardized, the above equation reduces to

$$1 = .49 + p_{2d}^2 \quad \text{or} \quad p_{1d}^2 = .51 \quad \text{or} \quad p_{1d} = .71$$

Thus 51 percent of the indicator variance is due to measurement errors, and the value of the coefficient on the arrow from the error term to the indicator variable is .71. Calculations for the remaining three indicators are similar

$$\sigma_{x2}^2 = 1 = .36 + p_{2d}^2 \quad \text{and} \quad p_{2d} = \sqrt{.64} = .80$$
$$\sigma_{y1}^2 = 1 = .16 + p_{1e}^2 \quad \text{and} \quad p_{1e} = \sqrt{.84} = .92$$
$$\sigma_{y2}^2 = 1 = .25 + p_{2e}^2 \quad \text{and} \quad p_{2e} = \sqrt{.75} = .87$$

4d. If $p_{\hat{x}\hat{y}}$ is unknown, the correlation between x_1 and y_1 would be written, using path analysis.

$$p_{x(1)y(1)} = (.7)p_{\hat{x}\hat{y}}(.4)$$

Solving for the unknown correlation between true scores gives

$$p_{\hat{x}\hat{y}} = \frac{p_{x(1)y(1)}}{(.7)(.4)}$$

Because all quantities on the right are supposed to be known, this provides a formula for estimating the true-score correlation. This procedure—dividing an observed correlation by validity coefficients to estimate the true correlation —is well known in psychometrics as the "correction for attenuation."

5a. The additional specification requires the addition of curved double-headed arrows to connect all the error terms. Each has a correlation of 0.30 attached to it. Application of path analysis to the revised diagram gives the following type of equation:

$$p_{x(1)x(2)} = (.7)(1.0)(.6) + p_{1d}(.30)p_{2d}$$

Numerical results are (p_{1d}, p_{2d}, etc., were estimated numerically in exercise 4c)

	x_1	x_2	y_1
x_2	.59	—	—
y_1	.28	.29	—
y_2	.29	.30	.44

These values are larger than when there were no correlated errors. Usually the errors on different questionnaire or interview items will be positively correlated because some of the same distorting factors operate throughout the data-collection period. Positively correlated errors of measurement always tend to increase the observed correlations among the items.

5b. The estimated correlation between true scores now is the following.

$$\rho'_{\hat{x}\hat{y}} = \frac{.28}{(.7)(.4)} = 1.00$$

This result might mislead us into concluding that the correspondence between attitude and information is perfect when, in fact, it is only modest.

5c. The validity coefficient for this indicator is 0.7, suggesting a fairly close relation between true and indicator scores over most of the scale. We can surmise, though, that the relation breaks down at the ends of the indicator scale. All extremely positive attitudes, no matter how extreme, must be coded 5.0; similarly all extremely negative attitudes are coded no lower than 1.0. Thus the joint distribution of true scores and indicator scores must look about as follows:

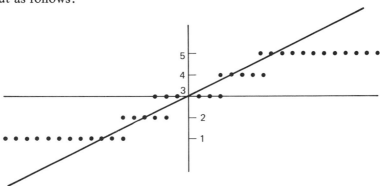

Over the middle range there is little relation between true scores and the measurement errors, but at the extremes the true scores clearly have a *negative* relation to the errors (e.g., the more positive the attitude, the more severely it is underestimated). Overall, this would create a negative correlation between true scores and measurement errors. This is generally true when a measurement scale is bounded so that extreme highs and lows are assigned attenuated scores. On the other hand, the resulting negative correlation will be small or negligible if few cases fall beyond the scale bounds.

6. In the system with a stronger reward mechanism but without feedback the variance of Z is

$$\sigma_Z^2 = [(2.0)^2 \sigma_Y^2] = [(2.0)^2 (1.0)^2 \sigma_X^2] = 4.0 \sigma_X^2$$

Comparing this with the parallel result in **4.20**, we see that the stronger reward mechanism has quadrupled the variance in statuses. In the system with stronger rewards plus feedback the variance of Z has the value

$$\sigma_Z^2 = \left[\frac{2}{1 - 2(-.25)}\right]^2 \sigma_X^2 = \frac{16}{9}\sigma_X^2$$

Here the variance is less than doubled. In the control system accomplishments are lavishly rewarded, but the extreme divergencies in status that would ordinarily result are moderated by linking success to lack of further accomplishments. This system might serve the functions of making persons content with their level of reward and, at the same time, of avoiding excessive social inequality. However, the control system has the dysfunction of wasting talent:

$$Y = X \text{ without feedback } (a = 1, c = 2, d = 0)$$
$$Y = \tfrac{2}{3}X \text{ with feedback } (a = 1, c = 2, d = -\tfrac{1}{4})$$

7a. The diagram indicates that the correlation between t_1 and t_2 provides an estimate of h.

$$\rho_{t(1)t(2)} = \sqrt{h}(1.0)\sqrt{h} = h$$

To compute this we obtain a large number of twins and measure them all on the trait. Then within each pair we arbitrarily call one twin's measurement t_1 and the measurement of the other t_2. Finally, the correlation is computed across twin pairs.

7b. If twins are raised together, it is likely that they will have experienced similar material and social environments. Consequently we would have to modify the diagram to show e_1 and e_2 as correlated to some unknown degree. Then, however, the correlation between t_1 and t_2 is a function of both genetic and environmental similarities and it no longer provides an unbiased estimate of heritability alone. To avoid this problem researchers try to find twins who were raised in unrelated environments.

7c. If intelligence is subject to any environmental determination at all, then theoretically it is possible to change intelligence as much as desired by environmental manipulations. To overcome genetic dispositions the environmental interventions may have to be drastic and expensive. Whether this is practical is a matter of social values. (Some behavioral geneticists do argue that a linear model is not entirely appropriate here. Environmental improvements, they say, would produce increases in intelligence only up to a point and then further improvements would have no effect.)

7d. The impact of measurement error can be seen by redrawing the diagram and distinguishing between true scores on t and the observed scores with error (as in exercise 4).

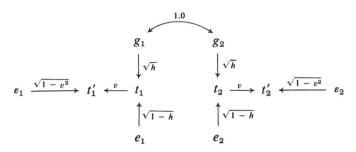

Now the correlation between the observed scores is

$$\rho_{t'(1)t'(2)} = (v)\sqrt{h}(1.0)\sqrt{h}(v) = v^2h$$

Because a validity coefficient is always less than or equal to 1.0 (it is the correlation between true scores and observed scores), the observed correlation will underestimate the value of h.

7e. A heritability is basically a variation on a standardized path coefficient. If a population's distributional characteristics are changing, the basis of standardization is also changing and heritabilities will change. In particular, an increase in environmental variance ordinarily will produce some increase in trait variance, whereas genetic variance presumably stays the same. Thus in the new population genetic variance will account for proportionately less of the trait variance and most heritability coefficients will decline.

8. For heuristic purposes let E stand for a composite variable representing all early-life determinants of aesthetic values and let **a** be the structural coefficient that transforms E to aesthetic values in the college years V. Let U stand for other determinants of V, notably including important happenings during the teen years. In a general population relationships might then be represented as

$$U$$
$$\downarrow$$
$$E \xrightarrow{a} V$$

In this case the correlation between E and V indeed would reveal something about the importance of **a**. In particular, the squared correlation, or coefficient of determination, is

$$\frac{\sigma_{EV}^2}{\sigma_E^2 \sigma_V^2} = \frac{a^2 \sigma_E^4}{\sigma_E^2 (a^2 \sigma_E^2 + \sigma_U^2)} = \frac{a^2 \sigma_E^2}{a^2 \sigma_E^2 + \sigma_U^2}$$

This quantity is large if **a** is large (assuming that the variabilities in early and teen experiences are roughly of comparable magnitudes). The above model, however, does not describe the population that was studied. Students are gated into the humanities partly on the basis of elevated aesthetic values and a humanities student who is low on E is probably high on U. One who is low on U is probably high on E. Thus E and U should be negatively related in this population, as indicated in the following diagram.

$$(-)\ \sigma\ \dashrightarrow\ U$$

$$E\ \xrightarrow{\ a\ }\ V$$

The negative covariance between E and U reduces the observed covariance between E and V.

$$\sigma_{EV} = a\sigma_E^2 + \sigma_{EU}$$

Accordingly, the correlation between E and V is also reduced. Indeed, the observed correlation in this population might be negligible even when the value of **a** is large enough to be theoretically and practically significant.

9. It is likely that musical interest in adolescence selects out those who will obtain professional musical training and experience. Thus a high level of interest predicts the occurrence of operations that yield a high level of skill. The early interest variable correlates with later skills not necessarily because it "causes" skill development but because it indicates who is subject to the professionalization operator that transforms talent into accomplishments. Few persons in the lay population are subject to the professionalization operator. Consequently the early interest variable provides little information about later development of skills.

CHAPTER 5

1. The variables can be organized into a recursive model only if we can arrange them into a hierarchical ordering of causes and effects. In addition, the disturbances for each variable must be uncorrelated with values of the sources for that same variable. In fact, the relationships can be specified as a system of causes and effects without loops; the relevant discussion is presented in the answer to exercise 5, Chapter 1. The question of independent disturbances raises several different kinds of consideration. By eliminating the possibility of loops, however, we have already eliminated one possible source of nonindependence. Further considerations are illustrated below.

Gates. Have we reason to suppose that cases in the population to be observed have been gated on the basis of any of the four specified variables? Conceivably. Sons of fathers with low occupational standings may have higher mortality rates. Sons whose own educations and occupational standings are low may not be found for interviewing. Such problems would tend to generate negative correlations between source variables and the disturbances of the gating variables. Ideally, they are corrected by extending analyses to all relevant cases, but this solution is not possible if differential mortality is involved. If the problems seem likely to bias parameter estimates seriously, then we must give up on recursiveness or restrict the population to cases in which father's education (the primary input) is high enough so that gating on the other variables would be negligible. We also must consider the possibility that some unspecified source variable joins with a specified source to form a gate. This idea can be illustrated. Suppose that aggressiveness is an unspecified source of son's occupational level. Suppose also that aggressive men with poor educations are more likely to be sent into military combat. The resulting attrition from the study population might generate a positive correlation between son's education and disturbances in son's occupational standing. The survivors among men with limited educations would tend to be relatively passive and thereby even lower in occupational level than expected.

Unspecified sources. If a variable that affects two or more of the specified variables has been left out, it will give rise to a problem of nonindependent disturbances; for example, a father's intelligence may be a determinant of his educational level and it may also be transmitted genetically to his son, indirectly affecting his educational level as well. Thus disturbances in son's education would be correlated with a determinant of father's education, creating a spuriously high correlation between father and son educations. If the intelligence variable cannot be brought explicitly into analyses, it may be deemed necessary to discard the notion of recursiveness in the model.

2. The model is as follows:

The variables are:

x_1: Father's education.
x_2: Father's occupational standing.
x_3: Son's education.
x_4: Son's occupational standing.

The first structural equation is

$$x_2 = p_{21}x_1 + p_{2u}u_2$$

This implies the regression of x_2 on x_1 and estimation of coefficients is (see **3.32** and **3.34**)

$$p_{21} = \beta_{21} = \rho_{21} \simeq .516$$

$$p_{2u} = \sqrt{1 - R_{2\cdot 1}^2} = \sqrt{1 - \rho_{21}^2} \simeq .857$$

The second structural equation is

$$x_3 = p_{31}x_1 + p_{32}x_2 + p_{3u}u_3$$

which implies the regression of x_3 or x_1 and x_2 to obtain the following parameter estimates (using the formulas in **3.33** and **3.34**):

$$p_{31} = \beta_{31\cdot 2} = \frac{\rho_{31} - \rho_{32}\rho_{12}}{1 - \rho_{12}^2} \simeq \frac{.453 - (.438)(.516)}{1 - (.516)^2} = .309$$

$$p_{32} = \beta_{32\cdot 1} \simeq \frac{.438 - (.453)(.516)}{1 - (.516)^2} = .278$$

$$p_{3u} = \sqrt{1 - R_{3\cdot 12}^2} \simeq (.309)^2 + (.278)^2 + 2(.309)(.278)(.516)$$

$$= .859$$

The final structural equation is

$$x_4 = p_{42}x_2 + p_{43}x_3 + p_{4u}u_4$$

and coefficients are estimated as

$$p_{42} = \beta_{42\cdot3} \simeq \frac{.405 - (.596)(.438)}{1 - (.438)^2} = .178$$

$$p_{43} = \beta_{43\cdot2} \simeq \frac{.596 - (.405)(.438)}{1 - (.438)^2} = .518$$

$$p_{4u} = \sqrt{1 - R_{4\cdot23}^2} \simeq \sqrt{1 - .381} = .787$$

3a. The regression coefficients for predicting I_1 from 0_1 and 0_2 would be estimates of the total effects $T_{I(1)0(1)}$ and $T_{I(1)0(2)}$ (see rule II.17). In the statistical literature they are called "reduced form coefficients." Note that it is appropriate to use ordinary least squares to estimate the total effects because I_1 and I_2 are recursively related to 0_1 and 0_2 in the reduced model. To determine whether we can estimate **a** from the reduced form coefficients we must define the expressions for the total effects. This involves applying Mason's principle (rule II.16) because there are six loops in the original system:

$$(I_1 D_1): \quad L_1 = a$$
$$(D_1 I_2): \quad L_2 = a$$
$$(I_2 D_2): \quad L_3 = a$$
$$(D_2 I_1): \quad L_4 = a$$
$$(I_1 D_1 I_2 D_2): \quad L_5 = a^2$$
$$(I_1 D_2 I_2 D_1): \quad L_6 = a^2$$

The total effects to I_1 are (parallel effects to I_2 are identical)

$$T_{I(1)0(1)} = \frac{k(1 - L_2 - L_3)}{1 - L - L_2 - L_3 - L_4 - L_5 - L_6 + L_1 L_3 + L_2 L_4}$$

$$= \frac{k(1 - 2a)}{1 - 4a - 2a^2 + 2a^2}$$

$$= \frac{k(1 - 2a)}{1 - 4a}$$

$$T_{I(1)0(2)} = \frac{k(-2a)}{1 - 4a}$$

Because the reduced-form regression coefficients estimate these values, we could derive an estimate of **a** by substituting their values for the total effects, dividing one expression by the other, and solving for **a** (an indirect least squares approach).

$$\frac{b_{I(1)0(1)\cdot 0(2)}}{b_{I(1)0(2)\cdot 0(1)}} = \frac{1 - 2a}{-2a}$$

$$a = \frac{b_{I(1)0(2)\cdot 0(1)}}{2(b_{I(1)0(2)\cdot 0(1)} - b_{I(1)0(1)\cdot 0(2)})}$$

Indeed, we really have two estimates of **a** because the regressions involving I_2 could also be used.

3b. If **a** stands for altruistic-exploitive actions and is negative, then L_1 through L_4 are negative and the system now has control loops in it. (The power system consisted entirely of amplifiers.) The total effects in the system with controls will be smaller. Consequently the regression coefficients should also be smaller in absolute magnitude, and the signs of $b_{I(1)0(2)\cdot 0(1)}$ and $b_{I(2)0(1)\cdot 0(2)}$ should be positive rather than negative. However, coefficient **a** is still identified by the above formula.

4a. Any conclusion that a variable does, or does not, provide an instrument for a relation derives from theorizing and the conclusion always remains vulnerable to theoretical debate. With this caveat, the procedures involved are illustrated below. All of the proposed instruments in this exercise are aspects of the natural environment. Because we intend to deal with small (nonindustrial) societies, it may be assumed that none of the environmental variables is determined directly or indirectly by the societal variables S, M, or I. Accordingly, the environmental variables meet one condition for serving as instruments.

The next question is whether every conceivable chain of relations from a proposed instrument to S always goes through M or I. Subsistence technology is probably dependent partly on length of growing season. A long growing season, however, might produce food surpluses to support a stratification system even if a society had a primitive subsistence technology. Thus the growing-season variable can have effects on S that do not pass through M or I, as measured, and length of growing season cannot serve as an instrument in this problem. A similar problem relates to soil fertility. Most of the effects of greater soil fertility would be mediated by impacts on level of subsistence technology, but if we were to increase the fertility of a society's land, it might gain somewhat in food surpluses and level of S, even if its subsistence technology were held constant. Thus fertility must also be rejected as an instrument.

Note that both growing season and soil fertility would be recovered as potential instruments if our materialistic indicator were a direct measure of food production. (Subsistence technology presumably is one of the determinants of amount of food production.) Unfortunately, level of food production is not easily coded from ethnographers' reports. Alternatively, perhaps we could argue that the "short circuit" effects mentioned in the above paragraph are negligibly small in the societies of interest or in some specially defined subset of societies. In this way, too, the variables might be returned to consideration as instruments.

Severity of habitat might be correlated with subsistence technology in that severer habitats are sometimes associated with less advanced technology (though there is no strict determinism). This weak relation would seem to absorb any strictly materialistic effects of a severe habitat on social structure. Yet a group might cope with persisting, predictable habitat threats (deserts, dangerous waters, or cliffs) by demanding strict discipline, and traditions of social discipline in turn might nurture the development of hierarchical social structures. Thus the variable as originally presented may have a link to S that does not pass through M or I, and so it cannot serve as an instrument.

On the other hand, we might focus on more erratic habitat threats in which defense must consist of individual vigilance rather than group discipline (e.g., poisonous or predatory organisms, sudden storms, and travel hazards like rockslides or cracking ice floes). Such conditions might have some inhibiting effect on the development of subsistence technology and thus affect S through M. These conditions might also encourage the development of acute perceptual sensitivity and analytic power [H. A. Witkin, "A cognitive-style approach to cross-cultural research," *International Journal of Psychology*, **2** (1967), 233–250]. If this is associated with what sociologist Pitrim Sorokin called a "sensate" orientation, perhaps it inhibits development of an authoritative moral ideology supported by religion, and thereby inhibits elaboration of a hierarchical social structure. Because it is difficult to imagine other chains of relations by which erratic habitat threats might relate to social structure, the refined habitat variable appears to be a feasible instrument for this problem. Its suitability then depends on the strength of its relation to M and I.

Accessible ore deposits would support the development of more advanced subsistence technology in the form of metal hoes, plows, and other implements, which in turn could substantially increase the surpluses available to support an elaborated social structure. Metallurgy is also likely to result in the development of improved weapons which might become part of the subsistence technology but might also lead to new power relationships and an elaborated social hierarchy. Consequently we have a direct relation with S that bypasses M and I and precludes the use of ore deposits as a means of identifying coefficients in the original structural equation. Rather than give up the idea, it might be useful to expand the original equation by specifying weapons as a determinant of hierarchical social structures. With a variable that measures weapons development explicitly in the model, ore deposits are revived as a potential instrument for the relation between M and S.

Unfortunately, though, even this would not be enough. Smelting of metals is likely to generate metallurgy specialists, and it could be argued that any refinement of the division of labor might enhance the development of a hierarchical social structure. Of course, we might include metal-working specialists explicitly in the model. Then, however, we would have added two new variables to the structural equation and would have to find still more instruments to identify their effects.

Of the four suggested variables, only one seemed to be a feasible instrument (after its definition was refined). One instrument is not enough to identify the two coefficients in the original structural equation. The options at this point (aside from abandoning the problem) are three.

(a) Continue the search for suitable instruments to use with the equation as originally specified.

(b) Redefine variable M as food production and reconsider growing season and soil fertility as instruments.

(c) Elaborate the equation to specify more of the determinants of S (e.g., weapons and metal specialists). The last requires definition of a still larger set of instruments, but the task may be easier once we are no longer restricted to variables that affect S only through M or I.

4b. As we have made clear in the above discussion, defining an instrument is a matter of theory rather than statistics. Thus the knowledge that length of growing season correlates zero with S (or I) is of no value in deciding whether it is an instrument for the $M \rightarrow S$ relation. In particular, a zero correlation with S does not necessarily imply a zero correlation with the disturbances of S in the specified equation.

5. Current attitudes or behavior involving alcohol do not affect a student's religious upbringing or age. Alcoholism could interfere with part-time work or precipitate a cutoff of allowance from parents. We might assume, however, that such a serious and obvious drinking problem is sufficiently rare in a student population to be ignored. (Alternatively, a respondent could be asked whether drinking had generated financial sanctions in order to eliminate any who have been subject to such operators.) Accordingly, the three proposed instruments are not affected by attitudes or behaviors, and so they meet one of the required conditions for serving. Next it is necessary to determine whether a proposed instrument's effect on one dependent variable is always mediated by the other.

A fundamentalist upbringing fosters antialcohol attitudes. Thus to be an instrument the variable must affect drinking behavior only by its attitudinal effect. Opportunities and models encouraging drinking would be absent in the fundamentalist home: children would be insulated from "ordinary" sources of drinking behavior and would be even less likely to drink than their attitudes would determine. Extremely fundamentalist parents might try to continue this insulation by insisting on restricted housing accommodations on campus, but, even determined parental efforts to control a student's associates may be ineffectual at a large state university after the freshman year, so analyses could be restricted to upperclassmen to retain the instrument. Extremely fundamentalist parents might also refuse to send their children to a large university so that the students would be gated on the religion variable. This would mean that the relationship between fundamentalism and attitudes would be underestimated but would not preclude use of the variable as an instrument unless the correlation became zero.

Amount of spending money would not seem to affect a student's attitude toward alcohol, though it might do so indirectly by influencing how much the student drinks. The main problem here is that amount of spending money probably is not linearly related to drinking behavior. Impoverishment would tend to reduce drinking, while even a small amount of pocket money might be used occasionally for a social drink. Variations beyond that would have little predictive value because extra money can be utilized in so many ways. Thus the variable that might be of some use as an instrument would measure austerity, disregarding gradations in financial comfort.

Students with austere budgets possibly avoid (or are avoided by) partying social circles in which drinking is regarded positively. Thus their financial conditions control the choice of associates who might influence attitudes apart from behavior. Here even the austerity variable cannot be used as an instrument unless friends' norms are considered as well.

Students can drink beer legally, but hard liquor is not made available to them by law until they are 21. Possibly the increased opportunities of those past the second legal age adds to overall drinking in the senior year so that chronological age would have a relation to behavior. There seems to be no purely psychological mechanism that relates aging to attitudes toward alcohol. We would be hard pressed to specify how taking on an "adult" identity would affect alcohol attitudes one way or the other. College friends ordinarily are in the same cohort, however, and all members of a social circle would ex-perince legalization of opportunity together. Consequently a student's age would correlate with variations in group norms as well as with individual behavior. Again we have a variable that might serve as an instrument only if we consider friends' norms explicitly.

Gating mechanisms may raise additional problems of defining instru-ments. In the case of students a great deal of entrance selection is followed by selection by attrition in which most of the gating is related to grade-point average. It seems doubtful that this gating has any direct relation to attitudes toward alcohol but there is some possibility that it is related to drinking behavior; for example, more neurotic students may be the heaviest drinkers and also may drop out because of poor grades. Then, if neuroticism were related to, say, religious upbringing, the latter variable would no longer be a servicable instrument. If some students drink to the point of becoming drop-outs, this phenomenon would tend to create a negative correlation between disturbances in the behavior variable and the values of its sources. However, it was assumed above that this phenomenon is uncommon.

At best, we now have one instrument that by itself is not sufficient to identify the two coefficients in the attitude-behavior loop. The other two variables could be returned to discussion if we considered group norms explicitly. However, relations between group norms and individual attitudes and behaviors probably are two-way, so at least one additional instrument would be required to identify the normative effects.

6. To estimate all coefficients we must construct two new variables, $\hat{V}$ and $\hat{Z}$, by regressing V and Z, respectively, on X and Y. Note that the variables are not standardized (some of the variances are greater than 1.0). Hence the formula in **3.29** is used to obtain regression coefficients.

$$b_{VX \cdot Y} = \frac{\sigma_Y^2 \sigma_{VX} - \sigma_{VY}\sigma_{XY}}{\sigma_X^2\sigma_Y^2 - \sigma_{XY}^2} = \frac{(1.0)(.283) - (-.113)(.3)}{(1.0)(1.0) - (.3)^2}$$

$$= .348$$

$$b_{VY \cdot X} = \frac{(1.0)(-.113) - (.283)(.3)}{(1.0)(1.0) - (.3)^2} = -.218$$

$$b_{ZX \cdot Y} = \frac{(1.0)(.235) - (.466)(.3)}{(1.0)(1.0) - (.3)^2} = .105$$

$$b_{ZY \cdot X} = \frac{(1.0)(.466) - (.235)(.3)}{(1.0)(1.0) - (.3)^2} = .435$$

To estimate **a** we construct $\hat{V}$ by using the first two coefficients above.

$$\hat{V} = .348X - .218Y$$

Using the procedures outlined in the statement of the exercise, we then obtain the following quantities:

$$\sigma_{\hat{V}}^2 = .123$$
$$\sigma_{\hat{V}Y} = -.114$$
$$\sigma_{\hat{V}Z} = -.020$$

From these and the given figures we calculate the regression coefficients estimating **a** and **e**.

$$b_{Z\hat{V} \cdot Y} = \frac{\sigma_Y^2 \sigma_{Z\hat{V}} - \sigma_{ZY}\sigma_{\hat{V}Y}}{\sigma_{\hat{V}}^2 \sigma_Y^2 - \sigma_{\hat{V}Y}^2} = \frac{(1.0)(-.020) - (.466)(-.114)}{(.123)(1.0) - (-.114)^2}$$

$$= .301$$

$$b_{ZY \cdot \hat{V}} = \frac{(.123)(.466) - (-.020)(-.114)}{(1.0)(.123) - (-.114)^2} = .500$$

The statistics for $\hat{Z}$ are defined similarly:

$$\hat{Z} = .105X + .435Y$$
$$\sigma_{\hat{Z}}^2 = .228$$
$$\sigma_{X\hat{Z}} = .236$$
$$\sigma_{V\hat{Z}} = -.019$$

The regression estimates of **c** and **d** are obtained by regressing V on $\hat{Z}$ and X:

$$b_{VZ \cdot X} = \frac{(1.0)(-.019) - (.283)(.236)}{(.228)(1.0) - (.236)^2} = -.498$$

$$b_{VX \cdot \hat{Z}} = \frac{(.228)(.283) - (-.019)(.236)}{(1.0)(.228) - (.236)^2} = .400$$

The original variances and covariances were generated by assigning the following values to the parameters:

$$a = .300 \qquad c = -.500 \qquad d = .400 \qquad e = .500$$

The differences between these and the above estimates are due to rounding errors.

7a. To estimate **a** we must construct the new variable $\hat{E}$ by regressing E on S and U. Because these variables are standardized, the formula in **3.33** may be used:

$$b_{ES \cdot U} = \frac{-.574 - (.226)(-.556)}{1 - (-.556)^2} = -.6490$$

$$b_{EU \cdot S} = \frac{.226 - (-.574)(-.556)}{1 - (-.556)^2} = -.1348$$

$$\hat{E} = -.6490S - .1348U$$

The relevant statistics involving $\hat{E}$ are obtained as in Exercise 6:

$$\sigma_{\hat{E}}^2 = .3421; \quad \sigma_{\hat{E}U} = .2260; \quad \sigma_{\hat{E}I} = .4094$$

The partial regression coefficient estimating **a** can be calculated from these and the given statistics. (We must now employ the formula in **3.29** because variable $\hat{E}$ is not standardized.)

$$b_{I\hat{E} \cdot U} = \frac{(1.0)(.4094) - (.569)(.2260)}{(.3421)(1.0) - (.2260)^2} = \frac{.2808}{.2910}$$

$$= .9649$$

Similarly, to estimate **c** we first define the new variable $\hat{I}$ and its relevant statistics:

$$\hat{I} = -.6262S + .2208U$$

$$\sigma_{\hat{I}}^2 = .5946 \qquad \sigma_{\hat{I}S} = -.7490 \qquad \sigma_{\hat{I}E} = .4093$$

Given these figures and the original statistics, the estimate of **c** is

$$b_{E\hat{I} \cdot S} = \frac{-.0206}{.0336} = -.6127$$

7b. Key quantities involved in obtaining an estimate of **a**, using the second model, are

$$\hat{E} = -.7563P - .3102M$$

$$\sigma_{\hat{E}}^2 = .5589 \qquad \sigma_{\hat{E}M} = -.1340 \qquad \sigma_{\hat{E}I} = .3412$$

$$b_{I\hat{E} \cdot M} = \frac{.3660}{.5409} = .6766$$

The parallel quantities for estimating **c** are

$$\hat{I} = -.5117P + .0658M$$

$$\sigma_{\hat{I}}^2 = .2819 \qquad \sigma_{\hat{I}P} = -.5270 \qquad \sigma_{\hat{I}E} = .3412$$

$$b_{E\hat{I}\cdot P} = \frac{-.0193}{.0042} = -4.6195$$

7c.   Coefficient **a** has a fairly large positive effect in both analyses. Coefficient **c** is negative in both analyses. The estimates are not of equal precision, however. In particular, each of the final estimates of **c** is obtained by dividing a very small number by another very small number. With such a small sample size it is likely that sampling errors in the statistics will be as large as the quantities used to estimate **c**. Thus the estimates of **c** might be quite different if we examined a different sample of SMSAs. The estimates of **a** are less vulnerable in this way. In particular, because we are dividing by a fairly large number in both cases the estimates will not be so affected by sampling variations. Hence we might have more confidence in their replicability.

Using more advanced analyses, we can estimate the probability that the true regression coefficients are different from zero, given just the values obtained from a sample. The procedures have not been presented in this book (they are discussed in econometrics texts). In general, though, testing the statistical significance of estimates lends greater objectivity to a consideration of estimation precision.

The estimates of **c** are unreliable because neither of the proposed instruments is adequate from a statistical standpoint. It is not too obvious from the original correlations that U and M are such weak instruments. As it turns out, however, their correlations with I are largely spurious within the context of these models; that is, once we control for S or P, there is little relation left between U and I or between M and I. Alternatively, we might view this as a colinearity problem. The correlation between the predictors (r_{SU} or r_{PM}) is too high in relation to the correlation between a predictor and the dependent variable (r_{UI} or r_{MI}). (We use the letter r to signify sample estimates of a true correlation ρ.) Note that a colinearity problem in 2SLS does not necessarily mean that we have extremely large correlations between predictors.

One of the estimates of **c** has an absolute value far beyond 1.0. This is theoretically and statistically possible. However, such values are sufficiently rare in practice to serve as cues for caution. In this case it does seem to signal an imprecise estimate of **c**, as noted above.

From a purely statistical standpoint the estimates of **a** seem to have some credibility. The two estimates are not exactly the same in value, but this is typical, and we could obtain a single improved estimate by using S and P together in a single 2SLS analysis. Alternatively, we might examine the difference between the estimates to help evaluate the relative worth of S and P as instruments, as illustrated below.

Whatever the statistical findings, the estimates of **a** and **c** might be wrong if the employment of S, P, U, and M as instruments is not justified theoretically. The theoretical adequacy of each instrument is discussed briefly below.

S: Minority group education and income do not affect a city's location; therefore one condition for using S as an instrument is met. Nonwhites (and whites, too) receive less education in the South, thus justifying the connection from S to E. We have presumed that lower nonwhite incomes are due solely to poorer educations, and this seems at least conceivable. Also, however, job discrimination may be more serious for racial minorities in the South. This provides a path from region to income that bypasses education, invalidating S as a proper instrument. If we have improperly used S as an instrument, we should expect to have generated a biased estimate of **a**. In particular, the correlation between S and I should be too strongly negative to be explained by E alone, and if r_{SI} is too strongly negative the estimate of **a** will have an exaggerated positive value. (This is most easily seen in terms of the identification procedure outlined in **5.12**. An indirect least squares estimate of **a** is

$$\frac{b_{IS \cdot U}}{b_{ES \cdot U}} = \frac{-.6262}{-.6490} = .9649$$

Thus the estimate of **a** is directly dependent on $b_{IS \cdot U}$, and this will have an excessively large negative value if r_{IS} has an excessively large negative value.) In fact, we did find that the estimate of **a**, using S as an instrument, was large compared with the estimate that used P.

U: We now know that this is an inadequate instrument from a statistical standpoint and there may be a theoretical explanation. It was assumed implicitly in the specification that unionization would have a significant effect on minority incomes, justifying the $U \rightarrow I$ path. In the original article, however, Hill presents two arguments about this relation. The neo-Marxist position is that unionization would increase minority incomes, and just the opposite is argued from the classical economic standpoint emphasizing competition among groups. Thus we may have operations that cancel and no sound theoretical reason to expect a definitive $U \not\to I$ relation either way.

The appropriateness of U's specification involves other factors. Unionization in a city probably does not directly affect educational levels in a racial minority; therefore the absence of a $U \to E$ path seems plausible. The given specification also implies that unionization is in no way affected by education or income levels in racial minorities. But perhaps educated minorities work to obtain the protection provided by unions ($E \to U$) or perhaps rising minority incomes are seen as a threat that stimulates white workers to unionize to protect their own jobs ($I \to U$). Different functions of unions for minorities are implied by these suggestions, but either way there is a possibility that the model may be misspecified. Such misspecification could create errors in estimating **a** as well as **c**; that is, if U is not a predetermined variable in relation to E and I, we should not have included U in the first stage definition of $\hat{E}$. (If we had left U out, we would have found a larger value of **a** than we did.)

P: The second model treated the percentage of nonwhites in a city as a source for the educational level of the nonwhite minority. The presumption is that schools in heavily nonwhite cities receive less support, provide poorer quality education, and foster dropping out.

High average education and income among nonwhites might encourage immigration of nonwhites to the city, and low education and income might produce emigration. Thus we might have both $E \to P$ and $I \to P$. It might be argued, however, that such effects are slight, sluggish, and correlated with white migrations as well so that for practical purposes P can be considered unaffected by E or I. Has P any effects on I that do not pass through E? One argument would be that if there is a large proportion of nonwhites the supply of labor for "nonwhite jobs" is large. This drives nonwhite incomes down. However, the inclusion of E and M should eliminate the problem. A low level of E is a more direct indicator than P of an oversupply of cheap nonwhite labor, and M is a reasonable indicator of the demand for blue-collar workers. Thus it seems fairly unlikely that changes in P will affect I aside from changes in E or M.

M: It is doubtful that minority group incomes have much influence on the amount of manufacturing in a city. Manufacturers have substantial capital investments and need to stay close to basic resources and markets, so in the short run, the amount of manufacturing in a large city is not much affected by normal variations in wages (white or nonwhite). For similar reasons nonwhite education levels should have little effect on the proportion of persons employed in manufacturing. Nonwhites conceivably could educate themselves out of factory work, but the jobs will remain and someone will take them. A large amount of manufacturing in a city might provide jobs that entice nonwhites away from school, thus lowering the nonwhite educational level. However, such an effect occurs through I and confirms the theoretical appropriateness of M as an instrument.

This discussion suggests that the instruments in the second model are more theoretically plausible than those in the first. Nevertheless, this is an appropriate time to restate the caveat: better theorizing might lead to different conclusions.

8. Using the formulas in **5.23**, we obtain an estimate of **a**:

$$\frac{\sigma_{PI}}{\sigma_{PE}} = \frac{-.527}{-.684} = .770$$

An estimate of **c** follows:

$$\frac{\sigma_E^2 \sigma_{PI} - \sigma_{EI}\sigma_{PE}}{\sigma_{EI}\sigma_{PI} - \sigma_I^2 \sigma_{PE}} = \frac{(1.0)(-.527) - (.709)(-.684)}{(.709)(-.527) - (1.0)(-.684)}$$

$$= \frac{-.0420}{.3104} = -.136$$

We again arrive at the conclusions that **a** is substantially positive and that **c** has a value less than, or maybe equal to, zero.

All of these results depend on quite a small sample of cities, and it might be objected that in no case did we have thoroughly satisfactory instruments. Thus to maintain absolute rigor we should refuse to conclude anything at all. On the other hand, we do reach essentially the same conclusions with three different models that involve somewhat different theoretical assumptions. Suppose, in addition, that this is the best information we have and that important policy decisions are soon to be made. Then wisdom might require transcending absolute rigor.

All three analyses suggest that improving the educational level of nonwhites increases average nonwhite incomes. All analyses also suggest that demands for higher wages will have effects limited to just average income at best. If average nonwhite income goes up, there is no indication that education will improve; in fact, there is a hint of the opposite: in American society, as constituted in 1960, high wages may have been enticing nonwhite youths away from continuing their educations. Thus working to improve nonwhites' educations would seem to be the best strategy for raising non-whites' overall socioeconomic status.

9. The estimate of the disturbance covariance based on imprecise measures can be defined in terms of the statistics for true variables:

$$\tilde{\sigma}_{UV} = \sigma_{YZ} - \frac{\sigma_{XZ}(\sigma_Y^2 + \sigma_F^2)}{\sigma_{XY}}$$

$$= \sigma_{YZ} - \frac{\sigma_{XZ}\sigma_Y^2}{\sigma_{XY}} - \frac{\sigma_{XZ}\sigma_F^2}{\sigma_{XY}}$$

$$= (\sigma_{UV}) - b\sigma_F^2$$

Thus the estimate is biased because (aside from sampling variations) it equals the true value minus the quantity $(b\sigma_F^2)$. The variance of errors in measuring Y is always positive. Hence the estimated covariance between disturbances will be too small when coefficient **b** is positive (perhaps even spuriously negative). The estimate will be too large when **b** is negative.

Unbiased estimates of disturbance covariances sometimes are examined to determine whether key variables have been left out of the system speci-fication. However, if variables were measured imprecisely, estimates of distur-bance covariances are biased (even though estimates of structural parameters are not). In particular, their values depend on measurement errors as well as on the true values of the disturbance covariances. Thus we could err in interpreting them simply from a theoretical standpoint.

This conclusion is generally true for more complicated systems estimated by the 2SLS procedure. The problem can be overcome by using instrumental variables, multiple indicators, and full-information estimation procedures to solve simultaneously for the structural coefficients, the disturbance covariances, and the indicator validities. (See the Jöreskog articles in the chap-ter references.)

CHAPTER 6

1a.

1b. Because levels of federal funding are directly dependent on G, we can suppose that the manifest function of the funding agencies is to encourage expansion of research on a topic. But examination of the flowgraph reveals that although the agencies do provide short-term amplification (a six-year return time), they also impose a long-term, or higher order, control loop on the system (with return time of ten years). Thus they serve the latent function of limiting the amount of research on a topic. This effect actually derives from the concern with growth. To the extent that concern is with sustained achievement rather than growth coefficient a'_{GP} approaches zero in value and the control loop disappears.

1c. The shortest return time for R is via loop (RP)—five years.

2a.

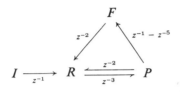

2b. The other two difference equations are the following.

$$P_t = R_{t-3}$$
$$F_t = P_{t-1} - P_{t-5}$$

2c.

Time	I	R	P	F
2	0	0	0	0
3	0	0	0	0
4	0	0	1	0
5	0	0	0	1
6	0	1	0	0
7	0	1	0	0
8	0	0	0	0
9	0	0	1	−1
10	0	0	1	1
11	0	0	0	1
12	0	2	0	0
13	0	1	0	0
14	0	0	0	−1
15	0	0	2	−1
16	0	−1	1	2
17	0	1	0	1
18	0	3	0	0
19	0	1	−1	0
20	0	0	1	−3

Note that the original impulse ultimately produces periods of sustained research activity. Note also that the control loop creates oscillations such that research and publications sometimes drop below their "average" level. The system appears to be unstable (compare years 6, 12, and 18). However, the heuristic choice of values for the coefficients did create unrealistic return effects for the loops.

3a. There are three equations:

$$Q_t = .50E_t + .10Q_{t-4}$$
$$I_t = .50Q_t + .05I_{t-1}$$
$$S_t = .10I_t + 1.05S_{t-1}$$

3b. The value of Q_t can be expressed in terms of earlier quantities:

$$Q_t = .50E_t + .10(.50E_{t-4} + .10Q_{t-8})$$
$$= .50E_t + .05E_{t-4} + .01Q_{t-8}$$

Note that the same process could be carried out again to give

$$Q_t = .50E_t + .05E_{t-4} + .005E_{t-8} + .001Q_{t-12}$$

In fact, this could be continued indefinitely to produce a single formula that would express the present value of Q as a weighted sum of past values of E. The same thing could be done for all the other variables in the system to yield a specification of the system in terms of time-series weighting patterns. The specification of any system can be converted to this form.

In this example it is clear that only the first two terms in the time series have sizable weights. Hence we could say that in this system present occupational level depends mainly on current qualifications, slightly on the credentials had four years ago, and only minutely on earlier conditions.

3c. Remembering that $Q_t = 0$ for $t < 0$ and $S_0 = -.25E_0 + .10I_0$, we get the following, at selected times, when education is set at 10:

t	E	Q	I	S
0	10	5.00	2.50	−2.25
1	10	5.00	2.62	−2.10
4	10	5.50	2.88	−1.58
10	10	5.55	2.92	−.15
15	10	5.56	2.93	1.41

3d. In this system doctor and high school dropout have about equal savings at age 38. Thereafter the doctor pulls ahead significantly.

4a. Attitude in a given year is obtained by applying the formula to the values of E, Q, I, and S in that year; for example, the attitude of a 36-year-old Ph.D. ($t = 10$) is

$$A = -.2(10) + .2(5.55) + .2(2.92) + .4(-.15)$$

The following is a graph of the results for both the Ph.D. and the dropout. (Points were calculated for every second year.)

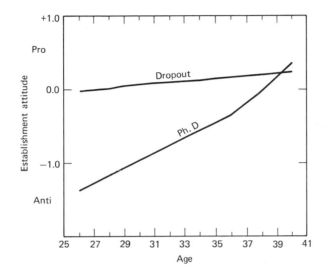

4b. Assuming that this system is operating on a population and that anarchists are strongly antiestablishment, we should search among the young educated (especially the unemployed) to find one. Assuming that progressives or liberals are neither for nor against the establishment, we might find them in almost any age group within the stable working class or among the middle-aged middle class. Persons who want to conserve the establishment might best be found among the elderly middle class. (Wealth without education, in youth and even more in old age, should also produce conservatives.) According to this model, it is doubtful that we would find many radicals of any kind in the stable working class. The time graphs for persons in this class stay near-neutral throughout their working careers.

5a. The formulas given in the problem can be used to estimate the values of I_t, L_t, and D_t from values of P_t, P_{t-1}, P_{t-2}, P_{t-3}, P_{t-4}, and P_{t-5}. Because

P has a value of 1.0 at all of these times, the estimates are simply the sums of the coefficients in each formula:

$$I_t = .50 + 0.0 + .08 - .03 + .02 - .01$$
$$= .56$$

$$L_t = 0.0 + .20 - .06 + .05 - .03 + .02$$
$$= .18$$

$$D_t = 0.0 + 0.0 + .08 - .03 + .02 - .01$$
$$= .06$$

5b. For a static analysis we ignore the zs in the flowgraph, in which case the values of the variables are

$$I = \frac{.5(1 + .32)}{1 + .32 - .16} \qquad P = .57$$

$$L = \frac{(.5)(.4)}{1 + .32 - .16} \qquad P = .17$$

$$D = \frac{(.5)(.4)(.4)}{1 + .32 - .16} \qquad P = .07$$

These results suggest that if the system input is held constant for six time periods we would make little error in assuming equilibration.

6a. The values of I_0 and D_{-1} can be defined from the values of P back through $t = -5$ by using the formulas given in exercise 5:

$$I_0 = .50P_0 + .08P_{-2} - .03P_{-3} + .02P_{-4} - .01P_{-5}$$
$$D_{-1} = .08P_{-3} - .03P_{-4} + .02P_{-5}$$

The definition is satisfied only when D_{-1} is large and I_0 is small or when $(D_{-1} - I_0)$ is large.

$$D_{-1} - I_0 = .08P_{-3} - .03P_{-4} + .02P_{-5} - .50P_0 - .08P_{-2} + .03P_{-3}$$
$$- .02P_{-4} + .01P_{-5}$$

$$= -.50P_0 - .08P_{-2} + .11P_{-3} - .05P_{-4} + .03P_{-5}$$

This quantity will be large when P_0, P_{-2}, and P_{-4} are small and P_{-3} and P_{-5} are large. Thus the "ideal" historical pattern for reformation in the system is as follows: a period of economic boom and then a recession, another boom followed by another recession, then a period in which the economy may do anything, followed by a severe recession in the present.

6b. We now want the quantity $(D_{-1} - L_0 - L_1)$ to be large.

$$(D_{-1} - L_0 - L_1) = .08P_{-3} - .03P_{-4} + .02P_{-5} - .20P_{-1} + .06P_{-2}$$
$$-.05P_{-3} - .03P_{-4} - .02P_{-5} - .20P_0 + .06P_{-1}$$
$$-.05P_{-2} + .03P_{-3} - .02P_{-4}$$

$$= -.20P_0 - .14P_{-1} + .01P_{-2} + .06P_{-3}$$
$$-.02P_{-4} + 0.0P_{-5}$$

Thus this second kind of reformation would be expected when there is a recession, an economic boom, then a period in which the economy does not matter much (so long as it is not in a severe recession), followed by two periods of recession.

Even here it is evident from the strong weighting of P_0 and P_1 (neither of which influences D_{-1}) that most of the changed legislation is due to economic conditions that weaken the influence of elites rather than to civil disturbances. At the same time it is clear that the overall pattern defining "reformation"—here, as in the first case—arises from oscillations in production surpluses. If surpluses could be held constant over time, the pattern defining a reform would not occur. Of course, such "findings" apply only to the system as specified. Inclusion of additional variables or changes in the structural coefficients and time delays could lead to different conclusions.

7a. The variance is

$$\sigma^2_{A(N)} = \sigma^2_{A(S)} + \sigma^2_{A(T)}$$

that is, the observed variance in attitudes is the sum of the variance due to stable differences among people, plus the variance among people due to recent experiences. Note that the second term does *not* measure deviations from stable attitudes. Rather it indicates the deviations from stable attitudes after they have been adjusted for any momentary trend in the population due to synchronized recent experiences; for example, everyone might recently have had experiences that produced positive transients. Then all attitudes would tend to be elevated from their stable components and transient variability around the average level of elevation might still be small.

The stable component would tend to be large in a society in which a variety of distinct socialization and pattern-maintenance programs is maintained. The transient component would tend to be small if people's experiences with the attitude object were rare, weak and impersonal, and synchronized. Thus we might guess that stable variance would predominate in a segmented, pluralistic society in which contact with the attitude object occurred mainly through the mass media. Transient variance would dominate in a group with a homogeneous culture in which people have frequent uncoordinated personal encounters with the attitude object.

7b. Selective exposure implies that persons' stable attitudes determine to some degree the kinds of experiences they have, and thus there would be some coordination between stable attitudes and transients. This might be represented as

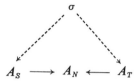

Now the variance of A_N is

$$\sigma^2_{A(N)} = \sigma^2_{A(S)} + \sigma^2_{A(T)} + 2\sigma_{A(S)A(T)}$$

Because the covariance is positive, the overall variance in net attitudes is increased (assuming that variability in recent experiences within the population is unaffected by selective exposure).

7c. Given the assumptions in this problem, the determination of net attitudes at time one and time two (ignoring selective exposure) could be represented as

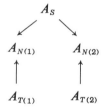

The correlation between net attitudes at the two times is

$$\rho_{12} = \frac{\sigma_{A(N)(1)A(N)(2)}}{\sigma_{A(N)(1)}\sigma_{A(N)(2)}} = \frac{\sigma^2_{A(S)}}{\sqrt{\sigma^2_{A(S)} + \sigma^2_{A(T)(1)}}\sqrt{\sigma^2_{A(S)} + \sigma^2_{A(T)(2)}}}$$

Assuming that variability in transients is the same at both times, this equation reduces to

$$\rho_{12} = \frac{\sigma^2_{A(S)}}{\sigma^2_{A(S)} + \sigma^2_{A(T)}}$$

Thus the correlation is equal to the proportion of variance in net attitudes that is determined by the stable component (provided that the stable components really do not change and the transients are uncorrelated over time).

Social conditions that would produce a large proportion of stable variance were indicated in answer (a). These same conditions will yield the most successful prediction of behaviors dependent on $A_{N(2)}$ from measurements of earlier attitudes $A_{N(1)}$.

8. The graph can be reduced to

$$U \xrightarrow{\ c(-)z^{-2}\ } D_B \ \circlearrowleft \ k(-)z^{-3}$$

from which we can write out and expand the difference equation for D_B:

$$
\begin{aligned}
D_{B(t)} &= k D_{B(t-3)} + c U_{t-2} \\
&= c U_{t-2} + kc U_{t-5} + k D_{B(t-6)} \\
&= c U_{t-2} + kc U_{t-5} + k^2 c U_{t-8} + \cdots
\end{aligned}
$$

We could interpret the end result as follows: the present level of conformity to a behavioral norm is a cumulative product of reinforcement history. This might suggest that a behaviorist approach provides a time-series perspective on the systems studied cross-sectionally by cognitive psychologists or by specialists in group dynamics.

INDEX

Absent arrows, 43-44, 194-195
Accountability, 11, 81. *See also* Explanation
Additivity of effects, 19-20, 31, 49-50, 63, 73
Advertising, 32
Age, 143, 199, 263, 277, 279
Aggregated effects, 7, 15, 18. *See also* Causal approximation; Flows
Aggregation procedures, 233, 238
Agriculture, 74, 199, 211-213, 275
Alcohol, 199, 277-279
Algebra of expectations, 86
Amplification, 27, 32, 64, 213-215, 217-218, 221-223, 249, 255
Arney, William Ray, 238
Ashby, W. R., 34
Aspirations, 15
Attinger, E. O., 34
Attitudes, 22, 36, 136-137, 142, 144-145, 199, 233, 241, 243-244, 247, 277-279, 289, 291-293
Authoritarianism, 11. *See also* Conservatism
Averroes, 1-2

Băianu, I., 34
Bertalanffy, Ludwig von, 34
Biased estimation, 158-159, 183-184, 189-193, 205, 230-231, 235, 286
Birkhoff, G., 34
Birth control, 36, 249
Birth rate, 36, 248-249
Blalock, Hubert M., Jr., 33-34, 108, 142, 195-196
Bohrnstedt, George W., 196
Borgatta, Edgar F., 196
Box, George E. P., 237

Branches, 41-42
Buckley, Walter, 34
Bunge, Mario, 33
Bureaucracies, 14

Cadzow, James A., 237
Campbell, Donald T., 33
Canonical analysis, 108, 191
Categorical algebra, 34
Causal approximation, 31, 36, 248
Causal inference, 3, 12-18, 26, 28-30, 33, 35, 44, 107-108, 141-142, 153, 192-195, 245-246
Causality, 1-18, 22-23, 25-34, 39, 55, 88, 115
Causal lags, 206-208, 223, 226-230, 235-236
Causal theory, applications, 73-76, 152
Causation, absence of, 13-17, 43-44
  analyzability, 7
  definition, 12
  materialistic basis, 4, 6-14, 219
Chain rule, 52, 55
Chains of causation, 7, 52-55, 57-61, 74, 115, 122, 226-227
Change, 3-4, 23-25, 31-32, 43, 59, 63, 73-76, 126-127, 208-218, 222-224, 227-232, 263
Change score, 239, 286
Chiang, Alpha C., 237
Coefficient of determination, 102, 105, 107, 151
Cohen, R., 33
Cohorts, 229-230, 238, 247, 279
Collinearity, 187, 282
Communications, 220, 225
Comparative statics, 258

Compatibility of components, 8-10, 12
Complex variables, 206, 208, 213
Components, 6-10, 32
  compatibility, *see* Compatibility of components
  contiguity, *see* Contiguity
  organization, *see* Organizing processes
Composite scores, *see* Linear composites
Computer programs, 105, 172
Conjunctive gating, 133
Conservatism, 36, 236, 241, 247, 289
Constant in equations, 20-22, 25, 49-51, 87
Construction of operators, 8-10, 148
Contamination, *see* Decontamination
Contiguity, 9-12, 14
Contributing path, definition, 128
Contributing-path effects, 128
Control systems, 14, 27, 32, 64, 136, 140-142, 145-146, 215-223, 254
Coordinating paths, 114-120
Coordinating-path effects, 120-122
Coordination of components, *see* Contiguity
Correction for attenuation, 267
Correlated disturbances, *see* Disturbance correlations
Correlation, *see* Statistical coordination
Correlation coefficient, *see* Product-moment correlation coefficient
Correlation matrix, definition, 262
Costner, Herbert L., 195-196, 238
Covariance, definition, 95-96, 98, 110, 200, 260. *See also* Statistical coordination
Crime, 14-15, 32, 74-75, 78-80, 143, 253-255
Critical cases, 73-74
Critical observation, 17
Cross-sectional data, 16, 83, 111, 160, 182, 225-226, 230-231, 233, 235, 237
Cross-sectional statics, 111
Culture, 14, 74, 199
Cycles, *see* Oscillation

Davis, James A., 64
Davis, Philip J., 108
Death rate, 13, 272
Decontamination, definition, 169
Deference, 35, 197-198, 245
Delay symbol, 207
Dependent variables, *see* Outcome variables
Determinism, 13

Developmental relationships, 4-5, 7, 15, 109, 245, 259
Deviancy, 142, 244
Deviation scores, definition, 87
Difference equations, 220, 228, 239, 287, 293
Diffusion processes, 199, 211-212
Disjunctive gating, 108, 133
Disposition, concept of, 4
Distributions, 82-98, 127
Disturbance, 28-30, 44-46, 50-51, 53, 66, 75, 94, 99, 114, 125, 132, 135, 137, 139, 143, 146, 235-237, 248
Disturbance correlations, 30, 102, 105, 114, 132, 135, 148-150, 152-153, 158-159, 161, 163, 168-169, 172-173, 177, 181, 193, 199, 203-204, 263, 271-272, 277, 286
Disturbance variance, 94, 125, 137, 139, 155-156, 170, 173, 236-237
Diversity, *see* Statistical diversity
Dogan, Mattei, 238
Double-negative amplifier, 249
Drugs, 35, 245
Duncan, Otis Dudley, 196
Dynamics, 32, 64, 73, 81, 204-244
Dynamic variance, 235-237, 291-292

Ecological correlation, 233
Education, 15, 35-36, 47, 77-78, 110, 137-139, 197, 201, 239-240, 245-247, 250-251, 261-262, 264, 272-273, 282-286, 288-289
Elaboration, 14, 16, 193-194
Ellis, D., 142
Endogenous variables, 52
Entwisle, Doris, 67, 77, 237
Epistemology, 33
Equilibration, 226-231, 243, 253, 290
Error variance, 101-103, 107, 110, 260-261. *See also* Residuals
Essentially constant signals, 227, 232, 234-236
Estimation error, 180, 182-194, 227, 230-231, 282
Estimation of parameters, 85, 148-197, 231, 234-235, 286
  theoretical assumptions, 152
Event configurations, 3, 8-9, 208
Events, 3-19, 22, 27

Evolution, 8
Exchanges, modelling of, 197-198
Exogenous variables, 52
Expectations, 4, 86-87, 90, 94-95, 97-102, 109-110, 131-132, 260
Experiments, 3, 12, 14-15, 29-30, 237
Explained variance, 94, 143, 146, 235-237, 262-263
Explanation, 7, 74-75, 248. *See also* Accountability
Exponents, 207
Exponential curve, 215, 218
Extrication, 71-73, 81, 174-176, 257

Factor analysis, 108, 191
Feedback, 31-32, 42-43, 213-223, 224-225, 227-228, 236
Fenton, Joann, 33
Field distortion, 10-11
Field gradient, *see* Contiguity
Fields, 9-12
Filter, 224
Flowgraphs, 25, 38-73, 75-77, 82, 112, 207-208, 237, 241
  absent arrows, 43-44, 257
  inversion, 73
  reduction, 52-53, 62, 167, 207-208, 212
  representation of variables, 38-39
  symbols, 39-40, 45-47, 207
  unlabeled arrows, 45-46, 68
Flows, 17-25, 246
Full-information methods, 181-182, 286
Functional analysis, 9-10, 146, 239, 269, 286-287
Fundamental, *see* Signals, constant component

Gating, 108, 132-135, 154-155, 271-272, 279
Genetics, 133, 146, 269-270
Gilman, B., 142
Goguen, J. A., 34
Goldberger, Arthur S., 108, 195-196
Government programs, 79-80, 206, 238-239, 253-255, 286-287
Graphs, *see* Flowgraphs
Graphs of distributions, 83-85
Grasmick, H., 142
Graupe, Daniel, 238
Group cohesion, 6

Grouping of observations, *see* Aggregation procedures
Growth, 9, 238, 240, 287

Hage, Jerald, 35
Hall, Arthur D., 76
Hamblin, Robert L., 238
Hannan, Michael T., 238
Hanson, Norwood R., 33
Hare, Van Court, Jr., 34
Hauser, Robert M., 196
Heise, D., 146, 196
Hempel, Carl G., 33
Heritability coefficient, 146, 269-270
Heteroscedasticity, example of, 258
Hibbs, Douglas A., Jr., 237
Hierarchical control, 223
Higher Order Feedback, 219-223
Hill, Richard Child, 201, 283
Historical analysis, 14-15, 18, 73-74, 82, 205, 225, 243, 290-291
Homeostatic control, *see* Control systems
Homogeneous flow, 17-18, 35
Homogeneous variables, *see* Homogeneous flows
Huggins, W. H., 77, 237
Hypothetical variables, 68-69, 128, 144, 173, 175. *See also* Causal approximation

Identification, 149-150, 152, 155-156, 181-184, 206, 225, 232, 237-238
  conditions for, 177-181
Identification problem, 150, 152, 165, 175-177, 190
Identity transformation, 46
Implication, 4-5, 8, 12, 19, 194
Income, 36, 46-47, 78-79, 109, 143-144, 201, 239-240, 247, 253, 258, 264, 282-285, 288-289
Independent variables, *see* Sources
Indicators, 144-145, 190-191, 193, 266-268, 286
Indirect effects, 13, 39, 42-43, 52-55, 73, 75
Indirect least squares, 168, 274
Ineffective operators, 14, 29, 111-112, 134, 194-195, 219
Inputs, definition, 52, 208-209, 223
Instability, 32-33, 63-64, 217-219, 223, 256

Instrumental variables, 15, 160-182, 184-
    185, 187, 190-194, 233-235, 275-279,
    282-286
Insulation, 14, 29, 278
Interactions, 47-48, 258
Interdiction, *see* Manipulations
International relations, 80-81, 255-258
Interval measurement, 19-20, 49. *See also*
    Measurement Scales
Intervening variables, 7, 52-55, 67-68, 75,
    154, 162, 227
Items, *see* Indicators

Jacobsen, R. Brooke, 238
Jenkins, Gwilym M., 237
Joint distribution, 85-95
Jones, Edward E., 33
Jöreskog, K. G., 196, 286

Kaplan, Abraham, 35
Kelley, Harold H., 33
Kerlinger, F., 108
Kish, Leslie, 195
Kmenta, Jan, 197
Kuhn, Thomas S., 33

Lagged variables, 184-185, 234-235
Lag period, 206-208, 210, 223, 226-231
Land, Kenneth C., 195
Least-squares estimation, 148, 195
Levels of analysis, 7, 11, 18, 31, 36, 207,
    248
Liberalism, 36, 236, 241, 247, 289
Limiter, 46-48, 134
Linear composites, 19, 28, 101, 200, 224,
    232
Linearity, 23-26, 40, 48, 50, 85, 92-94, 96,
    98-100, 135, 153, 206-207, 224-225,
    232, 258-259
Longitudinal data, 127, 184-185, 206, 225,
    232, 237
Loops, 42-43, 51, 56-73, 112, 119, 123, 130,
    140-142, 153-154, 159, 161, 167-168,
    174-177, 181-184, 193, 227-231, 252
    dynamics of, 63, 73, 213-223, 228-231
    elimination of, 68-73, 112, 167, 174-175
    identifiers, 56
    nests of, 57-58, 70
    see also Feedback
Lord, Frederic M., 196

Lorens, Charles S., 77
Lorrain, Francois, 34

MacLane, Saunders, 34
Manipulations, 3, 15, 55, 59, 63, 75-76, 79-
    80, 143, 147, 263
Marital adjustment, 14
Mason, Samuel, 62
Mason's Principle, 62, 64, 213, 274
Matrix algebra, 108, 172, 181
Mayer, Thomas F., 238
Mean, 85-87, 233. *See also* Expectation
Measurement error, 144-145, 147, 185,
    188-189, 191, 196, 203-204, 266-268,
    270, 286
Measurement problem, 188-191, 193, 232-
    233
Measurement scales, 19, 22-23, 45, 48-50,
    77-78, 85, 87, 106, 125-127, 252, 265
    bounded, 268
Meggers, Betty J., 74
Migration, 37, 246
Military, 35, 80-81, 246, 255-257
Miller, Jerry L. L., 238
Missing arrows, *see* Absent arrows
Modeling systems, 13, 38, 82, 285
Morale, 14
Multicollinearity, *see* Collinearity
Multiple causes, 5, 27-30, 41, 50, 52-54
Multiple correlation coefficient, 105, 156,
    188
Multiple effects, 30-31, 41, 53-54
Multiple regression, 30, 103-107, 155-158,
    168-173, 176, 200

Naroll, Raoul, 33
Necessary conditions, 1, 4-5, 8, 12, 180
Negative coefficients, 20-21, 26, 41, 55, 64,
    136, 139, 210, 249
Negative relations, 21-22, 26, 55, 92, 96,
    135-136, 138-139, 210-211, 213, 249
Negative values of variables, 22
Nesselroade, John R., 238
Nested loops, *see* Loops, nests of
Nodes, *see* Flowgraphs, representation of
    variables
Nonlinear relations, 46-48, 85, 92, 96, 100,
    219, 269, *See also* Linearity
Nonrecursive systems, 160-183
Nonstationary systems, *see* Stationary Systems

Normal distribution, 85
Normative zero point, 36, 246-247
Norms, 36, 244, 246-247, 278-279, 293
Novick, Melvin R., 196
Number of observations, 84, 90, 185-186,
    190, 285
Nunnally, Jum C., 196

Occupations, 35, 77-78, 110, 133, 139,
    143-144, 197, 236, 239-240, 245-246,
    250-251, 261, 264, 272-274
Open-path effect, 60-65
Open paths, 59-60, 64-65
Operators, 6-18, 26-27, 29, 32, 34-36, 39,
    81, 111, 135-136, 206-207, 209, 219,
    226-227, 245, 247, 249
  evolution of, see Evolution
  ineffective, see Ineffective operators
  taxonomies and typologies, 9
Ordinary least squares, 155-160, 169-171,
    173, 181, 185, 191-193, 274
Organizing processes, 8
Oscillation, 27, 32, 213, 216-217, 223, 230,
    288, 291
Outcome (dependent) variables, 40, 49-52,
    67, 73-76
Over-identification, 174-175

Panics, 6, 14
Parameters, definition, 22, 149
Partial-fraction expansion, 242
Partial regression coefficients, 104-106,
    155-156
Path analysis, 112-132, 134, 148-151, 165-
    166, 189-190, 200
Path coefficients, definition, 125
Path diagrams, 112-114, 124-126, 172-175
Path endpoints, definition, 115, 128
Path identifiers, 116, 128
Path origin, definition, 115
Pedhazur, E., 108
Piaget, Jean, 33
Point variable, see Homogeneous flow
Police, 78-79, 253-255
Policy decisions, 75-76, 79-80, 238-239,
    248, 253-255, 285-287
Politics, 79, 241, 253-254
Pollution, 13
Poole, Roger, 33
Popper, Karl R., 33

Population, 32
Power, 37, 80-81, 197-198, 255-257
Powers, William T., 35
Predetermined variables, 169-170, 232
Prediction, 75, 94-96, 99-107
Prisons, 142-143, 263
Probability, 85
Production of effects, 3, 7-8, 11
Productivity, 13-14, 18, 212, 223
Product-moment correlation coefficient,
    definition, 96-98, 102, 106, 259
Proportionality of effects, 19-20, 49

Race, 15, 37, 201-203, 282-286
Random assignment, 30. See also Gating
Rates, 18
Recursive systems, 153-160, 193, 210-213,
    227, 236
Reduced form, 67, 74-76, 136
Reduced form coefficients, 67, 274
Reese, Hayne W., 238
Regression analysis, 98-108, 150-153, 155-
    159, 259-260. See also Multiple regres-
    sion
Regression coefficient, definition, 100-101
Regression lines, 99-100
Relational tables, 44
Relevant feedback, definition, 62
Religion, 199, 276-279
Reorganization of systems, 219
Research design, 193-194
Residuals, 101-105, 107, 155-156, 170,
    260-261
Response characteristics, 208, 225
Restriction of range, 134
Return difference, 265
Return effect, 58-59, 62-64, 252
  units of, 252
Return time, definition, 219
Rokkan, Stein, 238
Rosenberg, Morris, 196

Samples, 85, 133, 152, 172, 185-188, 195,
    266, 272, 278
Sample size, see Number of observations
Sampling error, 185-186, 191, 282
Scattergram, 88-94
Science, 80, 238-239
Scores, see Linear composites
Second-order systems, 219-223

Secrecy, 15
Selective exposure, 244, 292
Self-loops, 43, 56, 62-63, 182-183
Semi-reduction of loops, 67-73, 112, 119, 130
Sex, 15, 18
Shielding, 14-15
Sigmoid curve, 212
Signal filter, 224
Signals, constant component, 232-236
    definition, 208
    time-varying components, 232-237, 291-293
Single-equation methods, definition, 181
Sinusoidal curves, 217-218
Skew, 109, 259
Slope, see Regression coefficient
Social control, 32, 136
Social exchanges, 197-198
Social interaction, 18, 245
Socialization, 18, 133, 291
Social mobility, 35, 111
Social status, 35-36, 111, 137-139, 144-145, 245, 265
Social stratification, 144, 198-199, 241-243
Social structure, 6, 32, 34, 198-199, 225, 276-277
Sorokin, Pitrim, 276
Source variables, 40, 49-50, 56
Specification, 154-155, 160, 162, 181, 191-194, 284
Specification errors, 191-194
Spurious correlation, 17, 30-31, 107, 115, 152, 184
Stability, 33, 49, 64, 81, 85, 215, 218-219, 223-224, 227, 242. See also Instability
Standard deviation, definition, 97
Standardized partial regression coefficients, 105-107, 151
Standardized variables, 97-98, 105-107, 124-127, 189, 270
Standard of living, 36, 248-249
Standard scores, definition, 97
Stanley, Julian C., 33
Statics, 49, 63, 85, 87, 111, 183, 205-206, 208, 214, 223, 227-228, 231, 237, 290
Stationary systems, 48-49, 230, 237
Statistical analysis, 12, 29-30, 81-112, 194
Statistical coordination, 31, 88-101, 107-108, 113-127, 133-135, 138-142, 153-

155, 157-161, 277
Statistical diversity, 87-88, 127-130, 133-138
Statistical inference, 85, 152, 194-195
Statistical tests, 85, 172, 194-195, 282
Status inconsistency, 36, 247, 289
Steady state, see Statics and Equilibration
Step-function, 209
Stinchcombe, Arthur L., 34, 76
Strength of relations, 26, 125-127, 135-136, 138, 140, 146, 185-188, 191, 195, 231, 245, 282
Structural coefficients, 22, 25-27, 37, 40, 55, 75, 77-79, 85, 101, 107, 120, 125-127, 155, 160, 168-171, 177, 236
    units of, 77-79, 250-252
Structural equations, 20, 22, 25-26, 51-52, 73, 82, 107-108, 169-171, 181, 255, 273
Subscripts, 39-40, 58, 60-61, 65, 95, 102, 120, 128-129, 184
Substantive analysis, 9
Sufficient conditions, 1, 4-5, 8, 12, 180-181
Summation rule, 50
Suppressor variables, 21-22, 247, 262
Surpluses, 36, 212, 241, 247, 275-276
Synchronization, 233, 291
System environment, 133, 135
System failure, 32, 219, 250
Systems, 27-34, 76-77

Taxonomy, 9
Technology, 32, 79-80, 199, 212, 275
Temporal order, 5, 12, 15, 73-74, 184-185, 245
Theil, Henry, 168, 195
Three-stage least squares, 182
Time scale, 206-207, 219
Time series, 234, 237, 288, 293
Time-varying inputs, 223-225, 231-237
Total effect, 62-63, 65-67, 274
Touching paths and loops, 61-66, 159, 254-255
Transfer function, 208, 219, 241-242
Transient, see Signals, time-varying components
Transmittance, see Total effect
True scores, 144-145, 188-189, 268
Two-stage least squares, 71, 168-176, 179, 181-183, 185, 188, 191-193, 200, 286

Typology, 9

Under-identification, 150, 166, 176
Unemployment, 35-36
Universal causes, 10
Unlabeled arrows, 45-46, 68
Unobserved variables, 188-191. *See also* Hypothetical variables
Unstable loops, *see* Instability

Validity coefficients, 145, 189, 268, 270, 286
Values, 147, 199, 270-271
Van de Geer, John P., 108
Van den Bergh, Simon, 1
Variables, definition, 22
Variance, definition, 87-88, 109, 200, 260.

See also Statistical diversity
Verbal theory, 25, 34-35, 38, 42-44, 51, 73, 75, 275, 285

Watts, Donald G., 237
Weapons, 35, 80, 246, 255-256, 276-277
Weighting pattern, 288
Welfare programs, 79
Werner, Oswald, 33
White, Harrison, 34
Witkin, H. A., 276
Wonnacott, Ronald J., 195
Wonnacott, Thomas H., 195
Wright, Sewall, 112, 142

Zero point, 36, 87, 246-247
Z transform, 242